RURAL U.S.A.: PERSISTENCE AND CHANGE

RURAL U.S.A.
PERSISTENCE AND CHANGE

edited by
THOMAS R. FORD

IOWA STATE UNIVERSITY PRESS • AMES

To the memory of six great rural sociologists and
past presidents of the Rural Sociological Society:

Edmund deS. Brunner	1889–1973
C. Horace Hamilton	1901–1977
Charles R. Hoffer	1892–1977
Walter L. Slocum	1910–1975
T. Lynn Smith	1903–1976
Carl C. Taylor	1884–1975

© 1978 The Iowa State University Press
Ames, Iowa 50010. All rights reserved

Composed and printed by
The Iowa State University Press

No part of this publication may be reproduced, stored in a retrieval system, or transmitted, in
any form or by any means, electronic, mechanical, photocopying, recording, or otherwise,
without the prior written permission of the publisher.

First edition, 1978

Library of Congress Cataloging in Publication Data

Main entry under title:

Rural U.S.A.

    Includes index.
    1. United States—Rural conditions—Addresses, essays, lec-
tures. 2. Sociology, Rural—Addresses, essays, lectures. I. Ford,
Thomas R., 1923–   II. Title.
HN59.R87   301.35'0973   77-27286
ISBN 0-8138-1345-X

CONTENTS

Part 6 • SOCIAL ORGANIZATION

Part 7 • THE FUTURE

PREFACE

SOMEWHAT more than a decade ago the Rural Sociological Society with the cooperation of the Center for Agricultural and Economic Development at Iowa State University sponsored the publication of *Our Changing Rural Society: Perspectives and Trends.* In that volume, edited by James H. Copp and published by the Iowa State University Press in 1964, a number of rural sociologists analyzed changes that were occurring in different segments of rural society and, in some cases, suggested topics for future study.

Because our rural society is indeed changing, the RSS recognized the need to update much of the information presented in the earlier volume and in 1974 commissioned a new survey of rural society in the United States. Probably less because of any special knowledge or abilities than because in an earlier presidential address to the RSS I had exhorted my colleagues to render greater public service, I was asked by the Council of the Society to direct the preparation of the new volume.

The ecological perspective employed in the organization of the book, it should be acknowledged, reflects the bias of the editor and does not constitute an endorsement of this particular approach by the Rural Sociological Society. For those who are unfamiliar with this particular analytic framework, a few words of explanation may be in order. Essentially, the perspective of human ecology focuses on the adaptation of humans to their environment, a process carried out largely by means of culture. It is this cultural adaptation that sets human ecology apart from other animal ecology. In keeping with this perspective, *Rural USA* presents, in Parts One through Three, a general overview and discussions of the rural environment and population, and then, in Parts Four through Six, discussions of human cultural response to the rural environment. For purposes of analytical simplicity we have maintained the more or less traditional three-part classification of culture into technological systems; value, belief, and normative systems; and social-organizational systems. Concluding the book, Part Seven departs from the traditional framework of ecological development to focus on rural social change.

During the preparation of this book, each chapter was sent in initial draft form to one or more members of the Rural Sociological Society for a

constructive review. The recommendations of the reviewers proved extremely valuable to both the editor and the authors of the various chapters.
The procedure also made the preparation of the volume much more of a
Society project than would otherwise have been the case. We gratefully
acknowledge the service provided by those reviewers whose names are
provided on a separate page and express our appreciation to numerous
other unnamed persons who assisted in various ways in the preparation of
this volume.

Thomas R. Ford, Editor

ACKNOWLEDGMENTS

To the persons named below who reviewed preliminary versions of one
or more chapters in this volume, the editor and authors express their
sincere gratitude.

CALVIN BEALE	GLENN FUGUITT	DUDLEY POSTON
ROBERT BEALER	GEORGE HILLERY	HARRY R. POTTER
J. ALLAN BEEGLE	BRUCE M. JOHN	PEGGY ROSS
THEREL BLACK	LARRY LONG	HARRY K. SCHWARZWELLER
STANLEY BRUNN	CHARLES P. LOOMIS	GENE F. SUMMERS
FREDERIC BUTTEL	DAN E. MOORE	WILLIS A. SUTTON
JAMES A. CHRISTENSON	HAROLD L. NIX	EVAN VLACHOS
A. LEE COLEMAN	NELDA M. NOLAN	EUGENE A. WILKENING
FREDERICK FLIEGEL	WILLIAM C. PAYNE	FERN K. WILLITS

Part 1
OVERVIEW

1 Contemporary Rural America: Persistence and Change

THOMAS R. FORD

FOR half a century or more, scholars have proclaimed the extinction of rural America or at least of any meaningful distinction between urban and rural society in the United States (Bender, 1975:185). A typical declaration of this nature is the statement by Friedman and Miller (1965:314) that "from a sociological and, indeed, economic standpoint, what is properly urban and properly rural can no longer be distinguished. The United States is becoming a thoroughly urbanized society, perhaps the first such society in history."

Of course, not even the most ardent rural sociologist is likely to argue that rural society exists in the United States as some independent system, but even though disagreement exists as to where the rural sector begins and the urban ends, it does not necessarily follow that we are unable to distinguish between "what is properly urban and properly rural." One does not have to be a particularly astute observer to detect that contemporary life in New York City and Los Angeles is still quite different from that in Bug Tussle, Oklahoma, or Gravel Switch, Kentucky. Considerably more remarkable than the mundane (but still valid) observation that people in small rural communities differ from those in the great metropolises is the pattern of gradient differences in social characteristics related to differences in community size.

The most intriguing feature of these ordered patterns of population characteristics, social and economic behavior, values, beliefs, and attitudes associated with community size is not their development but their persistence. The graded differences have continued long after the dissipation of social forces that originally were thought to account for them (such as the dissimilar occupations of rural and urban residents) and after the development of new influences (such as rapid transportation and the

Thomas R. Ford is Director of the Center for Developmental Change and Professor of Sociology, University of Kentucky.

3

mass media) that many social scientists thought would eliminate rural-urban cultural distinctions.

AN ECOLOGICAL VIEW OF RURAL-URBAN DIFFERENCES.

The persistence of rural-urban differences has not been a complete surprise to those sociologists who have utilized an ecological approach in the study of human society, an approach introduced in the United States by C. J. Galpin, one of the pioneers of rural sociology. In oversimplified terms, human ecologists see social forms arising from and modified by human cultural adaptation to environmental circumstances. Taking into account all of its aspects, including human population density, the environmental milieu of the city is appreciably different from that of smaller towns, villages, and rural areas. So long as these environmental differences persist, differences in social life will also persist.

The Rural Environment. The "natural environment" is often cited as one of the major advantages of rural over urban life, and many a migrant to the city has yearned for the sight of green fields, the smell of fresh-cut hay, the sound of a clear-running brook, or simply a deep breath of clean country air. But it is questionable whether tilled fields are any more "natural" than a city park and whether the rural streams are ever so sparkling and free of human pollutants or the air so fresh in reality as in nostalgic recollections. By and large, rural residents have been little more beneficent in their relations with nature than the denizens of our concrete and asphalt jungles. Indeed, profligate waste and destructiveness have marked the exploitation of our land and other natural resources since the earliest white settlements in America. Land, water, minerals, and other physical resources are still relatively abundant, but the increasingly rapid rate of their depletion has largely destroyed the myth of their inexhaustibility.

Paradoxically, the rapid urbanization of our society, which by 1970 had concentrated almost three-fourths of the population on only 2 percent of the national land area, may have served to conserve some of our resources. At the very least the urbanization process has made it possible to maintain a vast amount of open space and a relatively constant population density in rural areas.

The availability of land is only one aspect of the rural environment. How the land is used is another major consideration which influences most other aspects and is a source of past, present, and probably future conflict. The conversion of land to agricultural uses was accepted as a God-given right if not mandate by most American farmers, at least up until the 1930s when the terrible dust storms in the Great Plains led many to wonder whether that particular land should ever have been put to the plow. Liberty Hyde Bailey, one of the chief directors of the Country Life Movement, a national effort to revitalize rural living during the early decades of the twentieth century, did question whether it was "necessary or advisable in the interest of all the people, that every last acre in the national domain be opened for exploitation or settlement in this decade or even in this century" (Bailey, 1913:53). For the most part though, like other conservationists of the period, Bailey was concerned with instilling a sense of land stewardship in all farmers and educating them in conservationist skills as a deterrent to destructive farm practices. Many of the ruinous procedures and deteriorated conditions deplored by conservationists in the first decade of this century have since been ameliorated. Soil-building practices are now in common use; erosion resulting from ill-considered tillage practices is relatively rare; and most of the cutover woodlands are once again covered with forest. But present-day environmental damage inflicted by farmers through indiscriminate use of herbicides and pesticides may be no less consequential than those of earlier generations. They are different, though, and in that difference lies the hope that we can recognize and correct our mistakes.

While damage to the earth resulting from agricultural malpractices may have been largely eliminated, the same cannot be said yet of the consequences of mining. The fuel crisis of the 1970s has been used as justification for delaying federal regulation of the strip mining of coal, an extractive process that has been responsible for the extensive destruction of land surfaces and vegetation as well as stream pollution and sedimentation in Ohio, Pennsylvania, West Virginia, Kentucky, Tennessee, and Illinois. Surface mining has moved westward where it has been used to mine oil shale as well as coal, despite vigorous opposition by a variety of environmentalist organizations.

Air pollution too has been increasing in rural areas as more power plants have been constructed and as more industries have shifted to rural locales. Mining, energy-producing plants, and manufacturing industries have also contributed to rapidly growing problems of solid waste disposal, which few rural areas are prepared to deal with. Traditional rural methods of solid waste disposal such as burning, strewing on unused land, or dumping in streams to be carried away with the spring rise are not model disposal techniques to begin with, and they are certainly inadequate to handle massive quantities of solid waste.

To date, the rural environment of the United States has not reached the depths of disaster gloomily predicted by ecological doomsayers only a few years ago, perhaps not so much because the predictions were wrong as because they aroused public concern and counteraction. The forestalling of imminent disaster should not be interpreted to mean that the danger is past. A number of serious environmental concerns, discussed in Chapter 2, remain, and some of these can be expected to reach critical proportions in the near future.

The Rural Population. Because of the tendency to equate rural population with people who live on farms, it comes as a surprise to many that the number of rural residents has not been steadily declining. The census count of the rural population has remained relatively stable at about 54 million for the past quarter century. The farm population segment has decreased drastically, of course, from an estimated peak of 32 million between 1910 and 1920 to about 9 million in 1975. And the steady shrinkage of the total rural population as a percentage of the total population — from 95 percent at the first census in 1790 to 26.5 percent in the 1970 census — has helped create the illusion that the rural population was also declining in absolute numbers.

Like any dividing line on a continuum, the Census Bureau's boundary between rural and urban population is arbitrarily set. Some social scientists in recent years have found it more satisfactory to separate the population into metropolitan and nonmetropolitan rather than into traditional urban and rural categories. Others maintain the urban-rural differences within the nonmetropolitan classification, keeping the traditional 2,500 population as the dividing line between rural and urban places.

Although it makes some difference in comparing population characteristics whether one uses an urban-rural or a metro-nonmetro classification scheme, the effects are not as significant as might be supposed. The residents of larger and more densely settled places, whether classified as metro or urban, will differ in predictable ways from the residents of smaller and less densely settled places, whether called nonmetro or rural. Rural families are still larger than urban families, although both have declined in size. The ratio of males to females remains higher in rural than in urban communities, but with fewer children and more older persons in the population, females are more numerous in all communities. In rural areas compared with urban ones, adults still have less formal schooling, smaller proportions of women are employed, family incomes are lower, and relatively more families are poverty-stricken. The rural population has made significant gains in all these areas, but it still lags behind the urban population. These differences have persisted even though the divergences have diminished in some cases.

The Technology of Rural Life. Agriculture and animal husbandry have traditionally been the predominant technological domains of rural society, and in terms of land resources utilized this is still true in the United States. As has been noted, a relatively small portion of the rural labor force is now engaged in agriculture, and the economic returns of farmers and farm workers are still generally lower than those of workers in other industries. Earlier in our history, as in many less developed countries today, the relatively low earnings of agricultural workers were often attributed to the inefficiency of the technology, which was heavily dependent upon human and animal energy. This was a dubious argument when advanced, since it overlooked the fact that wage increases in other industries were generally achieved only after decades of labor strife, the organization of unions, and the passage of legislation favorable to labor. It is an even less valid proposition today when the productive efficiency of farm labor measured in output per man-hour has increased over the past quarter century more rapidly than that of manufacturing workers (U.S. Bureau of the Census, 1975: Tables 583 and 1063).

What farmers have long recognized but have generally been unable to cope with is that their earnings have been governed more by total agricultural production relative to demand than by their productive efficiency. Periodically, the net effect of greater efficiency in the production of a commodity has often been a lower return to farmers because the higher total production resulted in a notable lowering of market prices. Only if production control were achieved could farmers expect to gain reasonable control over their earnings. Direct efforts by farmers' organizations to control production have rarely proved successful, while government programs directed toward this end (primarily those of the Agricultural Stabilization and Conservation Service) have had only moderate effects, partly because of their limited support by farmers themselves. Increasingly, however, large private enterprises are gaining control of various agricultural commodities in an organizational revolution that may ultimately have as much impact on production as did the technological revolution.

Although agriculture still dominates the rural economic scene, it is by no means the only activity nor the only one that has experienced major technological changes. In forestry the growing stock of sawtimber increased 25 percent between 1953 and 1970, the volume of products harvested grew steadily, and gross sale value nearly tripled (U.S. Bureau of the Census, 1975: Tables 1106 and 1109). The amount of timberland during this period increased by only 1 percent, indicative of the more efficient utilization of the available land.

Extractive industries have also become much more mechanized in their operations during the past quarter century. The average bituminous coal miner today produces three times as many tons of coal per man-day as his counterpart in the 1950s, a consequence of the introduction of continuous mining machines and other mechanized equipment in the deep mines and a major shift to surface mining techniques. As in agriculture, mechanization of mining operations has been accompanied by substantial reductions in the number of employees. Despite the rapid expanison of mining operations in response to the oil crisis of the mid-1970s, the number of coal miners employed in 1975 was still less than half the number employed in 1950 (U.S. Bureau of the Census, 1975: Table 1158).

The most remarkable technological shift in rural areas, though, has not been in the traditional agricultural and extractive industries but in the spread of manufacturing industries to the country. While employment was declining on farms and in the mines, "rural and partly rural nonmetropolitan counties gained manufacturing jobs at a rate of 4.6 percent annually between 1959 and 1969, or more than double the rate in metro

counties" (Haren, 1974:31–32). By 1970 the proportion of the employed
labor force working in manufacturing industries was as high (about 24
percent) in nonmetro as in metro counties, although some of the nonmetro
workers were actually commuting to jobs in metro areas. Even in the
completely rural counties that were not adjacent to a metropolitan area,
17 percent of the employment was in manufacturing industries (Hines,
Brown, and Zimmer, 1975:36). In 1969, three-fourths of the manufacturing establishments with less than 100 workers located in nonmetro
counties were located in counties that were entirely rural (Haren,
1974:32).

The expansion of what has long been considered urban technology
into rural areas and the consequent closer occupational similarity of rural
and urban workers lends support to the plausible argument that rural-
urban differences are rapidly disappearing. But as previously noted,
traditional differences have proved remarkably enduring, and social and
economic studies have generally shown that the impact of industry on rural
areas has been far less momentous than earlier anticipated.

Rural Values and Beliefs. The influence of technology on social
behavior is always mediated by the basic values and beliefs of the society,
although these are also affected by technological change. Virtually all
comparative studies of the values and beliefs of rural and urban people
have shown similar patterns of difference. Rural people are generally more
traditional, clinging longer to older views and resisting new ideas. This is
not to say that rural values and beliefs do not change or that they are
fundamentally different from those of urban society. It does mean that
new ideas and behavior are much more likely to be adopted first in the
cities and are accepted only later by rural communities, by which time the
city people have moved on to something else. The result, as Fischer
(1975b:1336) notes, is that "there is a lag in social change as successive
'waves' diffuse from the urban center to the rural periphery."

At an earlier period, rural traditionalism was usually explained by the
relative isolation of rural people and their limited social contacts as a
consequence of low population density. This explanation is less valid now
for rural society in the United States, since virtually all of our rural
residents are able to receive the latest news and views of events in the world
via radio and television at the same time as urban people. Most rural
people also have access to metropolitan areas via good highways, and many
are able to reach suburban shopping centers as quickly as city residents.
Furthermore, there are few rural people today who do not have regular
contact with friends or relatives in metropolitan areas.

A more plausible ecological explanation than social isolation for the
persistence of rural traditionalism is that population size, density, and
diversity are significant determinants of the generation and acceptance of
new ideas. In heavily populated urban centers a new idea is much more
likely to acquire what Fischer (1975a:421) refers to as the "critical mass" of

normative support required for it to flourish. Rural communities, even with the same proportion of creative individuals and nonconformists, will rarely have the absolute numbers of supporters needed to sustain radically different innovations of thought and behavior. The subcultures of the metropolis (including those of rural migrants) are the seedbeds of cultural mutants, only a small proportion of which survive long enough to be transplanted to and thrive in rural environments.

Whatever its explanation, the persistence of rural-urban differences with respect to a wide variety of values and beliefs is documented by data from numerous polls and surveys summarized by Larson in Chapter 6 of this volume. Although the data analyzed by Larson are not adequate to measure changes for any substantial number of values and beliefs, the available evidence does show shifts relating to social equality, racial views, religious beliefs and practices, and family size preferences. In all cases the rural population has moved in the same direction as the national population, more rapidly than the urban population in some instances and more slowly in others. In the latter instances, rural-urban differences have sometimes become greater than they were a generation ago, but this does not preclude a narrowing of the gap in the near future. Even so, little in the available evidence indicates an early extinction of traditional disparities.

Social Organization. As with values and beliefs, the social organization of the rural sector appears to move continuously toward that of the urban sector without ever quite catching up, at least with respect to most aspects of social life. People in rural communities are still more likely to share bonds with their neighbors or at least to know who their neighbors are, but the existence of "gemeinschaft" communities strongly united by common values, beliefs, kinship, interests, and activities is largely a romantic myth. Their virtual extinction in the United States was noted some 50 years ago (Sorokin, Zimmerman, and Galpin, 1930:331), and there is some question whether they ever existed to any appreciable extent. Associational forms of social organization have long predominated in our rural society, and recent organizational changes have been more often changes of degree—toward more and increasingly complex formal associations—than changes in the basic structural type.

Two possible exceptions to this generalization might be found in the changing organization of the agricultural economy, to which earlier reference was made, and of rural local government as it has responded to requirements imposed by federal legislation and administrative agencies.

It was earlier noted that farmers have long been disadvantaged in their economic activities because of their inability to control total production of any commodity. While the virtues of the family farm as the last bastion of competitive individual enterprise were being extolled, American farmers found themselves economically outmaneuvered by both those organizations that bought their produce and those that sold them goods and services. Their own large-scale organizational efforts to counter large corporations, beginning with the Grange shortly after the close of the Civil War, were at best only partly successful. Instilled with the values of independence and self-reliance, American farmers were never able to sustain for long the spirit of unity and cooperative endeavor recurrently generated by farmer protest movements. Most of the larger farm organizations have given up or reduced their efforts of direct aid to farmers in favor of securing advantageous legislation through lobbying efforts (Rogers and Burdge, 1972:297). Only the National Farmers' Organization persists in dramatic protest activities, such as the destruction of farm produce or livestock when prices have fallen below production costs, and these tend to be more ritualistic than effective in achieving desired ends.

What is proving effective in bringing farm prices under control— although not necessarily under the control of the farmer—is the rapid development of various forms of commodity production contracts and vertical integration arrangements. As the number of commercial farms has declined (from 3.7 million in 1950 to 1.7 million in 1969), production has become increasingly concentrated in the larger farms. In 1969 less than a third of the largest farms—those with sales in excess of $20,000— accounted for more than three-fourths the total value of farm products sold, and only one-eighth of the farms accounted for 57 percent of the sales. This concentration makes it much easier for processing agencies or other corporations to control production. By 1970 more than half of all citrus fruits, 80 percent of seed crops, 85 percent of processed vegetables, 90 percent of broilers, 95 percent of fluid milk, and 98 percent of the nation's sugar beets were produced under contract (Harshbarger and Stahl, 1974).

It would be erroneous to suppose that the rise of large commercial farms and the changing organization of agricultural production and marketing came about only as a passive consequence of small farmers deserting their farm operations for more profitable economic enterprises. As the authors of one recent study of economic concentration in agriculture note:

The trends toward greater economic concentration in agriculture and more market coordination have not developed by chance, but by the deliberate efforts of private individuals, businessmen, both large and small, various public institutions and the Federal government to make agriculture more efficient and profitable through the use of new technology. While considerable progress has been made, it has nonetheless left deep scars on thousands of families who could no longer cope with the changing economic environment (Harshbarger and Stahl, 1974:25-26).

Viewed in economic perspective, what is unusual about agriculture is not the trend of economic concentration but the fact that it was so long in developing. Perhaps this is simply another example of the rural lag in the adoption of accepted urban ways, prolonged in this case by the romantic image of the family farm as a way of life instead of a business enterprise.

The gaining of corporate control over agricultural enterprises has undoubtedly been economically advantageous for many farmers by providing
greater stability to the marketing system and reducing the risks of farm
operations. At the same time, past records of oligopolistic industries in this
country must breed some uneasiness in the minds of both farmers and the
consumers of farm products as to how the power to control the production
and prices of food and fiber will be used if vested in a small number of
corporations.

A second qualitative change in rural social organization is to be seen
in the changing functions of local government. Just as agriculture has
finally adopted many of the organizational characteristics long found in
other industries, so too has rural local government recently begun to
accept practices in common use for some time in urban government and
many other institutional areas. Traditionally, local governments in rural
areas largely limited their activities to meeting community needs for
schools, roads, hospitals, and the like, which individual families normally
could not provide themselves. Not infrequently the response to need was
guided by the principle "best is least," applied to both the action taken and
its cost. For many of these "amateur governments," as Roscoe Martin
(1957) termed them, the devising of long-range plans not only exceeded
their capabilities but was viewed as intrinsically socialistic, un-American,
and abhorrent.

Two related sequences of events compelled local governments in rural
areas to become more active in planning and administering services. First
was the rediscovery of rural poverty in America in the late 1950s, which led
to the recognition that rural communities lagged considerably behind
urban communities in the quality and quantity of most services provided
their residents. Following hard on the revelations of widespread economic
problems in rural areas and the inability of rural communities to deal
effectively with their difficulties came a plethora of federal programs to
remedy the situation. Common features of many of these programs were
the requirements that communities provide comprehensive area
development plans and proposals for development projects, which few
rural communities were able to prepare in accordance with complex
agency guidelines. Understandably, the leaders of many rural communities opposed the planning stipulation on philosophical as well as
practical grounds, but increasingly the devising of comprehensive plans
was recognized as necessary. Some leaders conceded that it was a rational
approach to solving local problems; others, more cynical, viewed it simply
as another bureaucratic obstacle to be overcome in order to secure federal
funds, which rural communities had come increasingly to rely on. In any
case, rural local government, at least in those communities that elected to
participate in federal programs, changed from merely maintaining
existing services to setting new service goals and developing plans to
achieve them.

Federally   funded   development   programs   brought   other   organizational changes to rural communities. In many areas a movement to professionalism in government developed, partly because amateur administrators were no longer able to cope with the complexities of federal agency requirements and guidelines and partly because some federal programs provided funds for professional staffing, at least at the multicounty level. Recognizing that many rural counties were too small or too poor to fund effective service programs, both the Economic Development Administration and the Appalachian Regional Commission encouraged the organization of multicounty districts and district development agencies. In some states, districts have become accepted as meaningful divisions for planning and development. In other states they are still viewed as merely nominal units whose professional personnel constitute a technical staff pool to serve individual counties that cling steadfastly to their administrative autonomy.

Whether or not they have maintained their independence from other local units, the institutions of rural communities have become more dependent upon state, regional, or national systems. These external systems assist in the financing of local operations but usually at the price of the local community's relinquishing control of many basic decisions. (This general process of vertical linkage is also evident in the contractual arrangements made by farmers with corporate agencies that help finance the operations but set production specifications.) "Revenue sharing" programs were presented by the Nixon administration as a "no-strings-attached" method of allocating federal funds to local communities, the use of the funds to be determined by local officials. However, the actual funds distributed through the revenue sharing program have never amounted to as much as one-fifth of the total federal aid to state and local governments (U.S. Bureau of the Census, 1975: Table 424).

Many of the more traditional federal programs designed to aid rural communities were packaged together in the Rural Development Act of 1972, which had as a general goal the improvement of the quality of rural life. Like most of its predecessors, the Rural Development Act has failed to have significant impact for a variety of reasons. First, as Schaller points out in Chapter 12, no clearly defined rural development policy exists to orient the various programs. Second, the USDA, which was charged with coordinating the various rural development activities, has been less than enthusiastic in the support of social programs, which are viewed as peripheral to its traditional primary mission of agricultural development. Finally, and partly as a consequence of the first two factors, the funding provided has been far less than needed to mount a serious rural development program. However, despite its limited accomplishments to date, the Rural Development Act is portentous of the changes taking place in rural society and the institutions designed to serve its members. It is a concession that the well-being of agriculture is not coincident with the well-being of rural people, and although the two remain closely related, programs designed to improve the conditions of one constituency do not necessarily benefit the other.

Changes in other aspects of rural social organization, considered in greater detail in later chapters of this volume, have largely paralleled national trends. Racial and ethnic discrimination in rural communities has abated somewhat, but is far from being eliminated. More than half of the nonwhite population living in completely rural counties in 1969 had incomes below the poverty level. Four years later 41 percent of the non-metropolitan black population was still below the poverty level compared with 11 percent of the nonmetropolitan white population and 30 percent of the black population living in metropolitan central cities (U.S., Congress, 1975:18). Mexican-Americans in rural America have fared somewhat better than blacks, but their average income is still appreciably below that of the rural white population. The most disadvantaged minority of all, measured in economic terms, is the American Indian population. It is also the only one of the three groups that is still predominantly rural, despite a considerable amount of urbanization between 1960 and 1970.

While women in rural America no longer constitute a numerical minority, they are still often subject to forms of discriminatory treatment associated with ethnic minority groups. Their plight is not a new one nor is it only recently recognized. More than half a century ago the Commission on Country Life (which itself included no women members) deplored the condition of farm women, noting that "whatever general hardships, such as poverty, isolation, lack of labor-saving devices, may exist on any given farm, the burden of these hardships falls more heavily on the farmer's wife than on the farmer himself. In general her life is more monotonous and more isolated, no matter what the wealth or the poverty of the family may be" (Commission on Country Life, 1911:104).

Since publication of the Country Life Commission's report, the roles of rural women have changed in various ways. In general the changes have been those experienced by the total society. Increasing proportions of rural women are now gainfully employed, but at salaries and wages that are generally lower than those of men; marriage is less likely to be viewed as a supreme achievement for a woman and divorce as less a moral trans-gression; women can have fewer children without being considered derelict in their duties, and enjoy sex without being considered wanton; and more of the duties of child socialization have been relinquished to others, although the mother still bears greatest responsibility for this function. The differences between rural and urban women are largely differences of degree, for the change is probably in direct relationship to size of place, as is true of many other aspects of social life. While the pace of achieving sexual equality in rural areas may be far too slow to suit the desires of feminist leaders, it is at least partly governed by the prevailing norms of the women themselves.

Finally, rural poverty, which attracted so much attention but generated so little fundamental change in the 1960s, remains more prevalent than urban poverty, including that to be found in the central cities of large metropolitan areas. However, the number and percentage of families, both rural and urban, living on poverty level incomes have decreased by more than half since 1960, partly because transfer payments have lifted many families out of the poverty status. Typically, a smaller proportion of rural than urban families receives public assistance, which to some extent reflects community differences in the rendering of public services. Despite the efforts of the Office of Economic Opportunity to insure "maximum feasible participation" of the poor in community action programs the agency sponsored during the 1960s, there is little evidence of consequent changes in the power structure of most rural communities.

FROM HERE TO WHERE? In the predecessor to this volume, published more than a decade ago, Larson and Rogers (1964:60) listed seven major changes in the rural society at that time:

1. An increase in farm productivity per man accompanied by a decline in the number of farm people
2. An increasing linkage of the farm and nonfarm sectors
3. Increasing specialization of farm production
4. Decreasing rural-urban differences in values
5. Increasing cosmopolitanism of rural people in their social relations
6. Centralization of decision making in rural public policy and agribusiness
7. A decrease in the importance of primary relationships (such as locality and kinship groups) and an increase in the importance of secondary relationships (such as formal organizations, government agencies, and business firms)

For the most part these changes are continuing, although Larson in his contribution to this present volume (Chapter 6) questions his and Rogers's earlier conclusion about the decreasing differences in rural-urban values. But in noting these differences, Larson and Rogers pointed out even in the earlier book that "American rural society in transition presents basic persistencies and stabilities, along with great and rapid changes" (1964:61).

Perhaps because we have come to expect social homogenization as the ultimate end product of our great and rapid changes, the most surprising feature of the current state of rural society in the United States is the distinctiveness it has maintained. Observing the trends of change in rural society toward the patterns of urban society, social scientists extrapolated these trends to conclude that the two sectors would sooner or later merge into one indistinguishable "mass society." Implicit in their reasoning was the assumption that the rate of rural social change would have to exceed that of urban social change, since it was obvious that rural society would have to catch up if the rural-urban gap was to be closed. So far the catching up has not taken place, and there are sound sociological as well as ecological reasons for believing it may never take place.

If human society is in continuous process of adapting to its habitat, as ecologists maintain, it is a reasonable expectation that there will be different cultural responses to the different environments of the city and the country. This conclusion appears so obvious as to be dismissed as a mere commonplace were it not being constantly challenged by the argument that the apparent limitations imposed by environment can be largely overcome by modern technology.

Unquestionably technological changes have had great effects upon the rural population. Nevertheless, the environmental situations of rural and urban people remain quite different in ways that have significant social consequences. As the populations of our great metropolises have grown larger and more dense, for example, the rural population has remained relatively stable as has the amount of open space, which is so much more accessible to rural residents. Even farm acreage was approximately the same in 1970 as in 1940, while commercial forest land increased during the period. And since rural-to-urban migration drained off most of the natural increase of the population, the ratio of rural population to the land remained remarkably constant.

To be sure, only a small minority of the rural population is now employed in farming and in timber-based industries, but the major occupational shifts of rural workers have so far not brought about the radical social and cultural changes that had been anticipated. Equally surprising, and often disappointing to community leaders who had looked forward to major social and economic benefits, have been the circumscribed effects of manufacturing plants located in rural communities.

Will the reverse flow of migrants from metropolitan areas bring about major changes in rural life? As yet we cannot say. Obviously much will depend upon the extent of the movement and its duration. The nature of the migration and the character of the migrants will also be of significance. To some observers the process is nothing more than the further extension of metropolitan expansion beyond previous suburban boundaries. Others interpret the movement not as a new phase of metropolitanization but rather as a rejection or partial rejection of metropolitan life styles. They cite in support of their view the expressed preference by a substantial majority of the population for nonmetropolitan residences (Fuguitt and Zuiches, 1975) and the flow of inmigrants into rural counties that are distant from metropolitan areas.

From the analysis of the characteristics of inmigrants to nonmetro areas (see Chapter 4 of this volume, by Zuiches and Brown) we know that they exhibit many of the same traits as outmigrants to metro areas. They are predominantly young adults with more schooling, higher occupational status, and higher incomes than the nonmetropolitan resident population. They differ from the outmigrants to metro areas in having only a small proportion of blacks, a characteristic that Durant and Knowlton (Chapter 9) believe to reflect the greater discrimination against minorities still found in nonmetropolitan areas.

The demographic characteristics of the new migrants tell us little, though, about their values and beliefs or about their life-styles. It is a reasonable assumption that in these respects, too, they differ from the older population of the localities into which they are moving. Inevitably the sheer infusion of large numbers of new migrants will bring about changes in the rural places where they settle, possibly converting some of them into urban places. If these inmigrants are no more than a vanguard of the latest wave of metropolitan expansion and the bearers of main-stream metropolitan culture, then we can expect some further narrowing of rural and urban lifeways. But it is also possible that the new migrants are not the bearers of the culture of the cities but rather dissenters from the urban way of life. Dissenters from the culture of the cities have always existed, of course, but these were generally bound to the city until financially able to retire. The growth and diversification of the non-metropolitan economy and the consequent broadening of the range of occupational opportunities have now made it possible for more of those who prefer smaller communities or the open country to live in rural places. It is not inconceivable that the type of community in which individuals and families wish to live will increasingly become the major determinant of where they do live. The reversal of the metropolitan-nonmetropolitan migration streams suggests that a growing divergence of urban-rural life-styles may emerge, as the process of internal migration sorts out those with different tastes.

Whether or not recent migration patterns continue, current trends hold the promise of a future rural society that can retain many of the desirable features of small community life while overcoming many of the economic disadvantages that have plagued it in the past. Whether this promise will be realized we cannot say. Social scientists are not soothsayers. They can point out plausible alternatives, as Coughenour and Busch have done for the future of rural society in the United States in the concluding chapter of this volume. They can provide pertinent knowledge needed to make well-informed decisions, as we have sought to do in this book. And by analyzing appropriate social indicators, social scientists are able to make some assessment of the progress we are making toward the achievement of societal goals. But ultimately it is the people of rural America who must choose the kind of society they wish to live in—the nature of the environment, the types of communities. It is they, too, who must assume the major burdens of costs and responsibilities required to carry their decisions to fruition. For to relinquish those decisions and to abdicate their attendant obligations is to destroy fundamental principles of a working democracy, principles as essential today as they were when this was a rural nation, two centuries ago.

Part 2
HABITAT

2 The Rural Environment: Quality and Conflicts in Land Use

EUGENE A. WILKENING
LOWELL KLESSIG

THE 1970s were heralded as the Environmental Decade. But in the first half of the decade, environmental quality with respect to air, water, minerals, wildlife, living space, timber, and the soil all declined (see Table 2.1). While other groups such as the Council on Environmental Quality (1974) have presented a less pessimistic view, all of the apparent concern for the environment in recent years has not yet reversed the declining quality of our natural environment. Furthermore, there is an indication that the concern for environment in rural and urban areas inevitably conflicts with desires for economic growth and profits and with the increasing worldwide demand for food and energy. Thus, the quality of the rural environment is closely linked with trends and conflicts in the larger society.

The following four principles may help to illuminate the nature of the problems of the rural environment and attempts at their solution:

1. *Problems of the rural environment originate externally in the larger society.* The uses and misuses of the rural environment are affected by decisions made by government agencies, corporations, labor unions, and by the aggregate demands of the largely urban population. Agriculture is pursued to satisfy the demands of a largely urban market. The waters of rural areas are polluted as much, if not more, by the effluent from nonfarm sources as from farm runoff. Open spaces in the country are

Eugene A. Wilkening is Professor of Rural Sociology and Lowell Klessig is Associate Professor, Environmental Sciences, Extension, University of Wisconsin, Madison. Professor Frederick Buttel of the Department of Sociology, Ohio State University, provided constructive comments on the manuscript.

Table 2.1. Ratings of environmental quality for the United States, 1970–74.

	1974	1973	1972	1971	1970
Air	34a	34	33	34	35
Water	36	37	39	40	40
Minerals	42	44	46	48	50
Wildlife	47	48	52	53	55
Living space	50	53	56	58	60
Timber	73	73	76	76	75
Soil	74	76	77	78	80

Source: *National Wildlife,* 1975.
a Rating of 100 would be ideal.

being acquired by urban people seeking temporary and permanent homes away from the city. The noise and litter that disturb the solitude and beauty of rural areas emanate from outdoor recreationists getting away from the constraints of urban life. Now nuclear and coal-fueled power plants are pushing into the countryside and crossing the rural landscape with transmission lines carrying the power to industrial centers. While most of the problems of the rural environment originate in urban centers, it should also be recognized that the initiative for environmental protection has also come primarily from urban residents.

2. *Problems of the rural environment are affected by the values and conflicting interests of those who use that environment.* Patterns of land ownership and use are closely tied to our values of individual freedom, local autonomy, and growth. These values have historical roots and continue to affect the way in which our natural resources are used and waste products are disposed of. Starting with a great abundance of natural resources, individuals and firms have been free to exploit our natural resources with few restrictions. Measures to conserve and to preserve these resources have run counter to values that support free enterprise and growth for the individual, community, and nation. As the public interest in the use of land and in the disposal of waste products has developed, conflicts have arisen between private interests and the public good. The resolution of these conflicts must occur through the political process.

3. *Economic recessions and crises in food and energy place constraints on achieving environmental quality.* An economic recession increases pressure against constraints upon growth and against costly measures to protect the environment. A recession may reduce demand for some resources, but will increase pressures for job-creating projects, regardless of the environmental impact. High energy prices may reduce demands for gas and electricity, but they will also intensify the search for marginal energy resources and the development of nuclear power. The international food crisis increases the pressure to use more erodable land and to apply greater quantities of fertilizers and pesticides.

4. *Public policies to meet specific objectives often have far-reaching, unintended consequences for environmental quality.* Many environmental

problems are the unanticipated consequences of policies designed for attaining other socially desirable goals. For example, federally guaranteed home loans for single family dwellings have facilitated urban sprawl, and various tax policies to support public services have dramatically influenced environmental resources. The environmental consequences of such public policies have just begun to be recognized.

RURAL ENVIRONMENTAL RESOURCES: USES AND ABUSES

Agriculture—From Soil Conservation to the Energy Crisis. L. C. Gray and his colleagues noted in the 1923 *Yearbook of Agriculture* the long-term tendency of American farmers to substitute land for labor. The *Yearbook* article attacked the Bureau of Reclamation for opening up more lands for irrigation, land frequently marginal for agricultural production (pp. 503–4). Marginal lands were also entering agriculture as immigrant farmers bought cheap cutover land from the timber barons.

The later abandonment of marginal farmland and the idling of cropland for the purpose of reducing surpluses and stabilizing prices reduced soil erosion and contributed toward general ecological diversity. These changes were given greater impetus following the dust storms of the 1930s, through the soil conservation movement (Bennett, 1964) and the institutionalization of this movement in the Soil Conservation Service and the Agricultural Stabilization and Conservation Service, with their various educational and financial assistance programs. By 1968, according to Clawson (1972:102), 36 percent of the cropland had either been "adequately treated" or had never required special treatment. In any case, the cropland of the U.S. is in much better shape today than it was in the 1920s. Contrary to Marsh's dire prophecy of 1864, much land that had been abandoned for crops has healed the scars of erosion and misuse. (This has been particularly true in the Piedmont of the Southeast where some of the worst erosion problems occurred. Since the 1930s more than half of the cropland in that region has been abandoned to grow up in weeds, shrubs, and ultimately trees.)

However, the record of adoption of soil conservation practices has been mixed. Frey's (1952) investigation of soil erosion control measures helps to explain the gap between the recommended erosion control measures and those actually followed. Only one-fifth of the farmers interviewed were following all recommended practices. Yet most farmers knew about the erosion control measures, and only 12 percent said they did not expect benefits from using more of them. Further questioning revealed that 40 percent explained that they were not prepared financially to make the shift toward forage production and livestock farming that the erosion control measures would have required. One-third mentioned competing demands for financial resources, and one-fifth said they might not be farming long enough to obtain the benefits of investments in erosion control measures.

A later study of 340 farmers in Illinois (Pampel, 1974) found that the adoption of commercial innovations was not related to the adoption of environmental innovations. While the adoption of commercial innovations was predicted by the amount of capital, amount of education, and commercial orientation, the environmental innovations were predicted only by age, with the older farmers adopting more innovations including reduced tillage of corn, rotation of crops, sod waterways, contour planting, terracing, and planting trees. These findings suggest that the older, more traditional farmers are most likely to be concerned with environmentally sound practices. Apparently, the concern for the maintenance of one's basic resources, including land and livestock, requires a different type of motivation than practices that have a more immediate economic payoff. Conservation concerns are likely to diminish as farming becomes highly commercialized and the work is done by hired workers or by tenant farmers rather than by the owner-operator. Large-scale agribusiness with its mechanized and specialized techniques has also had detrimental effects upon the natural environment (Wong, 1974). Mechanized tillage has resulted in the elimination of terraces and strip cropping and continuous cropping of cash crops has increased soil losses and the use of fertilizers and pesticides.

Within the Department of Agriculture, and even within the Soil Conservation Service, programs with conflicting goals have been promoted. The Soil Conservation Service built farm ponds and flood control impoundments at the same time that it was draining wetlands and channelizing streams — practices that ultimately increase the flood threat downstream. Other USDA programs were paying farmers to reduce the number of acres planted, while vast amounts of money were being spent on new technology to increase yields per acre. The specialized approach to the problems of agriculture, forestry, and land use has produced conflicts among the agencies responsible for these problems (Hardin, 1952) and a general failure to consider the total impact of policies and programs on the ecosystem.

The food surpluses of American agriculture since World War II are being changed by an increase in the demand for feed grains for livestock in Europe and the food-deficit countries in Asia and Africa. The increased price of oil imports from the Middle East has also stimulated a need for increased agricultural exports. These conditons are moving our agricultural policy toward the maximization of production with unintended, but dramatic, environmental consequences including: (1) increased cultivation of marginal lands; (2) increased grain production and reduced pasture and hay acreage; (3) further drainage of wetlands and field ditching and tilling; and (4) removal of fence rows, windbreaks, terraces, grass waterways, and strip-cropping to facilitate use of advanced technology for planting, fertilizing, irrigating, harvesting, and other more intensive farming techniques. These practices will tend to increase soil erosion and water pollution and reduce wildlife habitat, plant diversity, and lands for recreation.

Concurrent with the increased demand for food is the increasing cost and decreasing availability of energy. The "energy crisis" may reverse or at least attenuate the central tenet of American agricultural progress — the substitution of land, capital, and mechanical energy for human energy.

American agriculture has become the most efficient in returns to labor and capital but the least efficient in the production of usable energy relative to the energy input. Heichel (1973) has compared the energy efficiency of different cropping systems in the United States in 1915 with those of the 1970s. The measure of efficiency is the ratio of digestible calories of energy produced to the calories of cultural energy (human labor, animal labor, electricity, and fossil fuel) used in the production process. The substitution of fossil fuels and other energy sources for labor has stimulated greater total energy yields, but less dramatic gains in digestible energy. Among the cropping systems lowest in energy yield in relationship to energy used are sugar beets in California, peanuts in North Carolina, and irrigated rice in Louisiana. For a number of modern cropping systems, a ten- to fiftyfold increase in the use of cultural energy has produced only a two- or threefold increase in digestible energy. Feedlot beef is among the most inefficient forms of protein production, since 2 to 10 units of plant protein are needed to produce one unit of animal protein, with a potential for nine units of water pollution as feedlot wastes are washed into streams.

Also measuring cultural and digestible energy, the Steinharts (1973) reported that U.S. agriculture uses 5 to 10 calories of cultural energy to produce one calorie of food. In contrast, more primitive cultures, using primarily hand labor, produce 5 to 50 calories of food for every calorie invested (see also Cottrell, 1955). The present food-energy equation is changing. Fossil fuels are becoming scarcer and the major limiting factor of human activity in the future will likely be energy, not time. Under these conditions, the decreasing energy efficiency of mechanized agriculture must be changed.

Energy-reducing practices such as minimum-tillage cropping are likely to be extended. Marginal land will be brought into production to offset the declining use of fertilizer. Better use of organic fertilizer will reduce dependence upon inorganic fertilizers, and the increase in subsistence food production may reduce the energy demands of highly mechanized agriculture. In any event, the increasing shortage of food and energy will have both positive and negative consequences for the rural environment.

Rural Living: Homes and Second Homes. While the social-environmental consequences of changing agriculture and energy availability will depend heavily upon world population trends, the quality of the rural environment will also depend on the behavioral patterns of the existing population regarding other uses of the landscape. One such pattern is rural and suburban residential development for people who work in the city (Real Estate Research Corporation, 1974) and the additional 5 to 7 million American families who own recreational property (Ragatz, 1974). Zuiches and Fuguitt (1974) have found that given their preference, people prefer to live outside of cities of 50,000 or more, but within 30 miles of a city of that size. As more urbanites have realized their dreams, they have contributed to the energy crisis and to the air pollution of the freeways. They have taken land out of crop production directly with their spacious homesites and indirectly through highway systems necessary for access to the best of both worlds. They have robbed the central city of its tax base and strained rural institutions with demands for police, fire, ambulance, and sanitary services which are most costly to provide for dispersed homes.

The expansion of permanent and second homes into rural areas presents special environmental problems as urban families search for a better quality of life. The commercial strip typically follows the commuter to his bedroom community, and the unplanned recreational community develops into a rural slum without basic social institutions and services.

Specific policies such as the federally guaranteed loan program for single family dwellings have had the unintended consequence of promoting sprawling suburbia. Each year about a half-million acres of land are converted to urban use and another half-million are converted to highways, airports, and reservoir sitings (Extension Committee on Organization and Policy, Subcommittee on Environmental Quality, 1974). At the same time, reliance on the property tax for local revenue has prompted local officials to permit residential and recreational development with tax base benefits but hidden costs of services.

Outdoor Recreation—Fragile Satisfactions. It is not only commuters and second-home owners who escape the city. The Friday night surge of urbanites to the mountains, lakes, streams, and forests for outdoor recreation has become a common pattern. As leisure time increases and the work world provides less opportunity for expressive and integrative activities, leisure activities become an important part of our life-style and deserve greater attention by social scientists (Cheek, 1972; Burch, 1974a).

The rural areas with most direct contact with urban people are in national, state, and local parks. Total annual visits to national parks are about equal to the population of the country, total visits to state parks are twice that, and those to city or county parks are about six times the population. The visits occur on about 50 million acres in the 50 states. A study of recreational demand and its impacts on the Upper Great Lakes Region estimates a 45 to 72 percent increase in recreation in that area from 1972 to 1980 (Cooper, 1973). Since the 1950s, visits to state and national parks have increased at a rate of about 10 percent per year (Clawson,

1972:77–79). Visits to Corps of Engineer recreational areas and TVA reservoirs have increased at a similar rate. But participation patterns may be altered as real income declines, energy prices rise, and the percentage of young adults stabilizes.

While an increasing number of Americans participate in outdoor recreation, many find problems rather than satisfaction. The conflict between landowners and hunters has received considerable attention by social scientists (Howard and Longhurst, 1956; Klessig, 1970; McIntosh, 1967; Munger, 1968; Stoddard, 1969). Forestry practices, public access to lakes, scenic versus improved roads, and regulation of snowmobiles and other off-road vehicles are other sources of conflict. In addition, friction may develop because of differences in values between the people who live in the hinterland and the people who visit the hinterland.

Since the Wilderness Act of 1964, we have formally set aside additional acres for wilderness, but the very people who fought to keep out the ranchers, lumbermen, and miners are now stumbling over each other's campsites. We have provided greater public access to lakes, but users with bigger motors have endangered swimmers, swamped canoeists, and disrupted fishermen. On streams, parallel conflicts have developed between trout fishermen, canoeists, and rafters. Burch (1974b) has suggested that the problem of the "carrying capacity" of recreational lands is more social than biological. While a person goes to the wilderness to be free of social constraints, "wilderness" is socially defined, and its use must be governed by social as well as biological norms. The search for solitude and beauty is widespread, but the rewards are fragile and must be protected (Klessig, 1973).

The impact of reservoirs is also one of the few resource developments receiving significant attention by social scientists. River flooding became more frequent as forests were cut over, grasslands cropped and grazed, wetlands drained, streams channelized, and highways and cities paved. Building dams appeared to solve the flooding problems and at the same time provided reservoirs for recreation in areas without natural lakes. The Corps of Engineers has built over 250 dams primarily for flood control. While the first dams were justified solely for flood control, they have increasingly been justified for recreational and other purposes in order to provide acceptable benefit-cost ratios.

The effects of reservoir construction upon the natural and human resources of an area are no longer regarded as all positive. The larger dams require moving people out of the valleys, sometimes involving whole towns and villages. The costs of the social disruptions of families and businesses affected by the dams have usually been given little attention (Wilkening and Gregory, 1941). The returns from land sold for a project were seldom enough to meet all the costs of relocation and adjustment. Evidence indicates that reservoir projects have brought increased economic gain to some communities (Saitta and Bury, 1973), but in others the boom never materialized after the construction ended and water and sewer systems were enlarged (Smith, Hogg, and Reagan, 1971). As with other types of developments, reservoirs in the long run have net costs and benefits in social as well as economic terms, depending upon how they are adapted to the natural, social, and economic conditions of the area.

Perception of the costs and benefits of impoundments vary widely (Becker and Burdge, 1971; Dasgupta, 1967; Peterson and Ross, 1971; Wilkinson, 1966). The organized opposition of citizen groups has been successful in halting or in stopping a number of dams (Bultena, 1974; Smith, 1974). However, these groups need the stimulus and expertise of outside persons in order to be effective in countering the efforts of government supported bureaucracies and business interests. Social scientists need to assess the effect of impoundments upon the economy, social institutions, and other aspects of the quality of life for both local residents and potential users of the area (Wilkening et al., 1973).

In any case, the boom in dam building has almost halted following the opposition of local farmers whose land is affected and of environmental groups striving to maintain the natural features of streams and rivers. Impoundments are another case of tampering with nature that may produce more environmental and social problems than they solve.

Forestry—Diversity or Efficiency. Throughout the early development of this country Americans viewed trees as unlimited virgin timber or as obstacles to cropping and grazing. Not until the middle of the 19th century was there concern for the destruction and lack of productive regrowth of forests (Udall, 1963:98-100). With the national forests established in the early twentieth century, a professional corps of foresters was trained. They provided the basis for the improvement of forestry practices on 142 million acres of public owned land, and 67 million acres of forest industry land. They have had less influence on the 151 million acres of farm woodlots and 149 million acres of privately owned recreation and miscellaneous forest lands. These woodlots grow substantially less timber per acre (Frutchey and Williams, 1965). Although improved stocking, genetic strains, and other timber stand techniques could more than double productivity, small private owners have been reluctant to adopt such practices because (1) the added returns are almost negligible for owners selling a low average annual output of forest products; (2) forest production is a long-term enterprise that does not fit into the shorter time span of the operations and plans of an individual landowner; and (3) most landowners receive noneconomic rewards from woodlots, such as hunting, recreation, firewood, and the like, which might be threatened by systematic silviculture.

With an estimated 80 percent increase in the demand for timber products between 1962 and the year 2000 (Clawson, 1972:137), the dilemma between the short-term private interest in the management of private property and the long-term public interest in maintaining adequate timber supplies will intensify. The application of improved management practices to maximize cellulose production often conflicts with the demands for grazing by livestock interests (Foss, 1960; Wengert, 1955), the demands for wilderness areas by preservationists, and the need for watershed protection for reservoirs. Some of these conflicts are fought out in government agencies, some in the courts, and some with the threat of violence on the part of the conflicting parties.

Mining—A Deepening Conflict. Our industrial society needs energy and minerals as much as it needs food, living space, recreation, and wood. While recycling and energy conservation could drastically reduce the amount of coal, oil, and minerals needed, mining continues to be an essential use of the rural environment. However, disregard of the desecrating effects of mining upon the landscape and local communities has been persistent.

Metallic mining has led to environmental conflicts on two principal fronts. Processing of metallic sulfide ores has produced classic examples of rural air pollution: Missoula, Montana before the clean-up there, and Sudbury, Ontario with the world's largest smokestack. The disposal of mining wastes—rock, tailings, and mine drainage—produces a different set of problems. A lawsuit against the dumping of 67,000 tons of tailings into Lake Superior each day by Reserve Mining Company has gone all the way to the Supreme Court but is still unresolved.

The major focus of environmental concern relating to mining has been on strip mining. Large firms have stripped and mined the coal with little regard for protecting the land or the streams from erosion and acid leakage. The profits of extraction have been siphoned off to the urban centers, while the maintenance of a stable, local economy and culture has been ignored.

Large areas in the Midwest and West are also underlain with coal, or shale oil, part of which can be surface mined. These areas include productive farm lands in Illinois and Iowa. Surface mining is already underway in those states as well as in Colorado, Utah, Montana, Wyoming, and the Navajo lands of the Southwest. While it is estimated that only about 5 percent of the 3 trillion tons of coal reserves of this country are strippable, this process is currently the most "efficient" method in many areas. Unfortunately, stripping may glean only 10 percent of the total coal deposits while making the costs of further extractions higher.

These physical resource problems are further compounded by legal institutions that relate to them. Ownership of mineral rights is unclear; broad-form mining deeds allow alteration of the land surface, and leases are drawn up by mining companies, which know the value of the mineral resource, while they are signed by small landowners, who have no working knowledge of mining or property rights.

Surface mining is another illustration of the inadequacy of the present institutional structure of private property to deal with the extraction and use of our natural resources. These resources are often located in areas where local government is not prepared to protect public interests in the face of large-scale developments (Caudill, 1971). Regional, state, and the larger public interests are involved; yet the mechanisms for balancing the local, regional, and larger public interest are not present within our existing institutional arrangements.

Transmission Systems—Rural Impact and Urban Use. While the institutional arrangements for auto transport on highway systems are highly developed in our society, attitudes toward highways are changing. New highways, especially interstates, have absorbed valuable farmland, disrupted farm operating units, and acted as barriers between communities. The siting of power plants, once welcomed by communities because of tax benefits, has now become controversial, and confusion prevails over what level of government and which agency in that level should decide on various permits. Who should decide whether or not the Navajo Indians in the Four Corners should have their air degraded in order that Los Angeles residents can keep their air conditioners running? Control over transmission lines and systems, oil and gas pipelines, the movement of hazardous substances on common corridors, and waste disposal sites has aroused controversy, as fewer people passively accept land uses that have harmful effects upon their natural and social environments.

Control over the movement of people, energy, and basic raw materials is a very effective way of directing the growth of a society. Highways, railways, pipelines, and power lines could be restricted to corridors that would then become the center for development and commercial activity. However, such restrictions have been bitterly opposed because most communities are not yet willing to give up their desire for unrestricted growth.

Ecosystem Integrity—Environmental Attitudes and Action. Attitudes toward the environment grow out of the experience with the environment and the use made of it. For the American pioneer, the clearing of the forests and the breaking of the prairie sod were great obstacles. Nature had to be subdued before the pioneer could grow his crops and begin a settled way of life.

The abundance of natural resources in America gave little incentive for its conservation or preservation. In the views of Tocqueville, the richness of the land and its natural resources in America were unequalled anywhere (Ekirch, 1973). Literature in the early nineteenth century presented a romantic view of nature and gave rise to an interest in the values of rural life, but it was naive about the economic realities that threatened those values. The prodding of European scientists and scholars like Schurz and Marsh (Udall, 1963) began to foster recognition of the significance of the wealth of the natural resources in America. However, the themes of expansion and conquest of the forces of nature were dominant, despite the warnings of those who foresaw the depletion of these resources and the need for their conservation and preservation.

Although conservation and preservation thinking was grounded in the writings of Catlin, Emerson, and Thoreau (Huth, 1957), these values did not reach the highest levels of decision making until President Theodore Roosevelt called the 1908 White House Conference on Conservation. Preservationists like John Muir, who had a different perspective than the President's, were excluded and formed the Sierra Club; the philosophical split between utilitarian users, such as Roosevelt and Pinchot, and aesthetically motivated preservationists has never healed.

The concern for environmental problems began to take the form of a movement in the latter 1960s and early 1970s. The utilitarian position commonly taken by farmers, miners, and lumbermen had become institutionalized in the federal agencies such as the Forest Service and the Soil Conservation Service. The preservationist position more likely taken by urbanites not directly dependent upon the land took form through such organizations as the Sierra Club, the Wilderness Society, and the National Audubon Society (Morrison, Hornback, and Warner, 1972). Environmentalists maintain that certain land, water, and wildlife should be protected for aesthetic and controlled recreational use and preserved to maintain the integrity of the ecosystem for people's future enjoyment.

Aldo Leopold, founder of the Wilderness Society, earned the title "Father of the Environmental Movement" with an environmental bible entitled *Sand County Almanac* in which he developed the land ethic:

All ethics so far evolved rest upon a single premise; that the individual is a member of a community of interdependent parts. His instincts prompt him to compete for his place in the community, but his ethics prompt him also to cooperate. . . . The land ethic simply enlarges the boundaries of the community to include soils, water, plants, and animals, or collectively: the land. . . . A thing is right when it tends to preserve the integrity, community, and beauty of the natural environment. It is wrong when it tends to do otherwise (1969:203, 204, 224, 225).

Leopold felt that the economic basis for the use of natural resources must be balanced with a moral obligation toward nature.

Environmental concern has clearly been stronger in some quarters than in others. It is perhaps not surprising that such concern grew most rapidly in the cities, where the quality of the natural environment had deteriorated most dramatically, rather than in rural areas (Yoesting and Burkhead, 1971; McEvoy, 1972; Dillman and Christenson, 1972). Buttel and Flinn (1974) reported that Wisconsin farmers were likely to consider environmental problems to be less important than other problems. With a national sample they found that awareness of environmental problems was positively associated with size of place of residence, but that support for environmental *reform* was only slightly correlated with place of residence. Age, income, and education were more important variables. Younger, well educated citizens felt the greatest moral obligation to nature. Other studies have shown that environmental movement and wilderness users are drawn disproportionately from upper middle class professions (Gale, 1972; Harry, Gale, and Hendee, 1969). Dunlap and Heffernan (1975), building on the work of Gale, show that a positive association exists between environmental concern and involvement in outdoor recreation. Their findings support Gale's conclusion that concern for those aspects of the environment is closely associated with specific recreational activities. For example, little association is evident between fishing and hunting and general environmental concern, except that each recreational group is concerned with enhancing the conditions for its particular activity (Fortney et al., 1972; Lambert et al., 1974).

In a series of studies, Heberlein (1972 and 1975) has shown a relationship between the recognition of social norms and the feeling of personal responsibility for littering behavior, the use of lead-free gasoline, and energy conservation. His findings suggest that people must not only be socialized to accept the general norms of conserving resources, but they must also develop the feeling that they have a personal obligation to do something about these problems. Without this, laws or regulations are not likely to affect behavior appreciably. This means that an awareness of the consequences of the behavior for the individual and his groups must become known. Only with these moral sanctions are financial subsidies and legal penalties likely to become effective.

However, the main thrust of the environmental movement has evolved from awareness to political conflict as the environmental movement has matured from teach-ins and clean-ups to the process of institutionalizing concern in laws, administrative codes, and court precedents.

PUBLIC POLICY ISSUES AND PROGRAMS RELATED TO THE RURAL ENVIRONMENT.

The nature of policy issues relating to rural environment or to any other topic depends upon an empirical situation, a conceptualization of the causal elements in that situation, a conception of the desired state of affairs, and an ideology as to how that state can be attained. We take the view that changing the individual will have limited effect upon people's relationship to the environment without changing the structural conditions for access to and the use of natural resources. This requires collective action and the imposition of restraints upon the individual in the interests of group survival and welfare. This process will involve the resolution of conflicts through a change of attitudes and values as well as through a system of coercive measures.

Our overall concern is with the social structures that can foster the enhancement and survival of human life and that are in turn based upon maintenance of the biophysical ecosystems of which that life is a part. Following is a list of the major issues related to the rural environment that must be dealt with in this process.

1. Commercial agriculture that responds to the economic forces of the market frequently conflicts with the public values of quality land and water resources. The farmer, faced with high costs of land, labor, and capital, has little choice but to utilize his resources to the limit unless

restrictions are placed upon all farmers. The issue is whether there should be economic incentives for encouraging farmers to follow soil and water protection practices or legal coercion prohibiting certain agricultural practices.

2. Another aspect of this problem is how to balance the increasing demands for food, fiber, energy, and minerals with the social and psychological needs for open spaces and natural settings. The issue is how we balance the sustenance and other material needs of people as biological organisms with their aesthetic and cultural needs as creative human beings.

3. Private property rights clash increasingly with the right to a clean environment through the protection of land, water, and forest resources. Public control over private property has been successfully resisted for the most part, but the sanctity of private property rights is being challenged, as exemplified by a recent ruling of the Wisconsin Supreme Court upholding the constitutionality of public zoning of private land:

An owner of land has no absolute and unlimited right to change the essential natural character of his land so as to use it for a purpose for which it was unsuited in its natural state and which injures the rights of others (Just v. Marinette County, 1972).

The issue is the extent to which the traditional and absolute right to private property will be modified in recognition that every piece of private real estate is part of a whole which it influences and by which it is influenced.

4. Multiple land use sets the stage for conflicts that are difficult, if not impossible, to resolve and that may reduce the quality of use for all purposes (Klessig, 1973). The issue is which uses should receive priority and how these particular uses can be allocated to prevent discrimination among groups with different interests.

5. Conflict also exists between present and future use of resources. According to Catton (1974), we are now harvesting "ghost acres," and we have the choice of how long we wish to continue this process at the expense of future generations. The Faustian bargain of selling the future for present indulgence is common. The issue is whether future options are foregone with highways, dams, strip mines, and other irreversible changes in land and water use, or whether options are preserved for future generations.

6. There is a constant tension between satisfying the needs of the individual versus those of the group, those of the community versus those of the region and the larger society. The issue is what the public interests are, and how these interests can be integrated into programs that allow for the protection of resources for the total society without the loss of local autonomy.

We discuss briefly here the major public strategies and techniques for coping with these policy issues.

Land Management through Public Ownership. About one-third of the nation's land is still under public ownership. The U.S. Forest Service manages 186 million acres of lumber, grazing, and recreational lands, and the Bureau of Land Management manages 465 million acres containing much of the nation's mineral and energy resources. While proprietary power offers the potential for sound management, vested interests such as those of lumbermen, cattlemen, oilmen, and miners have developed effective lobbies to protect their interests in the public lands.

Additional lands are being brought under federal control as scenic rivers and parkways. State ownership of lands for parks and wildlife protection continues to increase. Private organizations such as the Nature Conservancy are purchasing strategic natural areas for preservation and scientific purposes. Public lands are likely to increase and have general public support, but the extent of such purchases is limited by the increasing cost of these lands as they are competed for by private developers and investors.

Tax Policies. Taxes may be used to promote or to discourage real estate development, to make other changes in land use, to encourage energy conservation, or to reduce water pollution. To encourage forest management, the state of Wisconsin contracts with forest landowners and pays most of the property tax in return for a severance tax when the timber is cut (Solberg, 1961). Several states (New York, California, Oregon, Wisconsin) are experimenting with preferential taxation for agricultural land, wetland, and other open space to prevent the forced subdivision of land on the urban fringe due to existing tax structures based on potential use rather than present use (Barrows, 1974).

Yet another method of achieving the same goal is the public purchase of development rights or scenic easements, which allow present land use to continue but prevent residential and commercial encroachment until the public agency deems it appropriate (Wengert and Graham, 1974).

Changing local property tax structures, through state aids originally designed to provide equal educational opportunity, can dampen the pro-development ardor of local units of government. In Wisconsin, state aid to equalize educational opportunities in public schools has reduced pressures on local communities to attract commercial, residential, and recreational development, since increasing the tax base per pupil would reduce the state aid.

Also, taxes on pesticides and on other polluting chemicals could be used to discourage their use and to pay for environmental costs to the community.

Grants-in-Aid and Cost-Sharing. Beginning with the Federal Water Pollution Control Act in 1956, technical assistance and grants have been provided for the construction of municipal and other waste treatment facilities. Federal assistance is also available for parks, mass transportation, and wildlife protection, and to private landowners for soil conservation practices, timber production, and wildlife habitat plantings. These grants provide support for policies without complete state or federal ownership and control.

Incentives are needed for the reduction of energy consumption. Information, technology, and credit are needed for the small farmer who tends to use less energy in the form of fossil fuels than large-scale farmers. The commercial farmer also needs assistance in shifting his technology to sounder environmental practices.

Education and Extension of Environmental Problems and Policies. Lack of knowledge of environmental programs and policies is a major hindrance to the solution of environmental problems. Education and information programs are needed for all ages and classes of people to provide a basis for both individual and public action.

While there are many modes of private and public educational delivery systems, the Cooperative Extension System provides one example. With proven effectiveness in transmitting information on technical agriculture to American farmers, it is now attempting to broaden its scope to include natural resources.

Regulatory Power. Due to the public nature of environmental problems, changes in individual knowledge and attitudes are not sufficient to bring about changes in behavior. There are conflicting public interests that can only be resolved in the legislative, executive and judicial bodies. Many laws and regulations regarding the rural environment have been enacted at the federal, state, and local levels. Zoning ordinances, sanitary codes, air pollution standards, water pollution permits, and environmental impact statements have probably received the most attention, but many others affect the use of land, water, plants, and wildlife.

The concept of zoning is very well established in property law, but it has normally been employed to protect residential urban home owners from incompatible uses of property. More recently, zoning has been extended to protect resources from overexploitation as well as to minimize user conflict in rural areas. It is being considered for use in the regulation of land use practices to protect water from soil and nutrients. The federal government has no zoning power, and a bill to provide money to states for land use planning was narrowly defeated in 1974. The states have delegated their zoning powers to local units of government and now are finding it difficult to reclaim them. Hawaii has the most extensive recent experience with state land use planning and implementation efforts. States are likely to develop standards and provide technical assistance to local units of government that are responsible for drawing up the ordinances and enforcing them. One study (Kronus and van Es, 1972) has shown that passing a law does not mean compliance with restrictions on the use of nitrogen fertilizer and other chemicals by farmers. Institutional arrangements for defining the relationships of the levels of government and of public and private spheres and for disseminating information about needed regulations are required for effective regulation of land use practices.

The passage of the National Environmental Policy Act in 1969 helped turn national concern from the quantity to the quality of life. The chief implementation device in the act was a requirement for an environmental impact statement for all federal or federally related projects. Although the law required that the nature of social impacts be specified in the statement, this has usually been superficially included, if at all. Currently, the Rural Sociological Society, the American Sociological Association, and other professional associations and groups are considering guidelines for the preparation and analysis of the social impacts of environmental decisons (Wolfe, 1974; Johnson and Burdge, 1975). In addition to the methodological and conceptual problems of doing social-impact analysis, there is no assurance that the statements will be used in making decisions. Yet these analyses provide the public with knowledge of the social consequences of planned interventions and provide sociologists with an opportunity to study the effects of such interventions.

Public Participation in Environmental Decisions. While the need for public involvement is being recognized, the actual mechanisms for citizen involvement are still crude. Clark and Stankey (1976) have developed a method for utilizing a wide range of public inputs into resource policy decisions. It combines the use of letters, surveys, testimony, and other forms of expression by the public with techniques for analyzing and interpreting these inputs. Hendee and colleagues of the Forest Service are working on methods of involving sociologists in resource management. But Twight (1975) shows that public involvement through local meetings may be counterproductive in obtaining support for Forest Service policies. When held in rural areas away from urban centers, such meetings attract primarily the alienated and those opposed to broad management policies. Other methods of increasing the extent and depth of citizen representation through workshops and quasi experiments are being tested (Hornback, 1975; Heberlein, 1976).

The evolution of planning and the question of type of public participation point out central dilemmas for a complex democratic, technocratic society. Can the specialization of experts and the involvement of citizens in both decision making and implementation be reconciled? Many competing interests are impinging upon the rural environment, and how it is used for the present as well as future generations will depend upon how these interests are integrated. The management of rural environmental resources for human well-being and ecosystem integrity will require the pragmatic cooperation of social and natural scientists, of representatives of local and broader interests, of private and public expertise. In sum, future institutional arrangements must harmonize individual needs with the collective interest.

Part 3

POPULATION

3 People on the Land
CALVIN L. BEALE

IN 1790 when the first census was taken we were overwhelmingly a rural nation, with 95 percent of the people living in the countryside or in towns of less than 2,500 population. Despite the vast space available to be settled, the emerging cities grew more rapidly than the rural population in every succeeding decade except one (Table 3.1).

From the time of independence until the Civil War, the rural population (as defined by the Census) grew by an average of 2.5 to 3.0 percent a year. After the Civil War, rural growth (and national growth) gradually slowed. By 1900, rural population increase had diminished to about 1.0 percent annually, as the supply of new lands dwindled and as growing rural towns reached urban size and were reclassified. The farm population composed about three-fifths of the rural total. Farm population reached a peak, apparently in 1916, and then, despite an ample number of births, declined during World War I as thousands of people left for the cities (Table 3.2).

Over the years, the urban population had consistently grown more rapidly than the rural. By 1880 the country had its first city of a million people as New York passed that mark, and by 1910 Philadelphia and Chicago had been added to the list. Yet it came as a shock in 1920 to realize that the United States was a predominantly urban nation for the first time in its history. The census for that year showed 54.3 million urban residents and 51.8 million rural.

Ironically, it was not until 1920 that interest in farm population developed sufficiently to have farm residents separately identified in the decennial census. Although the farm element of the rural population was diminishing after World War I, rural-nonfarm people increased. This latter population has always been rather heterogeneous and thus somewhat difficult to characterize. Some of it consisted of people in ex-

Calvin L. Beale is Leader, Population Studies, Economic Development Division of the Economic Research Service, U.S. Department of Agriculture.

Table 3.1. Urban and rural population of the United States, 1790–1970.

Year	Total		Urban		Rural		Percent of Total	
	Population	Percent change from preceding census	Population	Percent change from preceding census	Population	Percent change from preceding census	Urban	Rural
	(mil)		*(mil)*		*(mil)*			
Current urban definition								
1970	203.2	13.3	149.3	19.2	53.9	-0.3	73.5	26.5
1960	179.3	18.5	125.3	29.3	54.1	-0.8	69.9	30.1
1950	151.3	...	96.8	...	54.5	...	64.0	36.0
Previous urban definition								
1940	132.2	7.3	74.7	8.0	57.5	6.3	56.5	43.5
1930	123.2	16.2	69.2	27.5	54.0	4.4	56.1	43.9
1920	106.0	15.0	54.3	29.0	51.8	3.2	51.2	48.8
1910	92.2	21.0	42.1	39.2	50.2	9.1	45.6	54.4
1900	76.2	21.0	30.2	36.7	46.0	12.5	39.6	60.4
1890	63.0	25.5	22.1	56.5	40.9	13.4	35.1	64.9
1880	50.2	30.2	14.1	42.7	36.1	25.8	28.2	71.8
1870	38.6	22.6	9.9	59.3	28.7	13.6	25.7	74.3
1860	31.4	35.6	6.2	75.4	25.2	28.4	19.8	80.2
1850	23.2	35.9	3.5	92.1	19.6	29.1	15.3	84.7
1840	17.1	32.7	1.8	63.7	15.2	29.7	10.8	89.2
1830	12.9	33.5	1.1	62.6	11.7	31.2	8.8	91.2
1820	9.6	33.1	0.7	31.9	8.9	33.2	7.2	92.8
1810	7.2	36.4	0.5	63.0	6.7	34.7	7.3	92.7
1800	5.3	35.1	0.3	59.9	5.0	33.8	6.1	93.9
1790	3.9	...	0.2	...	3.7	...	5.1	94.9

Source: U.S. Censuses of Population.

Table 3.2.   Farm population, 1880–1975.

Year	United States			South	Rest of Nation
	Farm population	Percent of total population	Percent of rural population		
	(mil)			*(mil)*	*(mil)*
1975	8.9	4.2	. . .	3.1	5.7
1970	9.7	4.8	18.0	3.8	6.0
1965	12.4	6.4	. . .	5.2	7.2
1960a	15.6	8.7	28.9	7.2	8.5
1955	19.1	11.6	. . .	9.2	9.9
1950	23.0	15.3	42.3	11.9	11.2
1945	24.4	17.5	. . .	12.7	11.7
1940	30.5	23.2	53.2	16.4	14.1
1935	32.2	25.3	. . .	17.2	15.0
1930	30.5	24.9	56.5	16.4	14.2
1925	31.2	27.0	. . .	16.8	14.4
1920	32.0	30.1	61.8	17.1	14.9
1915	32.4	32.4	. . .	. . .	. . .
1910	32.1	34.9	63.9	16.7	15.4
1900	29.9	39.3	65.2	14.2	15.6
1890	24.8	39.3	60.6	10.7	14.0
1880	22.0	43.8	61.0	. . .	. . .

Sources: Banks, 1976; Banks and Beale, 1973; and Truesdell, 1960.
aIncludes Alaska and Hawaii, beginning 1960.

tractive industries other than agriculture—such as mining, timber work, or fishing. A key element comprised the residents of the thousands of rural towns that served the farming population. Some of the rural-nonfarm population was located around small manufacturing plants, such as textile or lumber mills. And a growing segment represented the suburbanites whose settlements away from the cities first flourished with the advent of the street car and interurban lines and were further stimulated by the commuting possibilities of the automobile. Here for the first time was a rural component whose direct affiliations were highly urban but whose residential values were not.

The Depression period of the 1930s had mixed effects on the size and location of the rural population. Rural people increased in number in many states, especially in the timbered and upland areas—such as the Appalachians—that might be called "back country." This growth seems to have occurred because conditions in the cities were so dire that the subsistence possibilities in the rural areas looked comparatively attractive. Outmovement was deferred until better times, and some return flow from the cities was received. On the other hand, the Great Plains region proved to be anything but a refuge area. Severe drought drove hundreds of thousands of rural people out. However, despite a sharp cutback in urban growth stemming from low birth rate and reduced migration to cities, the urban areas of the nation as a whole still increased in population more rapidly than the rural during the Depression (8 percent vs. 6 percent).

World War II radically altered the whole frame of reference for rural people. Beginning in 1940, the defense buildup, economic recovery, and compulsory military service that followed the fall of France combined to produce a tide of movement out of the countryside. We do not know what the precise dimensions of rural-urban migration were in this period, but we can say that from 1940 through 1944 a net of 8 million people left the farm population in an unprecedented outpouring. The number of people on farms dropped from 30.5 million to 24.4 million. Although there was some return to farms in the year after the war, the exodus soon resumed in somewhat reduced volume, and the rural population for the first time consisted primarily of nonfarm residents.

From 1947 to 1962, adjustments in farming proceeded very rapidly. Enlargement was the pervasive theme. Farmers acquired the ability to handle more acreage through mechanization and struggled to stay ahead of dwindling profit margins by increasing their volume. So there was much consolidation of farms. At the same time, the cities prospered. Although brief recessionary cycles occurred, urban industrial and business expansion was heavy. This expansion required much more labor force than was available in the cities, especially when new workers had to be drawn from the small birth cohorts of the 1930s. Recruits from the farms were essential to this urban growth. More than 16 million net outmigration from farms occurred, and the population remaining on farms was only a little above 14 million people by 1962.

The year 1962 was the last that saw a million-person net migration from farms. After 1962, the annual rate of net outmovement continued to average better than 5 percent a year until the end of the decade (Fig. 3.1), but from such a diminished base the absolute volume of migrants could only decline. By the end of the 1960s, the reduced exodus from farms had ceased to have any significant further impact on the growth of urban areas, and farm people had come to amount to less than a fifth of all rural people.

Loss of farm population was universal but not evenly distributed. It was clearly linked with concentration of people on small farms or on

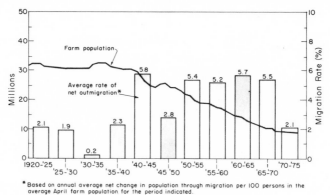

Fig. 3.1.   Farm population and migration, 1920–75.

previously unmechanized tenant farms. In 1940, more than half of all people on farms were in the South. A fourth of the southern farm population (4.4 million) was black, and the blacks were almost entirely tenants on cotton and tobacco farms, or, if owners, had places too small to support a family above the poverty level.

The tenants and small-scale owners who were most vulnerable to farm modernization trends either left farms in large numbers or else were not replaced by their children when they died or retired. Farm population in the South as a whole dropped by a remarkable 77 percent from 1940 to 1970, with a 90 percent drop among blacks. Even the smallest regional decline, in the north central states, was 54 percent. Among individual states, the least affected was Iowa, in the heart of the Corn Belt, where farm population dropped by 42 percent. Today Iowa has the largest farm population of any state (544,000 in 1970).

Over the last half century, the total rural population has remained surprisingly steady. The figure has rounded to 54 million in each of the last five censuses, except for 1940 when it hit 57 million under the former procedure that did not define metro suburbs as urban. In effect, the growth of the rural nonfarm population has equaled the drop in the farm population.

The stationary level of the national rural total conceals major internal changes (Table 3.3). Here a geographic look at the data is helpful. Several regions had extensive growth. One such region consists of the area surrounding the belt of major cities that stretches from Washington, D.C. to New England and then westward across the Lower Great Lakes to southeastern Wisconsin. Here a majority of the rural people live within the bounds of metropolitan areas and, although rural in residential setting, often relate to the large cities for work or services. This area has a sixth of

Table 3.3.   Rural population change in selected areas of substantial decline or growth, 1940–70.

Area	Rural Population		Percent Change 1940–70
	1970	1940	
	(thous)		
Declining areas			
Great Plains	2,412	3,536	−31.8
Western Corn Belt	2,822	3,648	−22.6
Southern Coastal Plain Cotton Belt	3,546	5,544	−36.0
Southern Appalachian Coal Fields	1,721	2,283	−24.6
Total	10,502	15,012	−30.0
Growing areas			
Pacific Coast and Southwest	1,614	1,112	45.0
Lower Great Lakes	5,369	3,824	40.4
Northeastern Coast	3,877	2,479	56.4
Southern Textile Piedmont	2,406	1,989	21.0
Florida Peninsula	758	323	134.3
Total	14,023	9,727	44.2

Source: U.S. Censuses of Population.

our total rural population, and the number of rural residents increased by nearly half from 1940 to 1970. Of 21 counties in the United States that contain over 100,000 rural people each, all but one are located in the area described above. In such counties, rural density may reach over 200 persons (or about 60 households) per square mile. Although some farming persists, the rural residents are overwhelmingly nonfarm.

A second area of rural growth has been the Southern Textile Piedmont. This upland region above the Fall Line extends from the Virginia–North Carolina border area to the Georgia-Alabama border. In effect, the new industrial South was born here in the post–Civil War period. Without any truly large cities except Atlanta, it has become an area intensely dependent on manufacturing, with many plants located in small towns. The rural population grew by about a fifth here from 1940 to 1970, despite the reclassification of much population as urban and a drastic cutback in farming.

The fastest growth of rural population has come in the Florida Peninsula. The numbers involved are much smaller than in the Piedmont or the northern industrial belts, but people living in rural locations increased by one and a third times from 1940 to 1970. Much of this is associated with retirement, of course, but Florida has attracted inmigrants of all ages to work in its largely service oriented economy.

Finally, one can note rapid rural growth all along the Pacific Coast and in the Southwest. The vast rural territory of this region tends to be sparsely populated as a whole, with some mountainous or desert areas virtually uninhabited, but the 30-year growth rate was 45 percent. Settlements are often clustered in valleys or related to water supply. Causes of growth vary, but mildness of winter climate, retirement, and the spillover effects of the major western cities all have been influential.

On the other hand, certain regions of the country in which the rural areas had been heavily agricultural experienced large declines in total rural population. Although the rural-nonfarm component often grew in such areas, it could not offset the extensive outflow of farm people. Thus, for example, the total rural population of the Great Plains — northern and southern combined — dropped by nearly a third from 1940 to 1970. This was and continues to be the agricultural area most remote from population centers.

An even higher rate of rural decrease was observed in the Cotton Belt sections of the Southern Coastal Plain, from South Carolina to East Texas. Here the 30-year decline amounted to 36 percent. Much of this loss reflected the exceptionally high outmigration of the black population to the cities, especially to major northern and western cities. In many counties, the rural white population increased in the Coastal Plains as diversification out of farming took place.

The third major farming area in which reduced numbers of farms precipitated overall rural population loss was the Western Corn Belt — that is, that part of the Corn Belt west of the Mississippi River. The changes were rather analogous to those in the Great Plains, but with more limited effect on total rural numbers. Rural people decreased by 23 percent in this prosperous farming territory.

A fourth area of comparative rural depopulation that merits mention is the Southern Appalachian Coal Fields. As the name implies, this area was dominated by mining rather than by farming. But the changes in coal mining employment were, if anything, more severe than those in farming. Coal lost much of its market in the postwar period and the coal mining industry also became swiftly mechanized. The attendant job loss, aggravated by the preexisting poverty of much of the area, impelled heavy outmovement. Thus, despite high fertility, the rural population fell by a fourth from 1940 to 1970.

In short, the United States reached the 1970s with its rural population about the same size it had been for several decades, but with much internal redistribution. This redistribution, in turn, reflected the steady movement away from rural dependence on extractive industries. In 1940, a slight majority of rural workers were still engaged in farming, mining, or timber work. As employment in all of these industries dropped it was replaced with jobs more typically associated with urban life, or by commuting. The result was not just a change in the social and economic basis of rural life, but also in the location of rural people.

SMALL TOWNS. In 1970 about one-fifth of the rural population lived in incorporated places of less than 2,500 inhabitants or in unincorporated towns of 1,000 to 2,499 people. The other four-fifths could be said to live in the open country, or in villages or other clusters of less than 1,000 people that have no incorporation. Statistics are not available to subdivide this latter group further, but an educated guess might be that 2 to 2.5 million people resided in the small unincorporated places. This would be no more than 5 percent of the rural total and would leave 75 percent in what might reasonably be called open-country settlement.

The "small town" has long had a reputation in the press and public mind as "dying" — to use the favorite adjective. A characterization of this nature is rarely acquired without some justification. There are indeed dying rural towns and even a parcel of dead ones. There have always been, at every stage of our history. Exhaustion of resources, political events, loss of transportation, natural disasters, decline of trading advantage, or other factors have been common reasons for change in a town's vitality. Many rural towns have declined in population in the modern era, but it can be shown that such loss has been characteristic only of the smallest places (Table 3.4). The majority of nonmetropolitan incorporated places of less than 500 people decreased in population in both the 1950s and the 1960s. However, this did not happen to the majority of larger rural towns. Thus at best the popular cliche should be the "dying *very* small town." The impression of universal small-town decline may be partly attributable to

Table 3.4. Population change in incorporated places, 1960-70.

Status[a] and size of Place[b]	Places			Population (thous)		Percent change 1960-70
	Total	Population gain 1960-70	Population loss 1960-70	1970	1960	
		(%)				
Total places	17,827	61.3	38.7	129,749	115,685	12.2
Metropolitan places	4,497	75.4	24.6	96,622	85,494	13.0
Central cities	256	53.9	46.1	60,790	57,658	5.4
Urban fringe	1,872	75.1	24.9	28,287	22,243	27.2
Not in urbanized areas	2,369	78.0	22.0	7,545	5,593	34.9
Nonmetropolitan places	13,330	56.6	43.4	33,128	30,191	9.7
10,000-49,999 people	673	64.6	35.4	15,140	13,714	10.4
5,000-9,999	731	66.5	33.5	5,612	5,122	9.6
2,500-4,999	1,145	65.3	34.7	4,454	4,042	10.2
1,000-2,499	2,562	63.7	36.3	4,390	4,018	9.3
500-999	2,600	60.3	39.7	2,030	1,861	9.0
Under 500	5,619	47.6	52.4	1,504	1,435	4.8

Source: Tabulations by the University of Wisconsin and Economic Research Service, USDA, based on 1960 and 1970 Censuses of Population.
[a] Metropolitan status as of 1963.
[b] Size of place as of 1960.

the fact that such towns have typically lost business functions, regardless of whether the population has dropped.

If one considers all towns of less than 2,500 population identified in the census (rural towns), their population increased from 8.9 million to 10.1 million during the 1960s, a gain of 14.0 percent. This growth was somewhat faster than total U.S. growth of 13.3 percent. Thus, far from dying, rural towns as a group were acquiring population faster than the nation as a whole, despite the large proportion of losers among the very small places. Inasmuch as the excess of births over deaths in rural towns is generally not high, the growth of 14.0 percent almost certainly involved some amount of net inmovement of people. This was particularly evident among places that were within metropolitan counties. Residence in rural towns within a metropolitan area but beyond the urbanized area has become increasingly popular. During the 1960s, rural towns of this description experienced a 40 percent gain in population.

Despite the emphasis placed in this discussion on the growth of the majority of rural towns in recent decades (other than the very smallest class), the major change in rural population that emerged in many areas in the 1960s occurred outside of incorporated places. In some sections this took the form simply of a shift from heavy population loss to minor loss. In other places, a moderate loss may have changed to a gain. All in all, the rural nonmetropolitan population of the United States outside of incorporated places went from 0.6 percent loss in the 1950s to a growth of 5.7 percent in the 1960s. Compared to the beginning of that decade, more people today are living in the open country or in villages and commuting to cities for work or for trade and services, even when the city in question is a nonmetropolitan place rather than a large center. Although data on the number of rural people who commute to urban places to work are not available, the Census does show that the proportion of employed rural people who commute to locations outside of the county in which they live has increased.

An additional factor leading to more open-country settlement is the growth of the retired population and the spread of rural retirememt areas outside of the conventional Florida and Arizona locations. Especially in scenic regions and/or along the shorelines of oceans, bays, lakes, and reservoirs, people by the thousands have been retiring to rural areas, often in open-country locations outside the rural cities and towns.

RURAL FERTILITY. Throughout American history birth rates have been higher in rural areas than in the cities. Benjamin Franklin observed the lower birth rate of the cities in 1751 (Grabill, Kiser, and Whelpton, 1958). And it has been shown that as early as 1800 the ratio of white children under 5 years old to women 20–44 years old was 56 percent higher in rural areas than in the small cities that constituted the U.S. urban population in that day (Grabill, Kiser, and Whelpton, 1958). Thus the relative growth potential of the rural population has been affected by birth rate and not just by migration. Both rural and urban fertility declined rather steadily from the time of the first censuses until 1940.

By 1940, at the end of the Depression, urban childbearing was below the level necessary for long-term population replacement, but rural childbearing was still above replacement. In the period 1935-40 it is estimated that childbearing in the U.S. urban population was only 73 percent of ultimate replacement needs, whereas that in rural areas was about 140 percent of replacement (U.S. Bureau of the Census, 1944). Thus rural fertility at its lowest historic level was high enough to exert substantial pressures for either rural population growth or outmigration as children came of age. The factors inducing migration led much of this potential growth to be channeled into outmovement to the cities. However, the comparatively large number of children per rural family did contribute to the size of the rural population at any given time, and differences in childbearing among rural groups contributed to differential patterns of regional growth or outmigration.

For two decades after 1940, the nation experienced a sharp resurgence in childbearing. The reasons for the upturn in births were complex, as demographers who constantly predicted an imminent end to it were to learn. Vastly improved economic conditions, wartime psychology, a lowering of the average age at marriage, and medically induced reductions in the incidence of involuntary childlessness all played important roles. Urban births increased more than rural. Thus an extended period of convergence of urban and rural birth rates began, unlike any known previous pattern.

By 1960 the revived birth rate had pushed the cumulative fertility of urban women somewhat above the replacement level, but rural fertility — which was already well above replacement — had risen also. As a result, a heavily disproportionate share of the childbearing that produced generational growth in the period came from rural people (Table 3.5). In 1960 rural women 35-44 years old comprised only 27 percent of all women of that age in the United States. However, they had contributed 66 percent of the childbearing from this cohort that was above replacement needs and that had thus contributed to the long-term growth of the total U.S. population.

After a third decade of higher (albeit waning) fertility in the 1960s, women 35-39 years old in 1970 — and thus 20-24 years old in 1955 — had experienced the highest fertility of any modern U.S. group even though they had not yet fully completed their childbearing. In this cohort, urban women had borne 2,866 children per 1,000 women, compared with 3,299 per 1,000 for rural women. The absolute urban-rural gap had been halved, and the level of urban fertility was nearly seven-eighths that of rural women. The "baby boom" had meant a 50 percent increase in urban fertility and a 15 percent increase in rural fertility. Although the rural population had a reduction in childless and one-child families, it also had

Table 3.5. Children ever born to women 35–44 years old in 1960 in the United States, by residence.

Residence	Women		Children Ever Born					
	Number	Distribution	Number	Per 1,000 women	Needed for parental replacement Per 1,000 women	In excess of replacement need		
						Per 1,000 women	Number	Distribution
	(thous)	*(%)*	*(thous)*				*(thous)*	*(%)*
Urban	8,988	73	20,351	2,264	2,084	180	1,618	34
Rural	3,348	27	10,058	3,004	2,084	920	3,080	66

Source: U.S. Census of Population.

a steady cutback in the proportion of very large families. Furthermore, the steady shift of rural families away from farming created a downward pressure on births, for no other occupation group has as consistently favored large families as have farmers.

Fertility data for somewhat younger women in 1970 indicate levels for both rural and urban women that are lower than those found for women of similar age ten years earlier. That is, women 25–34 in 1970 do not appear likely to equal the childbearing of women then 35–44, and married women under age 25 were lagging considerably behind the pace set by the group ten years older than themselves when they were very young. In these changes, the urban-rural differentials appear to have been maintained.

Since 1970, there has been no direct evidence of the relative trend of births in rural and urban areas. After a minor upturn of births nationally in 1969 and 1970, the trend turned downward again early in 1971, continued so until mid-1974, leveled out for more than a year, then resumed its decline in September 1975, nine months after the acute economic recession of the winter of 1974–75. The post-1970 decline was contrary to expectations, given the fact that the number of people of prime child-bearing age was growing steadily. It is not the purpose of this discussion to deal with the reasons for the post-1970 trend, but they could hardly fail to be related to factors such as the increased availability of abortion, the rise in age of marriage, and the heightened desire of women for roles other than motherhood.

The current movement of urban people into rural areas may introduce a larger component of people with urban family-size preferences. However, it seems clear from the journalistic literature on the subject as well as from field visits, that some of the urban-to-rural movement occurs among families looking for a more secure environment in which to rear their children. If there is selectivity of this nature, the present migration trend might not act to narrow the remaining difference in family size in the two populations.

Even though absolute levels of urban and rural fertility are no longer radically different, they are still wide enough to have implications for population growth, since only the children born in excess of replacement lead to eventual growth of population. Among U.S. women 35–44 years old in 1970, those in rural areas had borne enough children to produce a 59 percent increase in population from one generation to another. The comparable rate for urban women was 37 percent above replacement in 1970. At the present time, it appears that rural fertility is still above replacement level, whereas urban fertility has been below ultimate replacement for several years.

RURAL MORTALITY. Urban-rural differences in fertility are typically clearer than those relating to mortality—the other component of change due to vital events. Common sense tells us that country life has been associated with clean air, exercise, and comparative freedom from disease whose spread is fostered by crowds. But the traditional rural oc-cupations of farming and mining are still dangerous jobs, access to medical services is limited and time consuming, and the danger of deaths from automotive accidents is greater because of higher average speeds at which accidents occur in rural areas. The effects of rural life on health and mortality are both positive and negative.

Kitagawa and Hauser (1973) investigated metro and nonmetro differences in age-adjusted death rates for the period 1959–61. They found that on balance the death rate was 5 percent higher in metro areas of the United States than in nonmetro areas. All of this difference occurred among whites. No difference was ascertainable for other races. Differences were most pronounced in the Midwest, where they ranged up to 10 percent higher in metro areas. The researchers offered no suggestions about the reasons for the metro-nonmetro pattern; the data were not shown by cause of death. Sauer (1974) found that the lowest death rates of all in our society tend to be concentrated in rural and small-town areas of the Great Plains and the Western Corn Belt.

The national metro-nonmetro difference in mortality has not been sufficient to have major effect on relative growth, and is not as wide as the relative difference in urban and rural fertility rates. However, the overall pattern of mortality and fertility in combination is in the direction of favoring greater potential growth of the rural (and small-town) population through larger families and somewhat longer life. This fact is often masked by the effects of high net migration rates.

Several hundred counties in the country have had more deaths than births in one or more recent years, and the great majority of these counties are nonmetropolitan. But in most cases, this seemingly morbid condition occurs because heavy outmigration of young adults in the last several decades has created an age structure in which the number of young couples eligible to have children is small compared with the number of older people available to die. Or, less often, the area concerned is a retirement county in which the influx of older people has resulted in more deaths than would otherwise have occurred.

POST-1970 CHANGE. Since 1970, it has gradually become ap-parent that rural areas have indeed turned a corner in their ability to retain or acquire population. In hindsight it seems as though it should have been obvious that such a day was upon us. After all, the main source of exodus had been the flight from farms. With the farm population just a third of its former size by the late 1960s, how could one expect the outflow of farm people to continue? And with the continued crises in the cities over racial conflicts, riots, pollution, crime, and drugs, how long could the traditional sources of attraction to cities outweigh the disenchantment and second thoughts that were bound to affect the decisions of individuals and businesses?

Yet the process of bringing to public attention the extent and consequences of past rural-to-urban migration had taken so long to accomplish, and the momentum of acceptance of the information was so strong by 1970, it was difficult to reorient the public to the situation.

Population change since 1970 cannot be measured on a strict urban-rural basis, but it is possible to combine county data in a manner that reveals the nature of the movement. At the time of this writing, the data extend to 1974 (Table 3.6). In this period, the nonmetropolitan counties of the nation grew in population by 5.6 percent, while the metropolitan counties grew by 3.4 percent. More than half of the nonmetropolitan increase came from net inmovement of people. These rural and small-town counties had a net influx of 1.6 million people in the four and one-fourth year period, whereas in the previous ten years (1960-70) they had lost a net of 3.0 million by outmigration. This is a sharp reversal.

Some of the growing counties are adjacent to metropolitan areas and their gains may be viewed as stemming in part from the ever-expanding sprawl of settlement around the cities. However, if one considers only those completely rural counties that are not adjacent to a metropolitan area — and which thus are the most removed from immediate urban influence — one finds that these counties increased in population as a group by 6.1 percent from 1970 to 1974, compared with a decline of 4.3 percent from 1960 to 1970. Thus the renewal of rural population growth extends to the very core of rurality and is not limited to counties that contain small cities or that are contiguous to metropolitan areas.

If in addition to completely rural nonmetropolitan counties one considers those that contain a small city of up to 25,000 people, a 1970-74 growth rate of 5.7 percent if found. Such counties were nearly stationary in population from 1960 to 1970, increasing by just 2.8 percent in that entire decade. They have shifted from 2.9 million net outmovement of people in the 1960s to 1.4 million inmovement in the first part of the 1970s.

These are dramatic changes, but it must not be thought that all rural areas now have population increase. From 1970 to 1974 there were still 516 rural and small town counties that were declining in population. Most of them were in the Great Plains, scattered from North Dakota to Texas. The Western Corn Belt and the Mississippi Delta also had noticeable clusters of declining counties. Many of the declining counties are associated with high continued dependence on agriculture or with high proportions of black population. There is still some force for outmigration in such settings. However, even these areas have lost much of the momentum of their chronic population drain. Counties with a majority of blacks or with 35 percent or more employment in agriculture in 1970 have had in the early 1970s only a fraction of the net outmovement of the 1960s.

Perhaps the major single cause of truly rapid rural growth is the spread of retirement areas and recreation areas. Both typically occur in the same localities. The steady increase in the proportion of Americans who have good retirement incomes, the gradual reduction in age of eligibility

Table 3.6. Population change by metropolitan status and selected county characteristics.

Item	Number of Counties	Population Number 1974	Population Number 1970 (thous)	Population 1960	Population Percent change 1970-74	Population Percent change 1960-70	Net Migration 1970-74 Number (thous)	Net Migration 1970-74 Rate[a] (%)	Net Migration 1960-70 Number (thous)	Net Migration 1960-70 Rate[a] (%)
Total United States	3,097	211,392	203,212	179,323	4.0	13.3	2,076	1.0	3,001	1.7
Metropolitan status of counties[b]										
Metropolitan	628	153,930	148,809	127,191	3.4	17.0	461	0.3	5,959	4.7
Nonmetropolitan	2,469	57,463	54,404	52,132	5.6	4.4	1,614	3.0	−2,958	−5.7
Adjacent[c]	969	29,780	28,022	26,116	6.3	7.3	1,010	3.6	−705	−2.7
Nonadjacent	1,500	27,683	26,382	26,016	4.9	1.4	604	2.3	−2,253	−8.7
Entirely rural	623	4,618	4,353	4,548	6.1	−4.3	190	4.4	−553	−12.2
Characteristics of counties in 1970										
10 percent or more net inmigration at retirement ages[d]	360	8,653	7,554	6,340	14.5	19.2	932	12.3	624	9.8
15 percent or more	200	5,284	4,464	3,530	18.4	26.5	739	16.5	640	18.1
10.0–14.9 percent	160	3,369	3,091	2,810	9.0	10.0	193	6.2	−16	−0.6
Senior state college	187	9,031	8,434	7,463	7.1	13.0	323	3.8	91	1.2
No town of 25,000 people	2,328	46,740	44,230	43,010	5.7	2.8	1,431	3.2	−2,886	−6.7
30 percent or more employed in manufacturing	638	20,143	19,257	18,193	4.6	5.9	356	1.8	−746	−4.1
50 percent or more black population	97	1,709	1,713	1,900	−0.2	−9.8	−67	−3.9	−454	−23.9
10 percent or more military population	29	1,192	1,204	969	−1.0	24.3	−91	−7.5	28	2.8

Source: 1970 U.S. Census of Population, and U.S. Bureau of the Census, *Current Population Reports*.
[a]Net migration expressed as a percentage of the population at beginning of period indicated.
[b]Metropolitan status as of 1974.
[c]Counties adjacent to Standard Metropolitan Statistical Areas as of 1974.
[d]Counties with specified 1960–70 net inmigration rate for white persons 60 years old and over, 1970.

for retirement, the longer joint life of couples after retirement, and the reduced practice of older people living with their children all contribute to a growing supply of older people who choose to move but retain their own households when they retire. Much of this movement is going into rural areas, which often are the same areas that are favored for second-home vacation residences. Areas attracting retirees are no longer concentrated in the warm-winter climates of Florida and the Southwest. An impressive spread of retirement-age populations to other parts of the nation has developed. In recent years such areas as the northern half of the Lower Peninsula of Michigan, the Ozark Plateau, the Hill Country of Central Texas, and the Sierra Nevada foothills in California have all developed multicounty retirement districts. Other smaller districts show up in the southern Blue Ridge Mountains, around Puget Sound, in scattered areas along the Atlantic Coast, in northern Minnesota and Wisconsin, and western Oregon. All told, 360 counties can be identified in non-metropolitan territory in which a net inmigration of 10 percent or more took place in the 1960s among white residents who were 60 years of age or older in 1970. It should be stressed that newer rural retirement areas are not solely attracting elderly people; the areas may be attractive for other purposes, such as manufacturing or service businesses.

Perhaps the second most common source of rapid population increase in rural and small city areas has been the growth of colleges and univer-sities, especially state schools, which tend to be larger and more rapidly expanding than private schools. These locations are not geographically clustered, but rather tend to be in scattered counties, with three or four in a typical state. The evolution of former small teacher's colleges into full-scale colleges and universities and the location of many land grant schools in rural areas has provided the base for this growth during a period of rapid increase in number of youth of college age and in the practice of attending college. By 1980, the demographic force behind this expansion will have spent itself, at least for the moment, as the smaller birth cohorts of the 1960s reach college age. But the effect of college growth on rural and small-city areas in the last 30 years is not likely to be transitory. These institutions seem unlikely to recede to their former size, and they have altered the general amenity status and attractiveness of many com-munities. Despite the partial topping out of college enrollments in the last several years, the 187 nonmetropolitan counties that contain a senior state college or university increased in population by 7.1 percent from 1970 to 1974. This growth is not only well above the national average, but when annualized is also well above the rate observed in the same counties during the 1960s.

Growth of manufacturing has been strong in nonmetro areas, and during the 1960s nonmetro counties with a strong manufacturing base were much more retentive of population than were nonmetro counties as a whole. In the 1970s, however, this trend has been greatly modified. The nonmetro counties most dependent on manufacturing (in which 30 percent or more of all workers were in manufacturing industries in 1970) grew demographically by 4.6 percent from 1970 to 1974. This was enough to absorb the equivalent of their natural growth of people and a small amount of net inmovement, but was distinctly below the growth of non-metro counties as a whole (5.6 percent).

The new pattern of population change is not a trivial one and however long it may last, it has already made an impact. Take, for example, those nonmetro counties that contain no city of 25,000 or more people. Such counties grew by just one-fifth of the national growth rate during the 1960s. If such a ratio had persisted in the 1970s, these counties—which contain more than a fifth of the entire U.S. population—would have increased by not more than 375,000 people. Instead, 2.5 million more people are living in them than were doing so in 1970. These are significant numbers for so short a period.

Although the changes cited since 1970 have been couched in metro-nonmetro terms for convenience, the critical point of inflection of trend is up within the metropolitan category. The nation's major metropolitan areas with over 2 million people each have shifted to net outmigration in the 1970s. As a class, those having between 750,000 and 2 million people are still receiving some net inmovement of people and thus are behaving demographically more like the nonmetropolitan counties. We are experiencing simultaneously a general shift of people down the scale of city size and out from the city limits.

The trend does seem to have momentum to it. Much of the change in residential and business location preferences in recent times is surely not just emergence of a positive view of the rural areas and small towns but is also dissatisfaction with conditions in the cities. If the cities were to make visible progress in solving their problems, it would seem almost certain that the impetus to the countryside and small towns would be reduced. At the moment the image of the large metro centers continues to deteriorate, as fiscal woes impair efforts to cope with the unintended consequences of modern urbanism. The continuing increase in formally retired people should also support a continuation of rural and small-town growth, so long as a meaningful fraction of this population is disposed to relocate away from the cities. In just the five years from the beginning of 1970 to the beginning of 1975, the number of retired workers receiving Social Security benefits increased by nearly 25 percent—five times the growth of the total population. The growth of retired federal civil service workers is even faster.

Perhaps the major potential force for slowing rural growth is the possibility at some time of a distinct shortage of gasoline or truly major increase in its cost. The events of the oil embargo period appear not to have curtailed the growth in rural areas, if one can judge from the population trend data of 1974 compared with 1973. Perhaps it was too short a test. It is indisputable, though, that rural people have a higher per capita use of gasoline than do urban residents, and that they lack the public transportation alternatives available in a crisis in metropolitan areas.

To the extent that concern for children motivates rural inmigration, this factor should gradually diminish over the next decade at least. Because of the successively smaller birth cohorts since 1961, somewhat fewer families each year now find themselves with school age children.

It is essential to remember that rural growth does lead partially to urbanization. Using the conventional census definition of rurality, we had 54 million rural people in 1970. Unless the trend to settlement in the open country becomes so pronounced that almost no growth of towns occurs, it is doubtful that we could ever have more than a few additional million people living under settlement patterns that would continue to be classified as rural. I suspect 60 million is an outside limit. Similarly the growth of nonmetropolitan cities transforms many of them into small metro centers.

When chronic rural deficiencies in such areas as electrification, water supply, sanitary facilities, heating systems, paved roads, secondary schooling, and telephone service have been essentially eliminated, the basic premises governing location of both employment and residence would seem to be changed. The present slowdown of urbanization and revived settlement in rural and small town places is not confined to the United States, although it may be more advanced here. The most developed nations appear to be entering a period of residential demographic transition whose future course cannot be seen clearly, but is almost certainly different from that assumed just a few years ago.

4 The Changing Character of the Nonmetropolitan Population, 1950–75

JAMES J. ZUICHES
DAVID L. BROWN

THE rapid growth of metropolitan areas and the slower growth or decline of nonmetropolitan areas have been persistent features of the American demographic experience. Differential rates of population growth between the two residence categories—especially as they have been influenced by rural-to-urban migration—have had a substantial impact on the characteristics of the population of both the metropolitan and non-metropolitan sectors. The selective nature of migration means that areas of origin and destination will further change in characteristics as people move between them. Selectivity by age, race, and socioeconomic status affects both areas, but outmigration has particularly been a major determinant of the population composition of nonmetropolitan areas.

Recent turnarounds in nonmetropolitan growth rates and net migration indicate that the United States may be entering a new phase in the relationship between metropolitan and nonmetropolitan sectors, and that the transition from an agricultural to a manufacturing and service economy may have outmoded the traditional models of migrant selectivity (Beale, 1975). With economic changes have come life-style changes and alterations in demographic behavior. These recent changes need to be

James J. Zuiches is Associate Professor of Sociology, Michigan State University; David L. Brown is Sociologist, Population Studies, Economics, Statistics, and Cooperatives Service, U.S. Department of Agriculture.

This work was supported by the Michigan State University Agricultural Experiment Station (Journal Article 7441) and the Economic Research Service, U.S. Department of Agriculture.

evaluated in the context of long-term trends affecting metropolitan and nonmetropolitan areas.

For this evaluation the metropolitan-nonmetropolitan distinction, rather than the urban-rural, has been chosen as the appropriate unit of analysis for two reasons: it represents meaningful dimensions of geographic, economic, social, and political space, and it permits statistical presentation of trends over comparable units. The official delineation of metropolitan counties for 1960 is contained in the U.S. Bureau of the Budget (1964). We have chosen to maintain constant boundaries according to metropolitan status in 1960 for our profile of changes from 1950 to 1970. (See Brown, 1976 for a discussion of metropolitan reclassification.)

POPULATION COMPOSITION. Our basic perspective and underlying hypothesis is that population composition is both a determinant and a consequence of population change. The range of compositional traits is limited only by one's imagination and available data, but key compositional characteristics are associated with most demographic events. Moreover, composition limits or provides the opportunity for other processes to unfold.

Fertility and Population Composition. Historically birth rates in rural and nonmetropolitan areas have far exceeded the level necessary for population replacement. Thus the nonmetropolitan population generally has had a broad base of children and young adults and consequently a large number of potential entrants into the labor force. Ironically, the periods of highest fertility in nonmetropolitan America have coincided with periods of contraction in the labor force needs of agriculture, mining, and other traditional rural and nonmetropolitan industries. Consequently, heavy and sustained outmigration has been necessary to adjust the imbalance between supply of and demand for labor resources in nonmetropolitan areas.

Currently the level of childbearing in nonmetropolitan America has declined substantially from previous levels. Yet it continues to exceed the level of generational replacement and consequently has implications for population growth — especially in the younger age groups. Hence nonmetropolitan America is faced with the traditional challenge of providing economic opportunities for young workers and their families or losing such persons through outmigration.

Migration and Population Composition. Migration has a much more general effect on population composition than does the birthrate. While fertility affects mainly age and racial composition, migration has an impact on demographic structure, socioeconomic status, and labor force composition. Migration is selective of the young especially. But most studies have shown it is also selective of the better educated, the higher occupational classes, the more capable young. Those who could contribute most to a place of origin most often leave and the benefits of their talents and training accrue to the place where they move.

CHANGES IN NONMETROPOLITAN POPULATION COMPOSITION, 1950–70.

The centralization of population and activities into metropolitan areas has had a substantial impact on the social, economic, and demographic characteristics of the nonmetropolitan population. This section of the chapter evaluates the patterns of convergence and divergence since 1950.

Age Composition. The age composition of an area's population is associated with the processes that contribute to population growth and change — fertility, mortality, and migration; with the demand for various community, health, and social services; and with other attributes of population composition, such as income and educational attainment, as well as the size, rates of entry and departure, and other characteristics of the labor force.

Historically the urban population's median age has exceeded that of its rural counterpart. The much larger proportion of children in rural areas produced this difference and has tended to obscure the fact that as early as 1910 rural areas exceeded urban areas in the proportion of middle-aged and older population (Bogue, 1959).

Between 1950 and 1970 the median age of the nonmetropolitan population was relatively constant at about 28 years (Table 4.1). However, a detailed comparison (Fig. 4.1) of the 1950 and 1970 age distributions reveals that important changes did, in fact, take place. Constancy in the median age is due to the counterbalancing effects of growth at the older and younger ages.

The most substantial changes occurred in the working ages, where persons aged 20 to 49 years declined both numerically and as a percentage of the total nonmetropolitan population. One explanation for this decline is that persons aged 30 to 49 in 1970 were born between 1921 and 1940, a period of low fertility. On the other hand, young adults aged 20 to 29 in 1970 were born during a period of rising birth rates, and hence increased numerically over the two decades. However, their rate of growth in nonmetropolitan areas was less than expected. Thus one can infer that migration from nonmetropolitan areas occurred among the young adult population. Reduction of the working-age population, then, may be attributed to outmigration and to low fertility experienced during the 1930s and 1940s.

Population growth among the elderly was also characteristic of nonmetropolitan counties during the past two decades. Growth at ages 65 and above accounted for a large component of all nonmetropolitan

Table 4.1. Socioeconomic characteristics of the United States population by metropolitan status, 1950–70[a].

Characteristic	United States			Metropolitan			Nonmetropolitan		
	1970	1960	1950	1970	1960	1950	1970	1960	1950
Median age	28.1	29.5	30.2	28.1	30.1	31.4	28.0	28.2	28.1
Dependency ratio[b]	62.4	67.1	53.9	60.4	64.3	48.3	66.7	72.8	63.2
Sex ratio[c]	94.8	97.0	98.8	93.8	95.8	97.7	96.9	99.5	100.4
Percent racial minority	12.5	11.4	11.5	13.5	11.4	9.5	10.5	11.4	12.0
Persons per household	3.1	3.2	3.4	3.1	3.2	3.3	3.1	3.4	3.5
Median school attainment[d]	12.1	10.6	9.5	12.2	11.1	10.1	11.4	9.4	8.7
Median family income	$9,590	$5,660	$3,073	$10,532	$6,303	$3,451	$7,828	$4,387	$2,300
Percent males in labor force[e]	70.1	77.4	77.0	72.0	79.2	79.2	66.4	74.0	73.5
Percent females in labor force	39.5	34.5	28.9	41.0	36.4	32.0	36.4	30.7	23.7
Percent white-collar occupation[f]	45.6	41.1	36.9	49.6	45.3	42.7	36.6	32.3	26.8
Percent extractive industry[g]	4.3	7.7	14.1	1.7	2.6	4.3	10.2	18.8	31.1
Percent manufacturing industry[h]	24.4	27.1	25.9	24.4	29.2	30.0	24.4	22.7	18.6
Percent service industry[i]	24.5	21.1	18.0	25.0	21.4	19.3	23.3	20.0	16.0

Source: U.S. Censuses of Population.

[a] Metropolitan as of 1963. Hawaii and Alaska included in all three decades.
[b] Persons under 18 years of age plus persons 65 years old and over as percent of persons 18 to 64.
[c] Males per 100 females.
[d] Persons 25 years and older.
[e] Employed and unemployed (but looking for work) aged 14 years and older.
[f] Professional, technical, and kindred; manager, official, and proprietor; clerical, sales.
[g] Agriculture, forestry, fisheries, mining.
[h] Durable and nondurable.
[i] Business, repair, personal, and professional services.

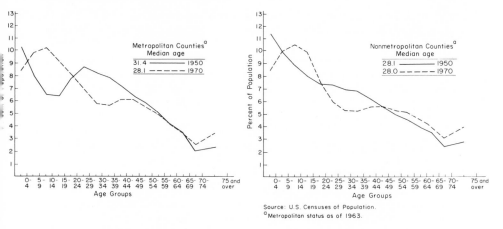

Fig. 4.1.   Age composition of metropolitan and nonmetropolitan counties, 1950 and 1970.

population growth between 1950 and 1970. The elderly grew by 2.3 million persons from 8.6 percent to 11.2 percent of the total non-metropolitan population.

Many nonmetropolitan counties, especially those in the Florida-California sun belt, have developed as retirement centers. Inmigration of retired persons to such communities is doubtless a contributing factor in the increased percentage of aged in the nonmetropolitan population. The extension of life expectancy is another contributing factor. In 1970, a person aged 65 had an average of 15.2 years of life remaining compared with an average of only 14.1 years in 1950 (National Center for Health Statistics, 1970; National Office of Vital Statistics, 1954).

Change was also evident among young persons less than 20 years of age. A larger proportion of the nonmetropolitan population was between 5 and 19 years of age in 1970 than was the case in 1950 (30.4 percent versus 26.7 percent). Persons aged 5 to 19 in 1970 were born in the period of high fertility that followed World War II, while their counterparts in 1950 were born during the Depression and prewar years. In contrast, the proportion of nonmetropolitan persons under 5 years of age in 1950 was higher than in 1970. This reflects the sharp decline in fertility that commenced in the 1960s.

A comparison of age structures of metropolitan and nonmetropolitan areas (Fig. 4.1) indicates similarities in the patterns of change between 1950 and 1970. Both sectors declined in the proportion under 5 years of age, increased in the proportion 5 to 19 years, declined in the proportion of persons in the prime working ages (20 to 49 years), and increased in the proportion of elderly. Secular demographic trends appear to have affected all areas, regardless of metropolitan status.

However, the metropolitan-nonmetropolitan comparison also indicates differences. Both categories grew in the proportion aged 5 to 19 years, but the rate of growth at these ages was substantially higher in metropolitan areas. Nonmetropolitan areas lost a significant proportion of their total natural increase between 1950 and 1970 through non-metropolitan-to-metropolitan migration. Another difference relates to the middle-aged and elderly population. Growth at ages 45 and above comprised a much larger component of total population growth in nonmetropolitan counties than in their metropolitan counterparts.

Sex Ratio. Traditionally the nonmetropolitan economy has demanded a preponderance of male labor. Consequently the sex ratio of such areas historically has been higher than that of metropolitan areas. But urbanization and reduced demand for workers in extractive industries have contributed to a steady decline in the sex ratio of nonmetropolitan America. The ratio of males per 100 females in nonmetropolitan areas declined from 100.4 in 1950 to 96.9 in 1970 (Table 4.1). The sex ratio in metropolitan areas also declined between 1950 and 1970 (97.7 to 93.8).

The national decline is related to the continued and growing disparity in length of life between the sexes. In 1970, a white male aged 65 had an average of 13.1 years of life remaining compared with an average of 17.1 years for a white female. In 1950 these figures were 13.0 years for a man aged 65 and 15.3 years for a woman (National Center for Health Statistics, 1970; National Office of Vital Statistics, 1954). The overall effect of change in the sex ratio at older ages is amplified because the elderly have increased as a proportion of the total population. Finally, the reduced numerical importance of international immigration, which is prepon-derantly male, has contributed to declines in the sex ratio.

Household Size. The average size of the American household declined by over 32 percent between 1890 and 1950, or from 5 members to only 3.4. Factors affecting this trend include reduced fertility (before 1945) and increased longevity, which tended to create a great number of small households occupied by elderly couples (Bogue, 1959). Traditionally, higher rural fertility meant that the size of rural households exceeded that of urban households (Grabill demonstrated in 1955 that rural fertility exceeded urban fertility in every decade from 1800 through 1950).

The number of persons per household in nonmetropolitan areas continued to decline from 3.5 in 1950 to 3.1 in 1970. The majority of this change occurred between 1960 and 1970 and reflected the rapid decline in birth rates in the 1960s. Moreover, the decline in household size is associated with the increased proportion of persons who live alone or with just one other person. The growth of such households is especially notable among young singles and among the elderly. Many elderly persons maintain their residences after their children have left home and/or after the loss of a spouse.

Comparing metropolitan and nonmetropolitan counties indicates that household size declined in both sectors, but at a faster rate in the nonmetropolitan areas. Therefore by 1970 average household size converged at 3.1 persons in both metropolitan and nonmetropolitan areas. The more rapid rate of decline in nonmetropolitan areas may be attributed to the greater proportional growth of older persons and to the outmigration of young families with dependent children.

Nonwhite Minority Population. The racial-minority population has been urbanizing since early in the nineteenth century, yet the proportion of the minority population classified as urban was less than that of whites in every decade until 1960 (Bogue, 1959). One outcome of this differential rate of urbanization is that the racial-minority component of the metropolitan population has consistently been less than that of its nonmetropolitan counterpart.

Between 1950 and 1970 the racial-minority component of the nonmetropolitan population declined from 12.0 percent to 10.5 percent. This decline reflects primarily the outmigration of blacks from southern agricultural areas to the metropolitan sector. During this period the nonwhite metropolitan population increased from 8.7 million to 18.4 million, or from 9.5 percent to 13.5 percent of the total metropolitan population. Much of this growth occurred in the core counties of large metropolitan areas and is associated with both inmigration of nonwhites and with high fertility. In 1970 the number of children ever born per 1,000 ever-married women aged 35 to 44 was 3,474 for the racial-minority population in metropolitan areas compared with only 3,040 in the total metropolitan population (Hines, Brown, and Zimmer, 1975).

Socioeconomic Status. Historically, nonmetropolitan areas have lagged behind metropolitan areas in objective measures of socioeconomic status and levels of living. Yet Carl Taylor observed in 1949 that rural and urban levels of living had become more alike. Reduction of status differentials between the residential sectors is associated with secular changes in the structure of the economy, changes that began at the turn of the century and affected all communities regardless of location. For example, Bogue (1959) demonstrated that in 1950 the proportion of professional, technical, and service workers was more than twice that of 1900 and the proportion of clerical workers three times its level at the turn of the century. On the other hand, farmers, farm laborers, and unskilled laborers comprised a vastly reduced share of occupations. Nevertheless, data from the 1940 and 1950 censuses indicated that substantial differences in socioeconomic status between the residence sectors persisted.

Three indicators of socioeconomic status—median years of school completed by the population 25 years of age and older, percent of the labor force occupying white collar positions, and median family incomes—

are discussed here. All three indicators show an increase in both metropolitan and nonmetropolitan levels since 1950 and a slight reduction in the differential between the residence sectors.

Median Educational Attainment. Median years of school completed in nonmetropolitan areas for persons 25 years and over increased from 8.7 in 1950 to 11.4 in 1970, or by 2.7 years compared with a 2.1 year increase in metropolitan areas. Hence, the differential in formal educational attainment between the sectors diminished from 1.4 years in 1950 to only 0.8 years in 1970. This differential results from the larger proportion of less educated elderly persons in nonmetropolitan areas as well as from lower levels of achievement.

Percent White-Collar Occupations. The proportion of the nonmetropolitan labor force engaged in white-collar occupations increased from 26.8 percent in 1950 to 36.6 percent in 1970. In metropolitan areas the proportion of white-collar workers also increased, but again at a somewhat slower pace, from 42.7 percent in 1950 to 49.6 percent two decades later.

Increased white-collar employment occurred primarily in the professional, technical, and clerical categories. Fig. 4.2 shows the changes in nonmetropolitan counties. Growth in these occupations is associated with the expansion of employment in professional service industries and with the increased labor force participation of women, especially in clerical jobs. In contrast to the growth of white-collar jobs in nonmetropolitan areas, employment in farm related occupations decreased (from 27.1 percent to 7.7 percent).

Median Family Income. Related to increases in educational attainment and occupational status is the growth in median family income. In 1950 in nonmetropolitan America it was $2,300, only two-thirds of the metropolitan median (Table 4.1). By 1970 median family income had increased to over $7,800 in nonmetropolitan areas, nearly three-fourths of the metropolitan figure. In addition to educational attainment and occupational status, family income is associated with an area's age structure, its rate of labor force participation by women, and the skill and wage level of its industry mix. (Adjusting for differentials in cost of living diminishes but does not eliminate income differences. In the spring of 1969, the cost of living for nonmetropolitan urban areas was 90.4 percent of the U.S. total, but median family income was only 79.4 percent of U.S. total [U.S. Department of Labor, 1971].)

Labor Force and Employment

Labor Force Participation by Males. The proportion of nonmetropolitan males participating in the civilian labor force declined from 73.5 percent in 1950 to 66.4 percent in 1970, and for metropolitan males

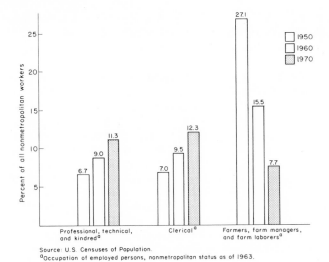

Fig. 4.2. Percent of nonmetropolitan labor force employed in selected occupations, 1950–70.

from 79.2 percent to 72.0 percent. One reason for these declines is the growing number of men who tend to retire at younger ages. Other factors include increased enrollment in colleges and universities (compared with 1950), larger proportions in military service, and perhaps a disaffection toward gainful employment among some segments of the young population. At the prime working ages little or no change had occurred in the proportion of white males participating in the labor force, although the participation of minority males did decline between 1960 and 1970 in such ages (Hauser and Featherman, 1974).

Labor Force Participation by Females. Labor force participation by women exhibits a secular trend that is similar for both the metropolitan and nonmetropolitan sectors. Between 1950 and 1970, the proportion of nonmetropolitan women participating in the labor force increased from 23.7 percent to 36.4 percent. In metropolitan areas the corresponding increase was from 32.0 percent to 41.0 percent. Thus, the metropolitan-nonmetropolitan differential diminished from 8.3 percentage points in 1950 to only 4.6 percentage points in 1970. Increased participation by women reflects a growing acceptance of nonhousehold labor for women, increased opportunities in a number of manufacturing industries such as textiles, electronics, and clothing, and the growth of employment in clerical and other support occupations.

Employment by Industry. The industry mix of the nonmetropolitan labor force has been substantially altered as a result of significant increases and decreases in various industrial categories. In 1820 over 70 percent of all American workers were employed in agriculture. One hundred years later, in 1920, this figure had declined to a little over a quarter, and by 1940 only 17.6 percent of the labor force was employed in agriculture (Ducoff and Hagood, 1949). The decline continued from 1950 and 1970. To summarize briefly from Table 4.1 and Fig. 4.3, nonmetropolitan employment in extractive industries (agriculture, forestry, fisheries, mining) declined from 31.1 percent to 10.2 percent of the labor force, or by over 4 million jobs; manufacturing employed almost a quarter of nonmetropolitan workers in 1970 compared with only 18.6 percent in 1950; and employment in service industries grew from 16.0 percent to almost one-fourth of all nonmetropolitan employees. Particularly impressive was the increase in the professional services sector, which grew by over 2 million jobs, a 146 percent increase over the 1950 figure.

Substantial change also occurred in the industry mix of metropolitan areas. Between 1950 and 1970 manufacturing declined in importance in metropolitan areas but grew in importance in nonmetropolitan areas. Service industries, especially professional services, gained in both sectors, and extractive industries declined dramatically.

Overview of Changes. Substantial changes in population composition have taken place in both metropolitan and nonmetropolitan America during the past two decades. In general the data indicate that similar changes have occurred in both residence sectors and that metropolitan-nonmetropolitan differences have diminished since 1950.

The trend in both sectors is toward higher levels of socioeconomic status, as indexed by educational attainment, white-collar occupational status, and median family income; greater labor force participation by women; greater employment in service industries (especially professional services); smaller household size; and a lower ratio of males to females. Both sectors experienced a decline in the proportion under 5 years of age, an increase in the proportion 5 to 19 years, a decline at the working ages

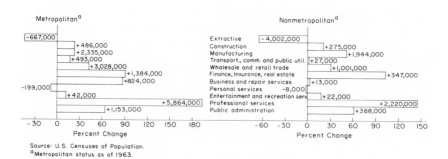

Fig. 4.3. Change of employment patterns in metropolitan and nonmetropolitan counties, 1950–70.

(20 to 49), and an increase in the proportion of the elderly. However, the rate of growth at ages 5 to 19 was substantially higher in metropolitan counties and at older ages higher in nonmetropolitan counties. Divergent trends were noted in racial composition (the racial-minority component increased in metropolitan counties and decreased in nonmetropolitan counties) and in the proportion of the labor force employed in manufacturing (it increased in nonmetropolitan areas and decreased in metropolitan counties).

THE CHANGING COMPOSITION OF MIGRATION STREAMS. The renewal of population growth in nonmetropolitan America, described by Beale in Chapter 3, is evident in sample survey data from the *Current Population Reports* as well (U.S. Bureau of the Census, 1975). About 6.7 million persons moved out of metropolitan areas between 1970 and 1975, and a little over 5.1 million moved out of nonmetropolitan areas, resulting in a net migration gain of about 1.6 million persons in nonmetropolitan America. (This figure is actually somewhat inflated because of changing metropolitan status. In its report the U.S. Bureau of the Census [1975] defines metropolitan areas as of the 1970 census. Since metropolitan status is therefore constant for the 1965–75 period, residents of new Standard Metropolitan Statistical Areas created as a result of the 1970 census and of counties added to existing SMSAs are not included in the metropolitan category. The discussion of nonmetropolitan growth due to net inmigration therefore overestimates the growth in the 1975-designated nonmetropolitan areas. In fact, 28 percent of all nonmetropolitan growth occurred in counties that changed definition between 1970 and 1975.)

Population redistribution is not unidirectional. Our analysis of the change in mobility rates from 1965–70 to 1970–75 indicates that two complementary demographic forces were operating to produce net inmigration to nonmetropolitan areas during the early 1970s. First, the number of migrants to nonmetropolitan areas increased about 23 percent over that of the late 1960s. This component has received national publicity and attention. (It parallels a 19 percent increase in the outmigration rate from metropolitan counties.) Second, outmigration from nonmetropolitan counties has decreased about 12 percent since the late 1960s, corresponding to a 14 percent decline in the outmigration rate. (See Tucker, 1976 for a similar analysis.) These areas therefore have retained many who in earlier years might have migrated to the cities. Both the increased retention of present residents and increased attractiveness to metro residents have combined to yield dramatic net migration growth in nonmetropolitan America.

Metropolitan-to-Nonmetropolitan Movers. Who are the recent inmigrants to nonmetropolitan areas? And what are their characteristics in comparison with the resident population? Persons of metropolitan origin who moved between 1970 and 1975 to nonmetropolitan areas (Column 3, Table 4.2) were younger and better educated than nonmovers (Column 1, Table 4.2). Only 4.8 percent of the inmigrants were black compared to 8.4 percent of nonmovers and 10.5 of within-nonmetro movers. Occupational status was higher among inmigrants than nonmigrants; fully a third of the recent inmigrants were employed in upper white-collar occupations whereas only 21 percent of nonmigrants held such positions. Conversely, recent movers were less likely than nonmovers to hold blue-collar jobs. Although recent migration to nonmetropolitan areas often is attributed to retirement, only 7.3 percent of the stream was over 65 years old, whereas 17.5 percent of the nonmobile population was over 65.

Compared with persons who moved but remained within the nonmetropolitan sector (Column 2, Table 4.2), recent inmigrants were more likely to be white, to be better educated, and to have higher income levels and occupational status. The remaining differences were not statistically significant. (Tests of significance were calculated for differences between the streams of migrants, and between migrants and nonmigrants. Nonsignificant results—less than twice the standard error—are specifically noted.)

Nonmetropolitan-to-Metropolitan Movers. Who is leaving nonmetropolitan America? Specifically, are nonmetropolitan areas losing their bright young people to metropolitan areas? The answer is a qualified

Table 4.2. Socioeconomic characteristics of the nonmetropolitan population by migration status, 1970–75.

Characteristic	Nonmetro Nonmovers	Within-Nonmetro Movers	Metro-to-Nonmetro Movers	Nonmetro-to-Metro Movers
	(In percentages except for Sex Ratio)			
Under 30 years	37.2	61.0	57.4	67.8
65 years and older	17.5	6.2	7.3	3.9
Households with 1 or more children	57.8	69.0	68.8	62.8
Sex ratio[a]	92.4	94.5	99.1	96.8
Black population	8.4	10.5	4.8	9.0
Completed 1 or more years of college	17.5	20.3	34.1	44.4
Income $10,000 or more, 1974[b]	44.7	39.0	47.3	48.6
Males in labor force	70.2	80.1	73.7	78.6
Males upper white collar[c]	21.5	20.9	33.0	41.2
Males skilled blue collar[d]	39.7	46.1	33.7	30.6
Males unskilled blue collar[e]	30.0	24.3	21.1	14.9

Source: U.S. Bureau of the Census, 1975.
[a] Males per 100 females.
[b] Income from all sources for married males, wife present.
[c] Professional, technical, and kindred, managers, administrators, except farm.
[d] Craftsmen, operatives, and kindred workers.
[e] Laborers, service workers, farm workers.

yes. Nonmetropolitan outmigrants (Column 4, Table 4.2) are younger and substantially better educated than nonmovers (Column 1, Table 4.2). Sixty-eight percent of the outmigrants between 1970 and 1975 were under 30 years old, and 44 percent had completed some college. They also had a higher rate of labor force participation and held jobs of much higher occupational status than nonmovers. However, income differences and racial and family composition differences between outmigrants and nonmigrants were not statistically significant.

Compared with persons who moved within or between non-metropolitan counties (Column 2, Table 4.2), outmigrants tended to be younger, to have completed substantially more formal education, and to occupy higher status occupations. On the other hand, these groups differed very little in sex and racial composition, family household composition, or in the rate at which they participated in the labor force. These data suggest that a substantial portion of the young adults in the non-metropolitan-to-metropolitan migration stream are recent graduates or transfers from colleges and universities located in nonmetropolitan areas.

The Interchange of Migration Streams. Distinct symmetries appear when one compares 1970–75 migration streams into and out of non-metropolitan counties. The young were highly represented in both the inmigration and outmigration streams, but nonmetropolitan counties experienced a significantly higher rate of outmigration of younger persons and a higher rate of inmigration of retirement-age persons. Similarly, the nonmetropolitan outmigrants were better educated, with 44 percent having completed one or more years of college. Only 34 percent of inmigrants had attained this educational level. Racial composition, the second significant difference, was predominantly white for both streams, but the proportion of blacks was much higher among outmigrants. Only a small percentage of the nonmetropolitan-destined stream was black, and this counterstream occurred mainly in the South.

Although the following differences are not statistically significant, they yield a composite profile that is of some interest. Females were more migratory than males, and the nonmetropolitan outmigrant stream was slightly more female dominated than the counterstream. By family composition, households moving into nonmetropolitan areas were more likely to have at least one child. Persons who migrated into metropolitan areas were earning higher incomes than nonmigrants or recent non-metropolitan inmigrants, but again the differences were not large. Nonmetropolitan male inmigrants held proportionately more blue-collar skilled and unskilled jobs than metropolitan inmigrants, who were more likely to be in upper white-collar occupations.

In general, although metropolitan-to-nonmetropolitan movers were older and had somewhat lower levels of education and occupational status than persons who moved in the opposite direction, migration streams to and from nonmetropolitan counties were quite similar in demographic and socioeconomic composition. However, compared with persons who resided in nonmetropolitan counties in both 1970 and 1975, inmigrants had distinctly higher occupational status, had completed more years of formal education, and were more likely to be white. Moreover, compared with nonmovers, inmigrants were substantially younger. These findings for the early 1970s are similar to those reported by Kirschenbaum (1971) and Fredrickson (1974) in their studies of inmigration to nonmetropolitan areas during the late 1950s.

Changing Composition of Migration Streams, 1965–75. Given this high degree of similarity in the characteristics of inmigration and out-migration streams, what is the net impact on the composition of the nonmetropolitan population? The impact depends on two factors: first, the selectivity of migrants and second, the actual number of migrants. Examining the selectivity enabled us to determine that a high degree of compositional similarity exists between inmigrants to and outmigrants from nonmetropolitan areas, except in the age and racial composition, and that migrants, whatever their origin or destination, are distinctly different in population composition from nonmigrants.

A summary statistic that indicates the net loss or gain by com-positional attribute (age, sex, race, and the like) is simply the difference between inmigration and outmigration. Figure 4.4 depicts expected and actual net migration by age, sex, and race, while Fig. 4.5 shows the same by education and occupation. These figures also include a useful measure of migration turnover, the interchange ratio, which is the ratio of in-migrants to outmigrants for nonmetropolitan areas. A ratio of 1.0 means a balance of inmigrants and outmigrants; ratios greater than 1.0 indicate a gain in the nonmetropolitan sector while those less than 1.0 show a loss to nonmetropolitan areas. We computed an *expected* ratio based on 1965–70 mobility (derived from U.S. Bureau of the Census, 1973) and an *actual* interchange ratio based on 1970–75 mobility (calculated from U.S. Bureau of the Census, 1975). The expected ratios and net migration for the dif-ferent subgroups reveal what would have happened to population com-position had the 1965–70 mobility rates continued. The actual ratios and net migration provide the contrasting recent situation.

By race and sex, Fig. 4.4 shows slight gains expected in non-metropolitan areas of white males, slight losses of white females, and substantial losses of blacks regardless of sex. Actually, nonmetropolitan areas experienced substantial gains of whites of both sexes and lower losses of black females than expected on the basis of mobility rates from 1965 to 1970. About 35 percent more whites moved into nonmetropolitan areas than out, and the expected loss of black females slowed primarily as a result of a decrease in outmigration. Rather than a net loss of population in nonmetropolitan counties, a net gain of 1.73 million whites occurred, with a net loss of 140,000 blacks.

If mobility rates by age had continued from the 1960s into the 1970s,

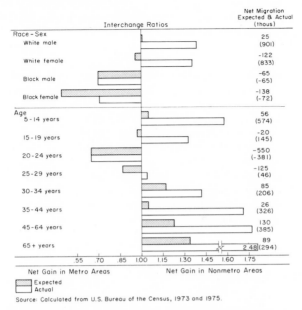

Fig. 4.4. Expected and actual net migration and interchange ratios for nonmetropolitan United States, by race, sex, and age, 1970–75.

nonmetropolitan areas would have experienced significant losses in the 20–24 and 25–29 age groups, slight gains in the under-15 and 30–45 age groups, and larger increases at older ages. However, the ratios for actual mobility show that only the 20–24 age category conformed closely with expectations. The youngest ages (5–14 years) and middle family ages (35–44 years) showed large nonmetropolitan gains over the 1965–70 expectations. Similarly, the retirement age category (65 years and older) also showed marked nonmetropolitan gains.

The positive net migration during the late 1960s was predominantly in the middle and older ages, but in the early 1970s the bulk of inmigrants was in two younger age categories: the middle working years (30–44) and under age 14. Net migration increased by a factor of 2.5 for those over 45, but had a five- to eightfold increase for the two younger age groups.

Educational attainment and current occupation are presented in Fig. 4.5. By educational attainment for those over 25 years old, projected net change based on the 1965–70 rates suggested small gains in non-metropolitan areas at all levels except for those with a college degree. Actual net migration was positive for all educational levels. Non-metropolitan areas primarily gained the less educated, and the ratios decreased as educational attainment rose. Table 4.2 showed that although 34 percent of the inmigrants had one or more years of college, 44 percent of the outmigrants had some higher education. Again, this may result from the outmigration of recent college graduates receiving their education in nonmetropolitan locations.

Figure 4.5 shows the occupational characteristics of recent inmigrant and outmigrant males over the age of 16. Based on the 1965–70 rates, a net loss for all occupations except farmworkers was expected. In fact, only for the professional and managerial categories did a net loss occur (−22,000). For all other occupations net gains occurred, with the bulk of the inmigrants (137,000) holding skilled blue-collar jobs.

Income and occupation reported by movers are often indicative of the result of a move rather than an explicit push or pull factor that determines mobility. Thus these substantial net gains in various occupational categories in nonmetropolitan areas imply a continuing increase in both white- and blue-collar jobs. Commuting, however, may still be an important factor in the explanation of employment-resident location patterns, since new nonmetropolitan residents may be commuting to work in metropolitan areas.

SUMMARY AND IMPLICATIONS. The process of population change is both a determinant and a consequence of population composition. Continuities and similarities are evident from decade to decade in the structural characteristics of metropolitan and nonmetropolitan populations, but changes in fertility rates, death rates, and migration rates

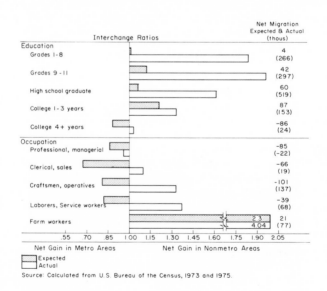

Fig. 4.5. Expected and actual net migration and interchange ratios for nonmetropolitan United States, by education and occupation, 1970–75.

over time have brought about a gradual convergence in compositional structures of the two residence sectors.

In the analysis of change from 1950 to 1970 a convergence in characteristics was evident for income, occupational status, educational attainment, household size, and labor force participation of women. Median age likewise converged, but differences persisted in certain age groups, for example the elderly. Moreover the racial-minority population increased in metropolitan areas but decreased in nonmetropolitan areas.

Analysis of migration streams between 1970 and 1975 indicates that further convergence in socioeconomic status is likely. Recent inmigrants to nonmetropolitan areas have a slightly lower socioeconomic status than outmigrants. However, inmigrants are of substantially higher status than nonmovers, which suggests that recent inmigration to nonmetropolitan areas will contribute to raising the income, education, and occupational levels of the nonmetropolitan population. On the other hand, recent inmigrants to nonmetropolitan areas are overwhelmingly white; thus, the 1950–70 trend of increasing metropolitanization of the black population probably will continue.

Within the nonmetropolitan sector population decline still persists in areas such as the Great Plains and the Mississippi Delta, in areas where military employment has decreased, in areas with high percentages of the labor force in agriculture, and in depleted areas dependent on extractive industries (Beale, 1975). But clearly high-growth areas and the characteristics of migrants contributing to such growth are closely related. Growing areas are associated with young populations of relatively high socioeconomic status and with high rates of labor force participation, especially in white-collar or professional activities–all attributes of the mobile population (Brown, 1975).

Although a great similarity exists between inmigrants and outmigrants, the nonmetropolitan sector is not merely replacing its outmigrants or serving as a bedroom suburb to metropolitan areas. Rather it has experienced a considerable expansion in economic opportunity. Its attractiveness extends to both retirees and young families. Both economic factors and attitudinal studies indicate a continued potential for nonmetropolitan growth. Residential preference studies by Fuguitt and Zuiches (1975) demonstrated the existence of a strong orientation to rural and nonmetropolitan environments. Furthermore, people having this orientation also had characteristics similar to recent nonmetro inmigrants. Compared with respondents preferring metropolitan areas, they were likely to be younger, with higher incomes and educational attainment, and they were more likely to be married and to work in white-collar occupations.

Population growth is generally desired by rural communities as a symbol of vitality and as a source of community pride. Growth may upgrade the skill level of the labor force, provide support for previously unavailable services and amenities, and generate necessary economic support for commercial and business enterprise. However, the consequences of unanticipated growth can be just as jarring as those associated with long-term, uninterrupted decline. In both cases, community institutions must adapt to changing size and composition of population.

As we have seen, increased numbers of the very young, the working ages, and those of retirement age are migrating to nonmetropolitan areas. An increase in young families creates demands for new housing and for fuel, water, sewers, and other services associated with housing. In addition, the age structure in growing areas is younger than that in declining areas. Consequently, growing communities should anticipate an increased demand for educational, health, and recreation services. Moreover, an increased number of children in a community increases the demand for certain types of consumer products such as baby food and accessories, toys, children's clothing, and school supplies.

Areas growing through the inmigration of retirement-age population can expect the demand for certain types of goods and services to increase as well. The economic position of elderly persons is determined by personal savings, pension plans, and, to a lesser extent, employment. Yet even with all these potential sources of income, poverty is more prevalent among the aged—and especially among aged minority groups—than in any other group in society. Thus the need for economic and community aid to the elderly is likely to increase in retirement areas. In sum, the changing age composition contributes to further demographic and nondemographic changes.

Finally, the long-term trend of metropolitan centralization and concentration seems to have stabilized, but renewed population growth in nonmetropolitan areas will pose challenging problems of a different nature. Further research into population distribution history and policies in industrially mature societies should be undertaken. The role of residential preferences in contrast to structural economic constraints in the mobility process should be considered. Moreover, the process through which the composition of population is transformed over time should be systematically investigated. The analysis of population composition as both a limiting and permissive factor will continue to provide a more refined insight into the structural changes of society. Only on the basis of such research can adequate policies for coping with future changes be developed.

Part 4

TECHNOLOGY

5 Rural Social Organizational Implications of Technology and Industry

ALVIN L. BERTRAND

RECENT developments in agricultural technology and rural industrialization help account for the growth and redistribution of the United States population. The behavior of rural people (and urban people as well) is undergoing constant adjustment and alteration as a partial consequence of these developments in rural technology and industry. Further, the rate of adjustment varies from one region to another. The contemplation of this change phenomenon and of what it portends highlights this chapter.

THE TECHNOLOGICAL REVOLUTION IN AGRICULTURE AND RURAL LIFE: 50 YEARS OF ADJUSTMENT TO INNOVATION. Former Secretary of Agriculture Clifford M. Hardin emphasized the importance of the technological revolution in agriculture by pointing out that it enabled "the individual farmer to increase productivity at a much faster rate than that of the industrial worker" (U.S. Department of Agriculture, 1970:xxxiii). The past half-century—the era of the revolution—has been one of constant social adjustment, especially in rural areas of the U.S. A number of serious problems can be at least partially attributed to the failure of policymakers and planners to predict and prepare for many of the direct and derivative consequences of technological innovations in agriculture.

Technological Trends in Review. Technology embraces far more than mechanical tools or machines, although popular definitions would

Alvin L. Bertrand is Boyd Professor in the Department of Sociology and Rural Sociology, Louisiana State University.

tend to restrict the concept to hardware. Intellectual tools, such as the knowledge of how to get farmers to adopt a new and improved practice at a faster rate or how to set up a more efficient horticultural experiment, are just as much technology as a new harvester or an improved pesticide. Technology also relates to applied or practical purposes (Mesthene, 1970:25). Unless there is an application of knowledge in the sense of improving efficiency in the achievement of desired goals, technology is not in evidence, although invention or change might be.

Historians note that the nature of farming had not changed much from the founding of the United States until about the 1920s. Sixty years ago, the majority of farmers were still largely self-sufficient with respect to what they and their livestock consumed, and horses and mules were the chief source of power. Production technology had not changed noticeably in the previous 100 years, with yields improving little if any over the course of this time. Farming was truly a way of life and was carried on with family skills and traditional wisdom handed down from parents to children.

Those who seek for a precise beginning of the agricultural revolution tend to agree that the advent of the general-purpose tractor in the late 1920s is the critical moment in time. In 1920, the peak year for workstock in the United States, almost 26 million horses and mules were counted as compared with 246,000 tractors. Ten years later in 1930 the number of work animals had decreased to just over 19 million — a loss of almost 700,000 per year — while tractors had increased to 920,000 — an increase of over 67,000 per year. By 1959 the number of farm horses and mules had dropped so low (less than 3 million) that a decision was made to stop counting them. In 1974 there were over 5.25 million tractors on farms in the U.S. plus a host of other self-propelled machines. The estimated worth of machinery and motor vehicles on farms was $43.6 billion in this same year.

The technological revolution in agriculture can be further dramatized by calling attention to the efficiencies that have developed on farms and in farming within recent years. Durest and Bailey, in an article prepared for the *1970 Yearbook of Agriculture* (U.S. Department of Agriculture, 1970:2–10), point out that the total man-hours utilized in farming declined from 23 billion in 1930 to 7 billion in 1968, a drop of over two-thirds. By 1973, the total hours used for farm work in the United States had dropped to 6.3 billion annually (U.S. Department of Agriculture, 1974. This is the source, unless otherwise noted, of agricultural statistics given in the remainder of this chapter). To highlight the mechanical aspect of the technological revolution in agriculture, in 1935 each farm worker had from two- to three-tractor horsepower available to him, while today each worker has in excess of 40-tractor horsepower at his service, and altogether U.S. farmers have tractors harnessing 212 million horsepower. An individual farmer supplied farm products to 52.4 persons in 1972, double the 25.8 persons supplied just 12 years previously in 1960 (Byerly, 1970:33).

The increase in production efficiency is manifest in yield trends as vividly as in the decrease in needed labor. In the last 50 years, the yield of wheat per acre has doubled, cotton lint yields have increased threefold, rice yields have more than doubled, tobacco yields have tripled, peanut yields have improved two and one-half times, soybean yields have doubled, and potato yields have more than tripled. In the cases of livestock and poultry, one man using modern systems can now handle up to 5,000 head of cattle, or he can operate a dairy enterprise of 50 to 60 cows, or he can take care of 60,000 to 75,000 chickens.

This brief account of the advent and effects of technology provides a perspective on the organizational adjustments that U.S. farmers have had to make in the last half-century. First, they had to adjust to the substitution of machines for animals as a power source. They also had to become accustomed to the use of hybrid seed, plus new and complex fertilizers, pesticides, and other soil and crop additives. They had to gain knowledge of use of water and of conservation techniques, of hormones, and of other things that improved the efficiency of livestock production. And they had to become expert in the use of finances, in marketing, and in politics — all in the span of the relatively few years since the 1920s. The consequence of this adjustment has been a drastic change in rural life.

The Trend of Commercialization. One of the most important changes brought by the technological revolution in agriculture is the highly commercial, thoroughly market oriented nature of farming enterprises. Fifty years ago much farm production was for home use; today almost all nonfeed and seed production goes through commercial channels. The market orientation is so pervasive that it is difficult to find a farmer who is not producing for a market of some type.

The commercial nature of farming is evident in a variety of ways. One is product specification and quality. Today's farmer makes an effort to determine what is wanted by the consumer before he invests in a production effort. Thus if the market is strong for a broiler of a specific age and weight, for eggs of a given color and size, for wheat with a minimum or maximum protein, or beef of a given finish, that is what he will produce. He is able to deliver according to quality standards because of the technology that has taken much of the guesswork out of production.

Commercialism is expressed also in wholesale or contract sales. In the past farmers were prone to sell directly to consumers and to do a considerable amount of the processing of animals and poultry themselves. Today the traditional type of farmers' market has all but disappeared, and poultry and meat animals are sold alive directly to processing plants.

A third manner in which commercialism is expressed is the trend away from ownership of all the land cultivated or used, especially by large-scale operators. In times past farm ownership was not only considered a wise investment but brought status and a feeling of security. The new "business view" is that ownership, when rental land is available, ties up investment and decreases opportunity to utilize capital to best advantage. This is why many modern farmers in the central Corn Belt, the wheat land in the Plains, and the cotton land in California and Arizona are likely to rent the land they farm. It is not unusual for a specialty-crop farmer to work out an arrangement with a general-crop farmer-owner to use his land for the growing season only, which allows the same land to be utilized during part of the year for other purposes (Bailey and Lee, 1970:11-12).

Custom work is another evidence of the commercialization of farms. In many areas it is possible not only to hire for specific operations, such as ground preparation, seeding, or harvesting, but to make arrangements for "package" deals as well. The latter practice is one where all necessary field operations are contracted for, which makes it possible for any landowner or renter to function as a farmer even though he is employed full time elsewhere.

A final indication of commercialization is the use of credit and the change in credit source. Increasingly, dealer credit has come into the picture as a means of financing goods and services. This practice is considered to be in the interest of the vendor as well as the farmer.

The Trend toward Larger Size and Smaller Number of Farms. It is logical that technology would have an impact on both the size and number of farms in the United States as well as on the value of products sold. Considering first the change in the size of farms, the average farm in the U.S. increased in size by 63 acres in the last decade for which records are available (1963-74). In 1974 the average number of acres per farm in the United States was 385. By contrast, in 1920, before mechanization became widespread, the average farm size was 148 acres; in 1930 it had grown, but only to 157 acres. The change in the size of farms in the United States can be depicted in another way. In 1940 only 264,000 of over 6 million farms were 500 acres or more in size. But in 1969, out of just over 3 million farms, 355,000 were at least 500 acres in size. During this period farms of under 50 acres decreased from 2,381,000 to 820,000.

The number of farms has also changed drastically in the last 50 years. In 1920 close to 6.5 million farms were counted in the United States. By 1974 considerably less than 3 million farms (2,820,570) remained in the nation. This represents a drop of around 70,000 farms a year during the past half-century, an overwhelming testimonial to the impact of advancing technology and to the changes in rural patterns of social organization.

Still another way to measure trends in number and size of farms is in terms of value of products sold. In 1960 about half of the farms in the nation marketed products worth less than $2,500; by 1969 the proportion of farms in this class was down to two-fifths. At the other end of the scale, farms with sales of $40,000 and over rose from 3 percent to 7 percent. In 1960 only 113,000 farms marketed over $40,000 worth of products; however in 1969 some 211,000 farms were selling goods worth this much or more. The number of commercial farms, those selling over $2,500, is still declining — from 1.8 million in 1964 to 1.6 million in 1969.

Ownership, Tenancy, and Labor Force Trends. A rather important change in the percentage of owners and part owners of farms in the United States has developed over the past 50 years, in spite of the growing practice of renting mentioned earlier. In 1920, 52.2 percent of the nation's farms were operated by full owners and 8.7 percent by partowners. Tenants made up 38.1 percent of the operators in that year. Ten years later, in 1930, the number of full owners was down to 46.3 percent, with partowners operating 10.4 percent of the farms. Tenants were operating 42.4 percent of the farms at this time. It is of interest that sharecropping was at its peak in this year, being practiced on 24.1 percent of the farms of the nation, mostly in the South.

The last Census of Agriculture available, for 1969, indicates that full owners now operate almost two-thirds of the farms of the nation (62.5 percent). Part owners operate one-fourth of the farms (24.6 percent). Sharecroppers have all but disappeared from the farm scene. They included only 7.4 percent of the farm operators in 1959 and were not considered numerous enough to count in 1964 and later census years.

On U.S. farms the last decade has seen a steady drop in the number of hired workers. In 1959 almost 2 million persons other than family members were employed on farms. By 1973 this number had dropped to less than 1.2 million. This trend is important in itself but becomes more so when it is considered that family workers also decreased at a rather sharp rate. In 1959 approximately 5.4 million family members were working on farms in addition to hired workers. Only 3.2 million were counted in 1972.

Trends in the Number and Distribution of People. The demographic trends related to agricultural technology are covered in great detail in other places in this volume. They are simply identified here in order to maintain a perspective for the reader. The main trends are population growth; redistribution of population from rural to urban places, with a recent trend toward migration to rural places; regional redistribution of population; and change in age distribution of the population.

Trend toward Shifts in Location of Agricultural Enterprises. Another technology related trend is the shift occurring in the location of agricultural enterprises. Two types of shifts have taken place. The first is the movement of specific crops; the second is the distribution of total harvested acreages. Illustration of the former is the migration of cotton production from one coast toward the other as new technology has entered the scene. Irrigation technology has made it possible for states like California, Arizona, and Texas to produce cotton more cheaply than is possible in the Mississippi Delta, where irrigation is not necessary. Irish potato production has tended to move from Maine and the East to the Pacific Northwest for technology related reasons. Soybeans have pushed cotton and other crops out in various places and have taken over in former wetlands, as drainage technology has advanced. As technology has made it possible to reduce the acreage needed for food production, the number of acres of harvested crops in some regions has been altered drastically. The populous eastern portion of the U.S. has experienced the greatest reduction in acres of crops harvested, in part due to to population growth but principally due to the poor adaptability of much of the land to mechanized farming (Barrons, 1971).

RURAL OR NONMETROPOLITAN INDUSTRIALIZA-TION: THE TREND OF THE PAST 25 YEARS. Since the early 1960s a number of federal legislative acts have been passed with the purpose of encouraging industrial development in rural areas of the United States. These statutes reflect a public policy view that has been crystalizing rather rapidly during the past 25 years. This view apparently derives its inspiration from two important factors: a "pull" for industry to move to the countryside, and a "push" for industry to move out of urban and metropolitan settings.

The pull factor is embedded in the growing conviction that rural-to-urban migration must be stopped and that the best means of doing this is to provide greater employment and income opportunity in rural areas. The push for moving industry out of the city into the country is bound up in what some have termed the "urban crisis." The ever-increasing problems of congestion, of environmental deterioration, of labor instability, and of skyrocketing costs have made industrialists investigate rural factory sites where such problems might be minimized. Maurice Fulton, president of the Fantus Company, explains one reason why executives who a decade ago swore they would not consider operation in a small town now have changed their minds:

We have one client with a plant in a big city and a new one in a small community. Both plants have the same machinery and both make the same product. All employees are a piecework basis. But the plant in the country out-produces the one in the city by one-third. Why? The answer is that in the city, you have a built-in attitude of job protection (North Carolina State University Policy Institute, 1970:70).

Of course, many other considerations enter into decisions about the location of a given plant. However in the eyes of knowledgeable groups — legislators, social scientists, businessmen, industrialists — rural industrialization is appealing enough to turn advice and decision making noticeably in this direction.

The Nature of Rural Industrialization. Gene Summers and some of his research colleagues at the University of Wisconsin have astutely observed that "the industrial development of a rural area within a technologically and industrially advanced nation is a process unlike the historical emergence of industrialized western societies" (Summers et al.,

1974:2-3). They go on to explain that industrialization per se must be conceived as an evolutionary process that derives its origin from scientific discovery and thus is a corollary growth of technological innovation. By contrast, rural industrial development is simply a redistribution in space of economic activity and technology already developed within a nation or society. Rural industrial development has not been treated extensively, although the work of Summers and his associates is a significant start in this direction.

A clear distinction should be made between rural industrialization and two other trends that have characterized industrial development in the U.S. within relatively recent years. One of these trends has been the much publicized shift of industry from the northeast and north central states to the states of the West and South. The second has been the movement of industry from central-city locations to the suburbs. Both trends remain in evidence, but they are distinct from rural industrialization. Although some of the industry that has moved south and west has located in rural areas, the reasons for moving to these regions and the reasons for choosing to locate outside of cities are quite separate matters.

By almost any measure the trend of rural industrialization has been most significant within the past decade and a half (1960-75), but it began some time before. Claude C. Haren points out that nonmetropolitan counties gained manufacturing jobs at the rate of 4.0 percent annually between 1959 and 1969, while metropolitan counties added such jobs at half this rate (Haren, 1974:9). By the end of this period the non-metropolitan counties of the nation had increased their share of the nation's manufacturing jobs to one out of every four. Some individuals who have spent a great deal of time studying rural industrialization forecast that this trend will not only continue but accelerate during the next few decades (Summers et al., 1974:3-9).

The Rationale for Rural Industrialization[1]

Federal Policies and Programs to Redistribute Population and Industry. Casting aside the issue of the appropriateness of government intervention in industrial location and population redistribution, it can be pointed out that the government has in fact made a rather massive effort to channel industry into what have been construed as depressed rural areas. The presumption is that industrial development will bring about increased economic opportunity and improve the quality of living there. In one way or another the provisions of the following Acts were designed to encourage capital investment in rural areas:

1. Economic Opportunity Act of 1964
2. Public Works and Economic Development Act of 1965

---

1. The discussion that follows draws upon the work of Gene Summers and associates at the University of Wisconsin.

3. Appalachian Regional Development Act of 1965
4. Rural Development Act of 1972

Other legislation with similar goals is currently under study by congressional committees and government agencies. They could well add to the large sums of money that have already been dedicated to the decentralization of industry.

Efforts of Local Communities to Attract Industry. It is indeed rare to find a town that does not have a committee (or other group) actively engaged in promoting industrial development in its particular community. (For an account of how and why industry came to five small towns in Kentucky, see Garrison, 1970.) In fact, so popular is this activity that a host of planners specializes in helping communities attract industry. At the same time, a number of "cookbook"-type publications are available on the subject of how to get an industry to come to town (for example, "How a ·Town Can Attract Industry" in the *1971 Yearbook of Agriculture*).

It is another part of the story that many communities have overextended or overcommitted themselves to attract industry and have only bitter experience to recount for their efforts. Nevertheless a strong conviction remains among the leaders of small towns that all their economic ills could be solved by an industry, and the attractive propositions made to industry no doubt have played an important role in rural industrialization.

Preference of Industry. Maurice Fulton, writing as president of a large diversifed company, states:

Many employers are growing disenchanted with big-city conditions. . . . The combination of journey-to-work frustrations, fear of physical attack, air pollution, and overpowering noise levels, coupled with high living costs and economic anxiety, is adversely affecting attitudes, work habits, and productivity (1974:69).

Summers and his colleagues (1974:2–11) identified four reasons for the preference of industry for rural locations: the lower cost of water and land; the tax exemptions and other inducements offered by local communities; the growing difficulty of attracting workers to plants in the central cities; and the belief that there is more of a "work ethic" among the residents of small towns and open country areas.

Preferences for small-town and rural location seem to be more strongly evident in the South than in other parts of the nation (Lonsdale and Browning, 1971). The nonmetro South added approximately three-quarters of a million manufacturing jobs in the 1960s. This represented more than half of all the manufacturing jobs accruing to the region during this period and one-fourth of all such jobs opening up in the nation (Haren, 1974:9).

Miscellaneous Factors. Several other factors have contributed to the rural industrialization trend. The first of these is the labor pool created by the decline in farm jobs as agricultural mechanization has progressed. Unless migration streams to urban areas are of sufficient size to carry off all those seeking work, the rates of unemployed and underemployed tend to rise in rural areas as technology invades agriculture related enterprises.

A second factor is the improved national, state, and local highway system. An interstate route is usually not far away from rural communities, and most connecting roads to these communities are hard surfaced and all weather.

A third factor that attracts industry is the increasing availability to rural residents of good schools, modern conveniences, and other cultural and social opportunities. In the past it was difficult to attract the more sophisticated workers to small communities because they were not able to enjoy the "style of life" they wished for themselves and their families.

The Problems of Rural Industrial Development. At least a partial myth exists among the planners for nonmetropolitan communities that "industry" will bring general economic and social betterment regardless of circumstances. The presence of this myth is evidenced in the intense competitive efforts of many small rural communities to attract industry. It is true that industry can bring benefits, but it is also true that industry can and does bring problems that sometimes override the positive aspects of their presence. The problems of industrial development in rural areas are of two distinct types. The first type includes all the difficulties that must be overcome before an industry can be attracted to a rural community. The second type arises after the industry has located within its environment.

The Problem of Attracting Industry. Obviously no sophisticated management team is going to choose a site for the location of a new plant without thorough investigation of the advantages of the particular area over others (see Holt and Pratt, 1974). Thus the community must provide assurance that both the physical and the social climate are compatible with the needs of the industry. Carl E. Annas of Burlington Industries, in explaining his company's policy for locating plants, comments on this point by asking this question:

For instance, does community leadership really want industry? This is a legitimate question and one that has considerable significance for us. Often a small group in a community may become enamored with the idea of getting new industry . . . when the broader leadership may be less than enthusiastic (Annas, 1970:18).

It is easy for the leaders of any community to say, "we have to go out and get a new industry for our town." But not all such leaders are cognizant of the tough job of planning that lies ahead. The following are specific problems with which communities that hope to attract industry must deal.

1. *The problem of a strong industrial development program.* This

84 A. L. Bertrand

problem is inherent in the difficulty of bringing together all the important resource people of the community into a cohesive, dedicated group. This group in turn must stand ready to do what is necessary for the preparation of the promotional and financial phases of the project. Too often it is impossible to get the full cooperation needed.

2. *The problem of projecting a strong community image.* Essentially this means that the community must show evidence of being a progressive, pleasant social environment. The people of the community must be seen as forward looking and interested in maintaining good schools, good health programs, and ongoing community improvement programs.

3. *The problem of providing an attractive, well-developed site.* Sites for industry must include more than mere geographic space. The terrain features must be right; the site must be accessible to utilities; transportation facilities must be adjacent; and certain satellite services must be available. The problem most communities face is the allocation of funds for the development of a suitable industrial site. It often is more politically expedient to invest money in projects with results that are more immediately perceived.

4. *The problem of providing the needed utilities and services.* When an industry is searching for location, it naturally wants to become operational in a minimum time. This means that the community seeking industry must have the potential for early if not immediate availability of water, electricity, sewage disposal, and other utilities the industry will need. In addition, services such as communication (telephone, telegraph, radio), banking, fire and police protection, and transportation must be available and adequate for the demand that will accompany industry.

The Problems Created by Industry. The consequences of industries locating in rural areas are often unanticipated or unplanned for. These consequences may represent problems that are unfamiliar and overwhelming to local officials. Some of the problems related to rural industrial development are discussed below (the following list is derived principally from the excellent article by Scott and Summers, 1974).

1. *The problem of leakage of economic advantage.* When a commuity goes through all of the processes needed to get an industry, it is with the anticipation that the economic benefits of the industry will remain largely in the community. This frequently does not happen, for a number of employees commute from outside the community and spend their income in surrounding towns. This is one reason that several adjacent communities need to work together in an industrialization project. A second reason is that persons living in the community but working elsewhere may now opt for employment in the new local industry. The net effect is that no additional money is put into circulation in the community.

Ralph Gray explains the economic leakage phenomenon as follows:

A city or county is not a closed, self sustaining unit. Workers cross county and city lines to report to their jobs, and they spend portions of their paychecks at retail centers other than where they work. Thus the benefits of a new industry . . . tend to radiate from the plant site (1962:21).

All in all, the possibility of going into bonded indebtedness to bring an industry in and then of losing a substantial portion of the economic benefit of the industry is a problem worth careful investigation.

2. *The problem of upsetting the stability of the local real estate market.* Some industries require rather large acreages for their operations. It is certain that land prices in areas adjacent to the location of the industry will be affected by such a large purchase. In the sale of large acreages, the agricultural economy is often disrupted. Land is revalued above its worth as farmland, and the farmers displaced by the original acquisition of industry cannot find land to work. Many may be too old or lack the skills to find other types of jobs. Even when an industry does not need a large amount of land, it is likely that real estate values around the plant will change, and this will cause speculation which may affect the stability of the community (see Scott and Chen, 1973).

3. *The problem of a rising cost of living.* Commonly small towns and villages serve as residence areas for older persons, many of whom are retirees. These individuals are likely to be living on minimum incomes and are vulnerable to any type of inflationary trend (Scott and Summers, 1974:79). One of the first impacts of an industry is to increase the demand for housing and for certain types of services. People also move from relatively low-paying jobs in grocery stores and the like to higher wage rates, as industry attracts the better workers. This causes prices to rise, as merchants have to pay more for their help. Since the low cost of living is the advantage that makes a rural community attractive as a place for retirees, welfare and relief loads may increase. The latter seems to be more of a problem for those persons not eligible for or able to take advantage of industry related opportunities.

4. *The problem of short-run, boom-type demand for facilities and services.* In many instances the incoming industry is relatively large and builds substantial quarters for its operation. Normally a contractor will bring a considerable number of workers with him when he takes on a contract of this type. This means that there will be pressure for housing and other accommodations for the period of the contract. Because of the short-term nature of these demands, local or outside entrepreneurs are usually not interested in investing in housing or other types of establishments. In fact, those persons who do overexpand in the hope the market will hold tend to create problems themselves.

5. *The problem of unbalanced employment.* Some industries hire mostly women, whereas others employ mostly men. In each instance certain developments may not be anticipated. When mostly women are employed average family income increases, but additional demand for such things as housing, restaurants, and furniture is small. Unemployment rates may also increase, because some men can remain in the community without jobs if their wives are working. Too, women normally not in the

employment force now are eligible to register as unemployed if they seek or lose a job.

A factory hiring mostly men will have quite different effects on the economy. An increase in demand for housing as well as for public services can be anticipated, since more men employed will usually mean more family units. However, per capita income and expenditures seldom increase at a rate sufficient to offset additional community costs for schools, streets, fire and police protection, and other services.

If the new industry hires men predominantly, the change in the local labor demand will affect wage rates and have repercussions on labor intensive enterprises. Workers will be attracted to the higher-wage, "easier" jobs, and vulnerable operations may be curtailed or dropped (In 1973 Durant studied this kind of impact of industrial development on farm enterprises).

The Potentials of Rural Industrialization. National policymakers, as well as the residents of rural communities, have generally considered industrial development a partial solution to rural outmigration and urban congestion. Since the obvious hope is that industrialization will reverse migration patterns and improve economic levels, it is well to look at what has actually happened in rural areas that have attracted industry. Some of the consequences have been summarized in a report by Summers and his associates (1974).

Rural Industrialization and Population Growth in Host Communities. This growth is almost always concentrated in the villages and towns nearest to the site of the plant. It is not normally of excessive proportion, although it tends to be a function of the size of the manufacturing plant or other type of industry. As might be expected, the source of population growth is generally inmigration coupled with unchanged or decreased outmigration. Nonresident workers usually commute for a period of time, then move closer to the site of their employment.

Population growth in host towns does not necessarily mean growth of host counties. In some instances the population of the larger area is simply redistributed or outmigration is slowed, or both. All in all, industrialization contributes to the solution of the problem of rural area depopulation, but not to the extent to which some planners anticipate (for a description of two case studies, see Ralph Gray, 1962).

Rural Industrialization and Increased Residential Mobility. Several studies show that the presence of an industry within a county is correlated with an increase in the number of moves per household. Plant employees as a group are considerably more mobile than rural dwellers in general. It is hard to say whether industrialization per se stimulates residential mobility, but it seems logical to expect persons seeking nonfarm jobs to be willing to move to advantageous locations for those jobs (see Irwin Gray's description of the inmigration of workers to a plant in West Virginia, 1969:26-30).

Rural Industrialization and Age Composition of the Population. Rural populations tend to have concentrations of older and younger people because of the usually high rates of outmigration of young adults and high birth rates. Research on the impact of industry on age distribution in rural communities indicates an increase of persons in the so-called productive ages, a consequence of employer preference for young workers (Maitland and Cowhig, 1958). This change has implications for overall community development, affecting the character, for example, of schools and social life.

The Economic Multiplier Effect of Rural Industrial Development. An often-heard argument for rural industrialization is that every dollar brought into a community will turn over several times and thus have a considerable "multiplier" effect on the local economy. Such effects are generated in two basic ways — by purchases of raw materials, supplies, and services directly utilized by the plant and by payrolls which diffuse through the local economy and indirectly create jobs. With regard to the first factor, studies indicate that very few small rural communities are able to provide the services or goods needed by a large plant. With regard to the second factor, it is usual for a considerable number of employees to be commuters from other communities. A multiplier benefit of some extent operates in the host community, but its effects are usually diluted (Garrison, 1972).

The Impact of Industry on Unemployment. A logical expectation of newly developed industry in a rural community is that it will reduce unemployment noticeably, but this does not appear to happen in a majority of instances. In fact the pattern seems to be for unemployment rates to remain approximately at previous levels, for several reasons. The opportunity for local employment slows outmigration, with the consequence of greater labor pools. More persons are stimulated to seek work once the opportunity structure is broadened, and many persons coming from outside the community may obtain jobs in the new plant. Finally, the plant may employ persons not previously considered a part of the labor force, such as women. This not only fails to reduce the ranks of unemployed males but tends to raise rates of unemployment when women lose their jobs or seek but cannot find work (for an often-quoted study of the employment effect of a new industry, see Irwin Gray, 1969).

The Impact of Industrialization on "Poor" or "Disadvantaged" Groups. Much of the legislation directed toward rural industrialization is inspired by the assumption that workers will be recruited largely from the ranks of the so-called disadvantaged. The latter include minority groups, the aged, and other individuals who normally have low incomes. Studies indicate that the type of industry has a lot to do with who will be employed. Industries with low skill requirements and low wage levels look for places with large pools of unskilled labor and do employ a number of persons in the disadvantaged category. However, even these industries usually pass over the hard-core unemployed persons (Till, 1974). Industries demanding high skills and educational levels employ very few individuals at the poverty level. With regard to specific minorities, such as blacks, hiring practices seem to follow those customary in the region. Rural industrialization is thus not a great answer to the employment of the disadvantaged.

Rural Industrialization and Improvement in Quality of Life. The majority of residents of recently industrialized areas tend to express positive feelings about the industrial development in their communities (Summers, et al., 1974:7-26). Feelings of this nature are indicated by statements to the effect that their community is now a better place to live. More specifically, residents who are positive about industralization say that the economy is more diversified, that rents and real estate values are favorably influenced, that schools, churches, and cultural activities improve, that new markets for agricultural products open, and that population ceases to decline. Those who express negative feelings are usually unhappy because prices go up, because labor is more expensive, because the peace and quiet of the community are disrupted to an extent, and because taxes and property values are higher. Generally, though, industrialization serves to raise the level of community morale and pride, especially when accompanied by obvious improvements in such things as health facilities, roads, and housing.

SOCIAL-ORGANIZATIONAL IMPLICATIONS OF TECHNOLOGY AND INDUSTRIALIZATION IN SUMMARY.

What is likely to be the continuing impact of agricultural technology and rural industrialization? A quotation by John Diebold of the Diebold Institute for Policy Studies sets the stage for a concluding statement:

Technology has always been important as an agent of change. However, the people who have created or applied new technology generally have thought last of all, if at all, of the real implications of that technology for society (Holmes, 1973:196).

Planners for agricultural and rural areas of the nation must be aware of and alert to the benefits and/or problems not only of technology and industrialization per se, but of their specialized application. Each of the related policies and programs adopted will have implications for social organization and will require alterations in the way people think and how they relate to one another.

Part 5

VALUE, BELIEF, AND NORMATIVE SYSTEMS

6 Values and Beliefs of Rural People

OLAF F. LARSON

WHAT are the value systems and beliefs of rural people in contemporary American society? How do these value systems and beliefs compare with those held by people who do not live in rural America? What are the variations within rural society? What changes in rural values and beliefs appear to be under way? These are the primary questions considered in this chapter.

The present account was originally to be derived entirely from existing studies. To this end, research literature since 1960 was reviewed to cover the period since preparation of *Our Changing Rural Society* (Copp, 1964), the predecessor of the current volume. (For a discussion of values and beliefs in that volume, see especially pp. 25-30 and 53-54). The review yielded a paucity of hard and comprehensive data. Therefore I elected also to glean such evidence as I could from the results of the repeated national surveys published in the 118 numbers of the *Gallup Opinion Index* (abbreviated hereafter as *GOI*) between June 1965 and April 1975.

The Gallup Poll sample, stratified geographically and by size of community, is designed to produce a national sample of the adult civilian population in the United States in private households. Answers of rural respondents have to differ by roughly 7 to 10 percent from those in other size-of-place categories to be statistically significant. The published dată do not permit calculating tests of significance.

Four size-of-place categories were used prior to October 1969, namely, rural (under 2,500 population); 2,500-49,999; 50,000-499,999; and places of 500,000 and over. At the upper size limit data were reported

Olaf F. Larson is Professor of Rural Sociology, Emeritus, Cornell University. Appreciation is expressed to L. Richard Meyers, graduate research assistant, for his help in the search of the research literature and for work with data from the *Gallup Opinion Index*.

for places of 500,000 and over and also, within that group, for places of 1,000,000 and over. Since then five size categories have been used, with the two larger groupings being 500,000–999,999 and 1,000,000 and over.

VALUES

Major Value Orientations. Values are used here in the general sense elaborated by Williams (1970). In brief, values are *"conceptions of desirable states of affairs* that are utilized in selective conduct as *criteria* for preference or choice or as *justifications* for proposed or actual behavior" (p. 442). In his analysis of 15 dominant value orientations in American society, Williams rarely mentions rural or farm people specifically. These themes rise above regional, class, and other variations. Deeply rooted as the values are in our cultural heritage—they derive from both those received and those established when the society was new, frontier, and predominantly rural—it is reasonable to assume that unless he included it in his discussion, Williams did not find evidence for notable rural variations from the general pattern.

A shorthand labeling of the American value themes that Williams isolated for analysis is as follows: (1) a stress upon personal achievement, especially secular occupational achievement, and success; (2) a stress on activity and work; (3) a moral orientation by which conduct is judged; (4) "humanitarianism"—emphasis upon disinterested concern and helpfulness; (5) emphasis upon efficiency and practicality; (6) progress; (7) approval of material comfort; (8) equality; (9) freedom; (10) external conformity; (11) science and secular rationality; (12) nationalism-patriotism; (13) democracy; (14) worth of the individual personality; and, to complete the list, (15) a value orientation that runs counter to and conflicts with the individual personality-linked values listed, namely, racism and related group superiority (1970:454–500).

Williams sought to make broad estimates of the direction of change in these main value patterns (1970:635–37; 1967). Stating that the changes should not be overstressed, he found for the period 1945–66 a "suggestion" of *lessened* emphasis on activity and work; achievement (at least prior to Sputnik I); humanitarianism as related to war; practicality and efficiency; progress; freedom; and racism. He found some evidence of *increased* emphasis on success; material comfort; humanitarianism (domestic); science and secular rationality; equality; conformity to social pressure; and, in the later part of the period, nationalism. For the other values he concluded there was no change or the evidence was indeterminate. Following a national survey in 1968 of a probability sample of adults, Rokeach (1973:328) concluded that equality and freedom were among the 4 values, out of the 36 he measured, that increased in importance over time, thus concurring with Williams' estimate of the direction of change for equality but not for freedom. A second national survey in 1971 afforded an opportunity to determine change and stability in the 36 values (Rokeach, 1974); stability was characteristic of the majority.

Rural or farm people receive special comment by Williams, directly or indirectly, for only five of the value orientations. The value on mastery of the physical world, an illustration of *achievement* (p. 456), clearly has special relevance for rural people and particularly for farm people. The emphasis on *work* which permeated the older agrarian culture and was a core element in the historic culture still exists "in practically the original quasi-religious form in some rural areas" (as well as among some other subgroupings) (p. 459). Likewise, scattered data suggest at least the possibility that the historic values that centered upon traditional *moral orientations,* instrumental *activism,* and group *conformity* are most prevalent in rural areas (and in low-income populations and entrepreneurial occupations) (p. 487). Further, *equality* as a value complex, through the conception of equality of opportunity, has had a role in the populist movements for economic reform, including especially the attempts of the farming population to check the power of "big business" (p. 478).

The complete set of 15 values has been used rarely, if at all, in any one empirical investigation involving rural people. One of the most comprehensive adaptations for survey use is a North Carolina study of a statewide sample of 3,115 household heads (Christenson and Yang, 1975). The adaptations resulted, however, in loss of strict comparability. Respondents were asked to place each of 14 items representing values (the exact wording is given in Table 6.1) in one of four categories of importance to them, from "slight" to "very great," corresponding to numerical scores of 1 to 4. Mean numerical scores determined the hierarchal ordering of the values. The values were classified into two groups, one designated as *social* values and the other as *personal* values. Honesty is an example of "social" values, while personal freedom illustrates "personal" values. Ranking and scores within the two groups of values were compared for four residential categories: farm; town (under 10,000 population); small city (10,000–49,999); and large city (50,000 or over).

No significant differences were found among the four residential groupings in their ranking of the two groups of values, leading Christenson and Yang to conclude that North Carolina constitutes a homogeneous cultural area from the place-of-residence perspective (although not from the perspective of other variables such as race and age). Some values, both social and personal, such as moral integrity and personal freedom, were clearly rated by North Carolinians as more important than others, as is shown by the summary for the two extreme size-of-place groups in Table 6.1.

The ranking of the 14 items by respondents in places with a population of under 10,000, which would take in all the rural-nonfarm population, was closer to that of the farm residents than to that of the people in cities of 50,000 and over. Low rank should not be taken to mean

Table 6.1.   Ranking of values by North Carolina farm and large-city residents.

Value	Value Type[a]	Farm		City of 50,000 +	
		Rank	Mean score	Rank	Mean score
Moral integrity (honesty)	S	1	3.57	1	3.63
Personal freedom	P	2	3.45	2	3.50
Patriotism (to country)	S	3	3.22	4	3.19
Work (your job)	P	4	3.20	3	3.29
Being practical and efficient	P	5	3.12	5	3.13
Helping others (humanitarianism)	S	6	3.01	7	2.94
Political democracy	S	7	2.99	6	3.09
Achievement (getting ahead)	P	8	2.82	8	2.90
National progress	S	9	2.70	9.5	2.74
Material comfort	P	10	2.66	11	2.65
Equality (racial)	S	11.5	2.44	12	2.58
Individualism	P	11.5	2.44	13	2.54
Leisure (recreation and taking it easy)	P	13	2.41	9.5	2.74
Equality (sexual)	S	14	2.18	14	2.28

Source: Adapted from Christenson and Yang, 1975.
[a]S = social value; P = personal value

that a value was of little importance. On the contrary, for the total sample only three values failed to be considered as of "great" or "very great" importance by the majority; these three were sexual equality, individualism (nonconformity), and racial equality. The North Carolina study provides empirical survey evidence that farm, small-town, and other residents in the state hold major values in a way generally consistent with that suggested by Williams' analysis.

Values of Youth.   In Schwarzweller's Kentucky study (1960) of high school seniors in eight rural high schools, several of the Williams value orientations were included. The Central Bluegrass and the Eastern Mountain regions were used for the study because they were assumed to be regions with contrasting cultural characteristics. However, with minor exceptions, the two regions had a strikingly similar pattern of value orientations. Schwarzweller suggests that the rural high school serves as a cultural bridge, with respect to values, between rural communities and the Great Society.

In a study by Clark and Wenninger (1963) public school youth in grades 6-12 in four contrasting types of communities — rural, a wealthy Chicago suburb, an area in an industrial city of about 35,000 near Chicago, and a largely black, predominantly lower socioeconomic-class area of Chicago — were asked to rate items representing each of Williams' major value orientations as of "great importance," "some importance," or "little or no importance" to them. The rural community youth differed significantly from those in all three other types of communities on nationalism-patriotism, moral orientation, and activity-work — in each instance having a larger percentage rating the value as of "great importance." Freedom was the only value that failed to show a significant difference between some pairs of communities. The values ranked highest by rural youth were achievement-success, nationalism-patriotism, and moral orientation, in that order. (It should be added, however, that the usefulness of these findings is limited by the difficulty of accurately representing value orientations in a word or brief sentence to meet the constraints of a questionnaire. I found the representations for democracy, worth of the individual, and racism especially dubious, perhaps accounting for the fact that all four samples placed democracy last among the 15 and that what was intended to signify racism was given such a high rating, even in the largely black area.)

Achievement and Success. In American society, education has been considered a means to occupational achievement and success. Educational aspirations could therefore serve as one indirect indicator of the comparative importance attached to the achievement and success value theme. This avenue of investigation, followed by numerous studies, should be borne in mind. However, the present review concentrates on those studies that focus directly on the values of achievement and success.

A study of 119 open-country household heads in an Arkansas low income county in the Ozark area found that being known in the community as a "successful man" received the lowest rank among the seven personal goals the heads were asked to rank (Folkman, 1962:22). The other six, from highest to lowest preference, were "providing a good education for my children," "owning my farm free of debt," "having lots of good friends in the community," "being one's own boss," "having modern conveniences in the house," and "having children settle nearby."

That Pennsylvania rural youth (high school sophomores) were more achievement oriented in 1960 and 1970 than their counterparts in 1947 might be concluded from their views on pupils who fail subjects in school, as reported in a set of carefully designed studies (Willits, Bealer, and Crider, 1973). However, youth concern with failure in school was not as strong in 1970 as ten years earlier, suggesting the possibility of a return to the trend for less emphasis on achievement.

Activity and Work. Job attachment (as measured by a scale on willingness to leave the present job) was significantly higher among open-country and small-village (less than 1,000 population) white male household heads in an 11-county area of western Illinois than among those living in larger places of up to 45,000 population (van Es and Brown, 1974). This held equally for both high and low level-of-living (measured by an 8-item scale of consumer durable items) households, with job attachment highest for high level-of-living rural households. Within the rural sample, job attachment was higher for farmers than for others.

A decrease in emphasis on work orientation by Pennsylvania rural youth between 1947 and 1970 is indicated by their responses to a question about criticism of young people "loafing uptown" (Willits, Bealer, and Crider, 1973). The decrease in work orientation was greater during the decade 1960–70 than during the preceding 13 years. Among different groups of rural young people, farm youth were more work oriented, by this indicator, at each of the three points in time than were their open-country nonfarm peers and village peers.

Moral Orientation. Some of the sharpest rural-urban differences are in the commitment to what is often stereotyped as the traditional morality associated with puritan ethical standards. Responses to some 20 indicator questions, illustrated in Table 6.2, point to this conclusion.

Examination of each Gallup Poll question judged relevant for the purposes of this chapter gave particular attention to the pattern of responses among the size-of-place categories. All survey questions offered respondents a choice of two or more response categories: "yes," "no," or "no opinion." Classification into one of five response types was based on the pattern for the category which drew a majority (or, in some instances, a plurality) for the national sample as a whole.

The contrast is most striking when the answers of rural people are compared with those of people in cities with populations of 1,000,000 and over. Rural people are markedly more in favor of increasing the difficulty of getting a divorce; they are more opposed to making birth control information available to anyone who wants it, to making birth control pills available to teenage girls, and to abortion to terminate normal pregnancy within the first three months. More rural people believe that premarital sex is wrong and find various expressions of nudity objectionable. They are more likely to find certain fashions in clothing objectionable, for example, the wearing of a miniskirt by a daughter (*GOI,* July 1967). Rural people are less opposed to national prohibition of the sale of alcoholic beverages. In all of these examples the rural–large-city differences range from 12 to 27 percent. It is also true, however, that for other indicators rural–large-city contrasts are not so great.

Responses for 10 of the 20 indicator questions are consistently related to size of community (a tie in the percentages for two adjacent size-of-place categories was permitted in identifying a pattern as consistent). This pattern is illustrated in Table 6.2 by the percentages in each size of place who believe premarital sex is wrong.

Table 6.2 also shows signs that rural people share with other Americans a weakening of commitment to some of the traditional ethical standards. Such a trend is demonstrated, for instance, in the smaller percentage who said in 1973, compared with four years earlier, that premarital sex was wrong and that three types of nudity were objectionable. What has to be pointed out, however, is that during the same period the rural–large-city difference *increased* for all four of these indicators (items 2, 7, 8, and 9 in Table 6.2), because rural people changed less than their most urbanized counterparts. The spread went from an

Table 6.2.   Moral orientation indicators by community size: United States adults.

Indicator Item (Year of Poll)	Rural	2,500– 49,999	50,000– 499,999	500,000– 999,999	1,000,000 and Over
			(% agreeing)		
1. Divorce should be more difficult to obtain (1968)	66	64	64	49[a]	44
2. Premarital sex is wrong					
(1969)	80	73	66	57	56
(1973)	61	50	44	41	34
3. Birth control pills should *not* be available to teenage girls (1967)	86	90	78	68[a]	62
4. Birth control information should be available to anyone who wants it (1968)	64	71	80	87[a]	88
5. Favor the U.S. Court ruling that a woman may have doctor end pregnancy during first 3 months (March 1974)	36	44	50	51	58
6. Abortion through third month should continue to be legal (Oct. 1974)	44	54	48	60	57
7. Nudity in Broadway plays is objectionable					
(1969)	87	87	78	72	75
(1973)	73	73	65	59	49
8. Nudes in magazines are objectionable					
(1969)	84	82	65	67	67
(1973)	67	67	53	44	. . .[b]
9. Topless nightclub waitresses are objectionable					
(1969)	82	83	70	72	81
(1973)	68	69	58	51	46
10. Oppose national law forbidding sale of beer, wine, and liquor (1966)	62	76	78	86[a]	. . .

Source: *Gallup Opinion Index.*
[a]Includes all places of 500,000 and over.
[b]Published figure (61) inconsistent with other data from same poll.

average of 13.5 percent in 1969 to an average of 24.0 percent in 1973. At the same time, two sets of answers shifted from an irregular to a rural-urban pattern, so that three out of four adhered to such a pattern. Such evidence clearly raises doubts about any contention that rural-urban value differences have been erased in the United States.

Further evidence that behavior departing from the puritanical Protestant stereotype of morality is increasingly accepted appears in the studies over time of Pennsylvania rural youth (Willits, Bealer, and Crider, 1973). However, the distinctions among farm, open-country nonfarm, and village youth in Pennsylvania were much more pronounced in 1970 than in 1947, because the change was less for farm than for other rural residents.

Humanitarian Mores. Numerous cases could be found to illustrate that humanitarianism is an important value pattern in rural America. Likewise, examples could be found in the rural arena to illustrate Williams' point that generosity in aiding persons in distress is also checked by conceptions of "justice" and "moral responsibility" (1970:464). Both the dominance of the humanitarianism theme and the tempering influence of other values among rural people are suggested by two Gallup survey questions (*GOI,* May 1969). A majority of the rural respondents, but a lower percentage than for any urban category, favored the government's giving free food stamps to all families with weekly earnings under $20. Just under one-half favored giving such stamps at a greatly reduced rate to families with weekly earnings of $20 to $60, whereas a majority in all urban categories favored such a policy.

Equality. In the political arena the equality theme has been gaining in dominance among rural people just as in American society generally, as measured by the results of questions in national surveys. The trend apparently has been to narrow the gap between rural areas and the nation as a whole. In 12 out of 14 inquiries the majority of rural people stated their willingness to vote for a qualified candidate for president (or, in one survey, for Congress) who was, depending on the survey, a Catholic man, a Jewish man, a woman, or a Negro man (*GOI,* September 1965, June 1967, April 1969, September 1970, August 1971, November 1971). At the same time, in eight of the surveys the data revealed a consistent rural-urban pattern, with the smallest favorable percentage found at the rural end of the continuum. Rural percentages were also lowest in four additional surveys that did not show a rural-urban pattern.

Size of place of residence was found to be significantly related to commitment to equal employment opportunities in a nationwide study of nearly 7,500 United Presbyterian elders and ministers (Nelsen and Yokley, 1970). For both elders (lay leaders elected at the local church level) and ministers, the percentage strongly approving equal employment opportunities followed a consistent rural-urban pattern, with least approval among those coming from rural areas (defined in the study as places of less than 5,000 population). The context suggests that equal employment opportunity referred specifically to blacks. (The responses include the 2 percent in the sample who were nonwhite.)

Like the majority of Americans, rural people assert publicly that in their community Negroes are treated the same as whites. In a consistent rural-urban response pattern, it is the rural group that has the largest percentage stating this perception (*GOI,* August 1967, July 1968). Likewise, it is rural women who have the most positive perception of women's equality; nearly three-fourths believe women get as good a break as men in the United States (*GOI*, September 1970). They do, however, concur with the majority who hold by a small margin that a woman with the same ability as a man doesn't have as good a chance to become a company executive. The prevailing perception by rural women that they get an equal break may explain why they typically express less support than any urban group for the Equal Rights Amendment to the Constitution; barely a majority favor such an amendment (*GOI*, March 1974, November 1974, April 1975).

Racism and Group Superiority Themes. Group superiority as a value runs directly counter to the cluster of dominant values represented by respect for the individual personality, equality, democracy, and freedom. The attempt as a national policy to strengthen the latter values is represented by school desegregation, the Civil Rights Act of 1964, expansion of voting rights, and the like. At the rural community level, behavioral and organizational manifestations of this policy may be seen in the schools, in the election of blacks to public office, and in the administrative merger of what was in a number of states a racially segregated Cooperative Extension Service.

Some erosion of racist values among rural people may be inferred from the fact that in the 1965 and 1967 Gallup surveys fewer than half of the rural sample said they would vote for a qualified Negro man for president if nominated by their party, but in the 1969 and 1971 surveys this changed to more than half. The same trend is suggested by Nelsen and Yokley's 1970 study of white Presbyterian elders and ministers. The young (under 45) rural elders and ministers were more likely than those 45 and over to be scored "liberal" on a civil rights scale.

No consistent pattern by size of community was found in a Gallup study (*GOI*, September 1969) that asked adults whether they had objections to sending their children to school with Negroes. Among the rural respondents, 87 percent said they would not object to a school where a few of the children were Negroes, 64 percent said they would not object where half were Negroes, but only 34 percent asserted they would not object if more than half of the children in the school were Negroes.

Empirical rural research evidence on the other major values isolated by Williams is not reviewed here because it is especially scant.

BELIEFS, BEHAVIOR, AND GENERAL OUTLOOK. Beliefs, in the sense used here, "concern what the believer takes as reality" (Williams, 1970:443). Beliefs may be evaluated as desirable or undesirable quite apart from whether they are demonstrably true or false. The review of research literature excluded studies concerned with beliefs and preferences about the rural environment as a place to live, about the rural physical environment, and about the rural "way of life."

Religious and Political Self-perceptions and Orientations. A larger proportion of rural people than of others rate themselves as "very" or "fairly" religious, claim political independence in the voting booth, and—for those willing to state a choice—would prefer a conservative over a liberal political party if there were to be two new ones. On all of these issues a consistent rural-urban pattern appears. The percentage comparisons for the rural and the large-city places of 1,000,000 and over are shown in Table 6.3.

Perhaps reflecting their sense of political independence, rural people are consistently less willing than others to declare their alignment along the conservative-liberal political spectrum. Although rural areas invariably have a larger percentage of residents who rate themselves as conservative in political beliefs than do large cities (*GOI*, July 1969, April and November 1970), the rural sector does not consistently live up to the image of being the most conservative politically. At times rural residents are surpassed in this respect by those in towns and small cities (population 2,500 to 49,999). Rural and town and small-city people agree in differing noticeably from those in large cities in the margin by which the self-designated conservatives outnumber the liberals.

Some Rural-Urban Beliefs and Behavior Compared. Rural people tend to differ from others in their faith in religion and in their religious beliefs, just as they differ in professed religiosity and in moral orientation indicators. To a greater extent rural people believe that religion can answer "all or most of today's problems," rather than being "old-fashioned and out of date" (Table 6.4). Like others, but more so, they disapprove by a wide margin the Supreme Court ban on reading of the Lord's Prayer or Bible verses in public schools.

In a study by Nelsen, Yokley, and Madron (1971) which used Gallup 1968 data, an index of orthodox religious beliefs was found for white Protestants and Catholics to be strongly associated with place of residence in a rural-urban pattern. Some 65 percent of the rural residents, as

Table 6.3. Rural–large-city comparisons of religious and political orientation indicators: United States adults.

Indicator Item (Year of Poll)	Rural	Large City[a]
	(%)	
Rate self as "very" or "fairly" religious (1974)	92	86
Have not always voted for candidates of the same party in past presidential elections (1972)	60	46
If two new political parties were formed, conservative or liberal, would prefer the conservative (1974)	43	34

Source: *Gallup Opinion Index.*
[a] One million and over.

Table 6.4.   Rural-urban comparisons of selected religious beliefs and behavior: United States adults.

Belief or Behavior (Year of Poll)	Percent Agreeing		Percent Difference	Response Pattern[b]
	Rural	Large city[a]		
Believe that religion can answer "all or most of today's problems," rather than being "largely old-fashioned and out-of-date" (1974)	69	44	25	R hi/LC lo
Disapprove of U.S. Court ruling that no state or local government may require reading of Lord's Prayer or Bible verses in public schools (1971)	72	62	10	R hi
Attended church during average week:				
(1966)[c]	44	47	−3	LC hi
(1970)	44	39	5	R hi
(1974)	42	35	7	LC lo
Catholics (1974)	53	49	4	LC lo
Protestants (1974)	41	32	9	R hi/U lo
Catholic women (1974)	62	51	11	LC lo
Catholic men (1974)	42	45	−3	R lo
Protestant women (1974)	45	32	13	R hi/LC lo
Protestant men (1974)	37	31	6	R hi
Have read any part of Bible at home in past year (1974)	71	47	24	R hi/U lo
Protestants only (1974)	76	63	13	LC lo

Source: *Gallup Opinion Index.*

[a]One million and over unless specified as 500,000 and over.

[b]R hi/U lo means a consistent variation by the five size-of-place categories. R hi/LC lo means that the highest and lowest percentages are for the two extremes in size of place but the pattern is not consistent for the intervening sizes of place. R hi or lo means rural has the largest or smallest percentage but the opposite is held by a place other than LC; LC hi or lo means the reverse.

[c]For 1966 LC includes all places of 500,000 and over.

compared with 40 percent in the large-city places, were classified as holding orthodox beliefs.

Church attendance is another story. In repeated surveys during the last half of the 1960s and in the 1970s, church attendance during the average week showed no significant difference by size of community. However, there is a hint that over the last decade a rural–large-city difference may be emerging, because the rural areas have resisted the nationwide downward trend in churchgoing. Thus the illustrative data in Table 6.4 show stability over the period 1966–74 in church attendance reported by rural adults, whereas the percentage of large-city attenders dropped. The declining attendance by large-city Catholics may account for the overall rural–large-city difference which is starting to appear.

Rural Protestants, and especially Protestant women, outdo their counterparts in all sizes of urban places in attending church (see Table 6.4). The same is not true of their Catholic neighbors.

Considering all religious faiths together, rural people exceed others in the percentage who read the Bible at home. The response by size of place falls into a consistent rural-urban pattern. The pattern does not hold for all place sizes among Protestants as a separate group, although such reading is reported by 13 percent more rural than large-city Protestants.

Rural people tend to differ quite markedly from large-city residents in some of their beliefs about citizenship and governmental systems (Table 6.5). For example, the idea of control of public expenditures by state and local governments rather than federal draws more support from rural than from large-city people. The revenue-sharing idea is an interesting case about which reactions were sought three times in a single year. Within 12 months, rural and large-city residents moved ever closer to agreement in favoring the idea, because the urbanites moved toward the rural point of view. Perhaps from the emergence of the issue the rural people were reflecting their belief in local control as against centralization, whereas

Table 6.5.   **Rural-urban comparisons of selected civic and governmental beliefs and behavior: United States adults.**

Belief or Behavior (Year of Poll)	Percent Agreeing		Percent Difference	Response Pattern[b]
	Rural	Large city[a]		
"Always" or "nearly always" vote (1970)	76	77	−1	Irregular
Registered in election district where now live (1970)	76	74	2	Irregular
Think state government spends taxpayer's dollar more wisely than federal (1967)[c]	56	36	20	LC lo
Favor returning 3 percent of federal income tax collections to state and local governments to use as they see fit				
(January 1967)[c]	79	57	22	R hi/LC lo
(May 1967)[c]	78	65	13	R hi/U lo
(August 1967)[c]	76	72	4	Irregular
Willing to serve on committee to deal with local problems, if asked (1969)[c]	61	50	11	LC lo
Never served on committee to deal with local problems (1969)[c]	89	85	−4	R hi/U lo

Source: *Gallup Opinion Index*.

[a]One million and over, unless specified as 500,000 and over.

[b]R hi/U lo means a consistent variation by the five size-of-place categories. R hi/LC lo means that the highest and lowest percentages are for the two extremes in size of place but the pattern is not consistent for the intervening sizes of place. R hi or lo means rural has the largest or smallest percentage but the opposite is held by a place other than LC; LC hi or lo means the reverse.

[c]LC includes all places of 500,000 and over.

many metropolitan inhabitants shifted from a "no opinion" to a supporting position.

The majority of rural Americans, 61 percent, assert they would accept if asked to serve on a committee which would deal with local problems such as housing, recreation, traffic, health, and the like. However, only 11 percent of the rural adults reported experience on such a committee. In this, as in "always" or "nearly always" voting and in being registered in the election district where they now live, the rural–large-city differences are small, even where there is a rural-urban pattern.

Some evaluative beliefs related to family reflect strong rural-urban differences. The family unit has long been held to be one of the distinctive features of rural society, with rural families characterized by their larger number of children and lower rate of breakup by divorce. Historically a regular pattern of fertility differences along the rural-urban continuum was observable. A decade ago this fertility pattern conformed with rural-urban differences as to the ideal number of children a family should have. This is no longer so. Since the start of the 1970s large families (four or more children) have gone out of favor in communities of all sizes. In this sharp shift, the traditional rural-urban differences have been greatly reduced, and the regularity of the rural-urban pattern has been broken up. In 1966, for instance, 48 percent of rural adults believed four or more children to be ideal, as compared with 31 percent in cities of 500,000 or more population (*GOI*, April 1966). In contrast, a 1974 survey found such larger families favored by only 22 percent of the rural and 16 percent of the largest-city respondents (*GOI*, May 1974). The magnitude of the shift away from larger toward smaller preferred family size has been distinctly greater for rural than other people.

One additional form of behavior—the use of alcoholic beverages—is of interest because of the contention by Lowe and Peek (1974) that it is symbolically representative of contrasting life-styles. They cite several national and state studies that found abstinence consistently related not only to size of community of residence but to size of community in which respondents were reared. Additional support for this relationship is found in a Gallup survey in which, in a rural-urban pattern, rural people were lowest in the proportion who reported they used alcoholic beverages (*GOI*, June 1974).

Satisfaction, Confidence, and Outlook. Other information from polls and surveys, while not dealing directly with values and beliefs, may tell us something about the state of mind of rural people in contemporary society—their satisfactions, confidence in U.S. institutions, and outlook on trends and the future.

Campbell, Converse, and Rodgers (1976) developed a composite Index of Well-Being as a measure of overall life satisfaction in connection with a national survey in 1971. With this measure they found "there is a substantial gradient of increasing sense of well-being with life as one moves from the inhabitants of the nation's twelve largest cities to those of more sparsely settled areas" (p. 51). Rural people, both blacks and whites, scored higher on this Index of Well-Being than city people (pp. 52–53). A substantial relationship was also found between level of community satisfaction and size of community, with rural areas highest in level of satisfaction (pp. 234–38).

On 21 questions pertaining to satisfaction with quality of life in the community, standard of living, family income, housing, and the job — asked in Gallup surveys between 1965 and 1973 — the percentage satisfied was larger among rural people than among those in large cities for every question. More than 4 out of 5 rural people were satisfied with the quality of life in their community and about three-fourths with their "standard of living" (*GOI*, October 1971 and December 1973), roughly three-fourths with their housing situation (six surveys, 1965–73), about two-thirds with their family income (five surveys, 1965–73), and some 82 to 90 percent with the work they were doing (six surveys, 1965–73). The rural–large-city differences in satisfaction did not mean that among the five size-of-place categories the rural places consistently had a larger percentage satisfied than did urban centers of all sizes. On the contrary, the highest satisfaction level was found in rural areas for only 10 of the 21 questions. It is also true, however, that with respect to income and housing, and possibly job satisfaction, the rural–large-city differences in satisfaction became greater around 1969–70 than before. In fact, there was far more evidence of a rural-urban or rural–large-city pattern in the 1970s than previously. The large-city contrast with all other sized places in frequency of satisfaction stands out. For 19 of the 21 questions, large cities were the residential group with the lowest percentage of satisfied people.

Another perspective on life circumstances is provided by how people rate their life — as "generally exciting," "pretty routine," or "dull." Fewer than half, 45 percent, in rural areas find life exciting (*GOI*, October 1969), while in urban places of all sizes those who find life exciting outnumber those who find it routine. Fewer than 1 out of 10 Americans, rural or otherwise, rate their lives as generally dull.

To what extent do rural people share in the pessimistic views about key institutions in American society which have taken hold in recent years? The evidence suggests that dissatisfaction and lack of confidence predominate with respect to all but the church and public schools among the set of institutions examined here. Even in the case of the two exceptions, a sizeable minority view exists.

Nearly three-fourths of rural respondents profess a "great deal" or "quite a lot" of respect for and confidence in the church or organized religion, a larger proportion than for any other residential category and 16 percent more than residents of large cities (*GOI*, July 1973).

Rural areas and the large cities are at the extremes in the strength of support for the public schools. About two-thirds of those in rural areas, but barely a majority in the big cities, assert "a great deal" or "quite a lot" of respect for and confidence in the public schools. Likewise, in 5 out of 7 national surveys between 1965 and 1973 a larger percentage of rural than other people expressed satisfaction with the education their children were getting, or thought the public schools were generally doing a good job. The rural–large-city margins ranged from 8 to 22 percent, with the exception of the 1965 survey, which recorded no difference.

For nearly all key institutions except the church and public schools, rural people have *less* respect and confidence than do their fellow Americans. The rural percentages for "a great deal" or "quite a lot" of respect and confidence are as follows (*GOI*, July 1973):

Newspapers	35 percent
Television	34 percent
Labor unions	26 percent
The U.S. Supreme Court	37 percent
Congress	39 percent

The rural–large-city differences range only from 1 to 14 percent, but in each instance it is among rural people that confidence in these institutions is weakest. The poor rating received by labor unions is balanced out by the fact that it was rural people who had the largest percentage, 34, according big business "very little" or no respect and confidence. This compares with 25 percent in large cities. Rural people are more likely than others to take a definite pro or con rather than a middle ground position on big business.

The most speculative, most volatile area of all in public opinion data is that concerned with general outlook on trends and the future. On the positive side, rural people are not far from unanimous in believing that life is getting better rather than worse in terms of knowledge and intelligence, reflecting man's rationality and technological achievements. About two-thirds also see life getting better in terms of health. In these appraisals, rural people do not differ in any consistent way from those who reside elsewhere (*GOI*, November 1968).

But these positive views of trends are not matched in some other, less tangible areas by rural or urban folk. Thus, of the rural people:

—74 percent believe life is getting worse, not better, in terms of peace of mind (*GOI*, November 1968);

—52 percent believe life is getting worse in terms of happiness (*GOI*, November 1968);

—81 percent believe life is getting worse in terms of morals (*GOI*, September 1968);

—64 percent believe life is getting worse in terms of honesty (*GOI*, September 1968);

—72 percent are dissatisfied, on the whole, with the honesty and standards of behavior of people in this country (*GOI*, December 1973);

—68 percent believe, taking everything into account, that the world is getting worse (*GOI*, March 1972).

Typically, rural residents are more pessimistic than others, by a narrow margin, in these views. But despite the critical evaluation rural people give to American institutions and despite their stated pessimism about societal trends in important areas of concern, 64 percent, nearly two-thirds, express "quite a lot" of confidence in the future of the United States (*GOI*, May 1974). Only 13 percent claim "very little" or no confidence in the nation's future.

When asked to give a more personal evaluation of the overall prospects for the future facing themselves and their families, something over half of those in rural areas expressed satisfaction with the outlook in three successive studies (*GOI*, October 1971, March 1972, December 1973). Rural-urban differences were narrow.

RURAL CULTURAL PLURALISM. The view given of major value themes in the rural sector of American society, following one specific framework for analysis, and the illustrations of beliefs and associated behavior gleaned from national studies are only suggestive of the pluralism revealed by closer examination. Some of this pluralism has high social visibility; some does not.

Typically, when this pluralism has high visibility, it is characterized by groups with distinctive life styles reflecting unique clusterings of values that set the groups apart as "cultural islands." Examples include the Amish, the Hutterites, the isolated polygamous illegal groups which claim a doctrinal base in the original tenets of Mormonism, the many American Indian tribes, and the communes which have sprung up as a part of the rural revivalist movement. But even "mainstream" local societies tend to have value patterns that give each a characteristic hallmark. Beyond the local societies, there is regional differentiation in the emphasis given to particular beliefs and value themes.

A review of rural pluralism would normally include discussion of blacks, the most numerous rural ethnic minority (4,213,000 in number, according to the 1970 Census of Population, and 7.8 percent of the rural total). However, comparative nationwide data by place of residence are lacking for blacks. One study has provided information of note: the statewide North Carolina sample reported on by Christenson and Yang (1975) underrepresented nonwhites, but the results have special interest, in the absence of better data, because somewhat over half of the North Carolina nonwhite population in 1970 was rural. The white-nonwhite differences were in the ranking of the importance of some of the "social" values rather than the "personal" values. Thus whites were more concerned with patriotism and political democracy, while nonwhites were more concerned with racial equality and humanitarianism. This is generally supportive of the point made by Williams (1975), based on an extensive review of the research literature, that when socioeconomic status is matched the only pervasive value difference is that black Americans give equality a higher priority than do white Americans.

Two other illustrative categories of rural pluralism have been chosen here for a severely selective review: farm people, now a decided minority numerically within the rural population, and rural communes, which, in the contemporary rural revivalist sense, were not to be found in any number before about 1968.

Beliefs and Values of Farmers. This section focuses on Gallup Poll data. Also relevant, but not discussed here, are recent studies designed to determine the extent to which farmers or the general population agree with the agrarian ideology, also given such labels as the "Jeffersonian creed," "agricultural fundamentalism," and the like. Examples of such studies are those made in Wisconsin by Flinn and Johnson (1974) for farmers and by Buttel and Flinn (1975) for the rural and urban population. For a discussion of research on values and goals of farm people in the context of agricultural policy, see Larson (1961). Also of interest is Gulley's *Beliefs and Values in American Farming* (1974), which draws upon the work of John M. Brewster to offer a historical perspective on contemporary farm problems in the United States.

Farm people, like others, have not been unanimous in their response to value indicator and belief questions asked in national surveys. A paradoxical statement best summarizes how the values and related beliefs and behavior of farm men and women compare with those of rural adults as a whole; they are the same but different. For most of the Gallup data examined for this chapter, the farmer response was closer to the total rural response than the rural response was to the national majority or plurality position. Although for any one survey the farm-rural difference might be accounted for by chance, in an overwhelming proportion of the items for which there were comparative data (71 out of 94) the farmer position was more distant than the total rural from that of the largest-size-of-place dwellers. Thus, the consistency of the direction of farmer-rural differences strongly suggests that they were real. Further, for 32 out of the 94 value, belief, and behavior items the farmer position was the most extreme of any of the occupational, age, community size, education, income, racial, regional, religious, political, or sex categories for which data were reported. (In the Gallup national probability samples, farmers numbered only about 100 just prior to 1974, when the *Gallup Opinion Index* discontinued publishing data on farmers as one of four occupational categories. The number of rural respondents in the total sample varies from poll to poll but has generally been in the range of over 400 to under 500 in the 1965-75 period.)

When Gallup Poll results for 1965-75 are compared with postwar national polls for 1946-50 (Beers, 1953) and polls for 1953-65 (Glenn and Alston, 1967), the following trends appear: an increase in the proportion of farmers committed to the racial and religious equality theme; a decrease in the proportion taking a "moralistic" position on such matters as women's attire and national prohibition; an increase in voter registration; and a holding firm in voting regularity, church attendance, and views on ready access to birth control information.

Despite such trends, the data for 1965–75 show that in 12 out of 14 surveys a smaller percentage of farm adults than other rural residents support the equality theme, as measured by willingness to vote for a qualified woman or Catholic, Jewish, or Negro man for president or Congress. A larger proportion of farmers (in 6 out of 6 surveys) held such behavior as premarital sex and displays of nudity to be wrong, and fewer opposed national prohibition. Fewer approved the type of humanitarianism represented by the food stamp program (two items), and fewer (in 11 out of 14 surveys) had respect for and confidence in major U.S. institutions.

The conclusion that contemporary farmers differ significantly from nonfarmers in a number of their predominant value and belief patterns is a reaffirmation of the conclusions reached by Beers with 1946–50 data and by Glenn and Alston with 1953–65 data.

Rural Revivalism and Communes. The diverse strands of the rural revivalist movement which has gathered momentum in the last decade contain elements of both the old and the new. Among these are reminders of rural romanticism, reaffirmation of key aspects of the Jeffersonian agrarian creed, the long quest for rural equity, and the withdrawal to a rural refuge as one expression of protest and disenchantment with the prevailing social system and associated life-style.

Manifestations of this revival are many. Symbolic of a widespread interest in things rural was the bringing back in 1975 of the magazine *The Country Gentleman;* the publication, as a result of surveys of reader interest, by the National Geographic Society of *Life in Rural America* (1974); and popular books on the traditional subsistence skills and crafts, such as *The Foxfire Book* (Wigginton, 1972). A host of periodicals like *The Green Revolution* and *The Mother Earth News* has sprung up or increased their following, with contents for the whole spectrum of rural refugees — for example, food production and processing skills and techniques, organic farming, philosophy of alternative life-styles, and social protest. Organizationally, rural revivalism is expressed in such ways as the growth of farmers' markets for disposal of craft products and food produced in excess of subsistence needs, the formation at the national level of organizations such as Rural America, Inc., to act as pressure groups for rural people, and the establishment in the House of the bipartisan Congressional Rural Caucus. Legislatively, the Rural Development Act of 1972 could be interpreted as another manifestation of the movement. Demographically, national surveys began to report in about 1968 an increase in aversion to large cities as the preferred place of residence (Fuguitt and Zuiches, 1975:493). That substantial numbers began to express their preferences by action is evidenced by the reversal of urban-to-rural migration recorded for 1970–73 (Beale, 1975).

Some part of this reversal is accounted for by the refugee participants in the rural revivalist movement who are identified with a counterculture, an alternative life-style. These are comprised of two broad categories: the individual nuclear family "homesteaders" and the group communes. There is no census of either category. One study roughly estimated the number of rural communes in 1973 at some 25,000 with 250,000 to 300,000 current residents (Jerome, 1974:18). Communes, as well as the individual "homesteaders," are most likely to be found in open-country areas marginal for conventional modern agriculture.

A "bewildering diversity" among communes, whose members are predominantly young and white with middle-class urban backgrounds, has been found by Jerome (1974:19). He asserts, "there is no satisfactory way to define a commune" (p. 7). In his study he discards his initial definition as too inclusive and develops a taxonomy reflecting his concern with the *new culture*. However, he states that contemporary communes in the United States are typically domestic units (homes) averaging less than a dozen adults plus attendant children (p. 4). He finds basic distinctions between rural and urban communes. Jerome identifies a number of useful distinctions between communes, for example, those organized for purposes external to themselves such as a craft or a cause vs. primarily an internal orientation of the members, creedal vs. noncreedal with respect to a specific set of beliefs, and organic vs. nonorganic with respect to diet and food-raising methods. It appears that antipathy to "the system," a distaste for the corporate and the big, self-sufficiency as an end, disdain for the modern home conveniences and most machinery, desire for acquisition of survival skills for autonomous existence, an ecological orientation, and an underlying assumption that rural is better are among the identifiable themes. The generalized model of a typical rural commune as sketched by Jerome suggests a fairly strong work orientation in most; little emphasis on governing structure—because group decisions are made by consensus; tolerance of a wide range of religious concerns; disregard of dress, undress, and other conventions associated with the puritanical Protestant model; and a vaguely dual (individual and group) ownership of income and things. "Anarchism" is the term used by Jerome as best characterizing the philosophical and political disposition of contemporary communes. Thus, this sector of the rural revivalist movement adds a new dimension to today's pluralism in rural society.

DISCUSSION. What can be concluded about the values and beliefs of rural people in contemporary American society, and about the other questions raised at the beginning of this chapter? The answers have been winnowed out of the research literature published since 1960 and the published results of national surveys dating from 1965. My answers to the questions are more specific and carry a different tone than they did in 1961 when, in taking a long-term perspective on trends in American rural society, I wrote with Everett Rogers, "Rural-urban differences in values are decreasing as America moves in the direction of a mass society" (1964:53). While asserting that there were still important rural-urban value differences which stemmed from historical, occupational, and ecological differentials, we could produce little documentation, and we warned that generalizations about rural-urban value differences must be accepted rather cautiously due to the lack of adequate research findings on the topic.

The limitations of research-based knowledge may still be lamented. Systematic knowledge is especially short on the diversities of value and belief within the rural sector. Despite these cautions, conclusions have emerged that (1) challenge any assumption that all the important rural-urban differences in values and beliefs are rapidly vanishing, if they have not already been obliterated by the forces of a mass society; (2) draw attention to the rich diversity within rural America, especially to the pattern of farmer-nonfarmer differences; and (3) suggest that rural society shares in the strains and tensions that bear on the cohesion of American society in general.

The following generalizations are offered as a summary:

1. *Rural America differs from urban, especially from large-city (defined generally as places of 1,000,000 and over) America, in the emphasis given to major values, in value related beliefs and behavior, and in general outlook.* A number of these differences are substantial and vary consistently by size of community from rural areas at one polar extreme to large cities at the other. Rural differences and consistent rural-urban patterns are more frequent for indicators of values and for the beliefs most closely related to those values than for behavior and general outlook.

For example, on the answers to the 136 questions judged to be relevant from Gallup national surveys during 1965–75, the rural respondents occupied one of the polar positions—most in favor, least approving, or the like—for 70 percent of the set; rural residents were at one pole and large-city residents at the other for 45 percent; and response varied consistently by size of place in what may be termed a rural-urban pattern for 29 percent.

Taking just the 43 value indicator and closely related belief questions, for 79 percent the rural respondents had one of the polar positions. For 54 percent rural and large-city, residents were at opposite extremes, and for 46 percent the answers followed a consistent rural-urban pattern by size of place.

The frequency of the rural and large-city distinctions is indicated by the fact that on 90 percent of 136 Gallup national survey questions analyzed, one or the other or both concurrently occupied a polar position.

2. *As values and beliefs change over time, rural and urban dif-*

ferences may simultaneously narrow in some respects and widen in others. Rural support for equality indicators has tended to increase, bringing rural and urban areas closer together on this value. On the other hand, while rural adherence to puritan orthodox beliefs has been weakening, urban values seem to have weakened further in this respect, so that while the trend is in the same direction in both rural and urban, the gap has widened.

3. *No unanimity, no solid front pro or con, exists among rural people on any statement from which values may be inferred or on any value related belief or behavior.* Cultural pluralism is a characteristic of rural America.

4. *Although farm men and women generally take a position corresponding with that which prevails among rural adults as a whole, they are more distant from the values and beliefs positions taken by the majority or plurality of large-city dwellers.* Farmers show an increase in the proportion committed to racial and religious equality. While moralistic views on such matters as national prohibition and women's attire have decreased, even within rural areas the farm-nonfarm differences in traditional morality may be widening because of the slower rate of change on the part of farm people.

5. *Rural adults generally take the same pro or con position as do the national majority or plurality on questions of values and beliefs.* They rarely were in complete disagreement with the nation as a whole on any of the 136 national survey items examined. This similarity extends to the tensions of the larger society.

From the very lack of unanimity within rural areas and from the differential rates of change among rural subgroups — as between farm and other rural people or between professional leaders and their clientele groups — we may infer the presence of strains within rural society. Conflict, alienation, and anomie — the value-problems in the cohesion of American society named by Williams (1970:637) — are not absent from the rural scene. At the same time, rural-urban differences, especially in matters ethical, moral, and religious, and the fact that only a plurality profess confidence in a number of major U.S. institutions (with confidence lowest among rural people) indicate strain within the larger society.

Values do have consequences for human behavior, including the governance of people and the solution of community and societal problems. For social systems, values are a factor in the determination of goals and the selection of means to achieve goals. Primacy given to values supportive of goal attainment and adaptation — values such as efficiency, rationality, and progress — clearly has guided the drastic changes made in the farming sector during recent decades. The results are well known: high productivity per worker, larger scale, reduced independence in decision making by the operator, fewer farms, fewer farm people. What would have been the consequences if similar primacy had been given to equity considerations or some of the other major value themes?

Public policy purposes at any given level—local, state, or national—are served by knowledge of the values and preferences of people as they relate to goals and means. Such information can aid in the decision as to whether a problem should be solved in the private or the public arena and on what level. Points of conflict can be more readily identified in advance of decisions to adopt specific goals and particular means, and steps can be taken for the resolution of conflict. (Statewide studies in Washington [Dillman, 1971] and North Carolina [Christenson, 1973, 1974a, 1974b] provide examples of one technique used to establish the preferences of different categories of citizens with respect to the allocation of public funds.) A more critical evaluation and perhaps a restructuring of organizational systems to increase their responsiveness to the people for whom they are intended should be aided by a better understanding of the people's values and beliefs. Administrators in charge of programs for rural people should recognize that while the values and beliefs of this minority group in our national population have changed in many ways, rural society has maintained a distinctiveness that cannot be shrugged off or disregarded.

Part 6

SOCIAL ORGANIZATION

7 Rural Community Change

KENNETH P. WILKINSON

WHILE the population of the United States is mainly urban (74 percent in 1970), a large proportion of the people, more than two-fifths in fact, live in smaller centers and open-country neighborhoods away from big cities. This chapter is concerned with changes occurring in such places over the past few decades. About one-half of the nation's urban places are outside the "urbanized areas" which contain metropolitan centers. The 3,840 places in this category accounted for 15.2 percent of the total population in 1970. Another 5.2 percent of the population lived in places classified as rural by the Bureau of the Census, meaning that they had fewer than 2,500 inhabitants. Of the 13,706 places in this category, 9,515 had fewer than 1,000 inhabitants in 1970. In addition, 21.3 percent of the total population in 1970 lived in rural areas outside the places enumerated in the census.

Changes have been occurring in many aspects of life in these smaller centers and rural places and areas. Other chapters in this volume deal with changes in population and in the functioning of various rural institutions. The focus here is upon changes in what might be called community interaction: people within a given locality must interact to some degree to meet problems arising out of their common life in the area. The range of issues addressed through such interaction, the degree of organization of collective action, and the level of success achieved in meeting needs and resolving issues are subject to much variation over time and among communities. Many changes in local interaction in recent years can be related to changes in the larger society and to the increased significance of the larger society in local life. Some of the more significant of these changes are described below as background for a discussion of changes within the rural community. The final section of this chapter contains an assessment of the future prospects for the rural community in an increasingly urban society.

Kenneth P. Wilkinson is Associate Professor of Rural Sociology, Pennsylvania State University.

GENERAL FORCES OF CHANGE AFFECTING THE RURAL COMMUNITY. A "Great Change" (Warren, 1972) has been occurring in society over several decades, with direct consequences for the vitality and significance of community interaction. The spread of rational philosophy and along with it the growth of science, applied as technology, have greatly increased economic and material productivity, especially of primary enterprise (for example, agriculture), increasing thereby not only levels of consumption but also population mobility. Among the easily recognized sociological correlates are urbanization, formalization, and secularization, and, clearly at the community level, a fundamental shift from a local to a regional or national emphasis in the organization of life. Complex organizational structures linking localities, and indeed nations, in highly specialized institutional interest fields have come to dominate many aspects of local life, offering efficiency, expediency, and sophistication. Formal contractual mechanisms have replaced informal ties as means of involvement of the individual in social organization. Agencies of local cohesion of an earlier era, such as the family, the church, the common plight, and the localized economy, have yielded in significance to the more powerful vertically arranged structures, such as government and bureaucratic organizations.

One important consequence has been a shift, made possible by technology, from a culture of survival to a culture of consumption. As a substantial proportion of the population has been freed from food production, energy has been released and made available for the pursuit of other social goals. A potential for creative expression of human values is present in western society at this time to an extent never before experienced on such a scale. Local cohesion throughout much of history has been heavily based on symbiotic interdependencies in the struggle for survival. Mutual protection — from human and natural enemies — required a closeness and orderliness among neighbors. Institutionalized norms developed to maintain local cohesion, often at the expense of the freedom of individuals to express their own potentials. Human ecologists have written of the bondage of "the independent community," that is, one without access to resources from other communities (Hawley, 1950). Migration of individuals from such communities was a traumatic event, undertaken usually either by large numbers at once or under extreme conditions, as when an individual was banished for violation of norms. The level of freedom from the threat of imminent starvation achieved by the masses in modern society makes possible a new basis of affiliation and collective organization. Community can now be created, rather than merely maintained as a protective device. Community organization can occur as an expression of human values and natural affiliative impulses, with pattern emerging from the expression of values rather than being imposed out of the contingencies of primary interdependency (see Allport, 1955). The potential has not been widely realized in the creation of intentional communities. Rather, the recent trends suggest that the transition from a society based on survival needs to one oriented to other needs is hardly occurring at all, despite the potential.

The major trend is toward increased significance of nonlocal forces in community life. As agriculture has become more rational and productive it has become more of a regional and national enterprise than a local one (Rodefeld, 1975). As industry has become nationally rather than locally controlled a bifurcation of local power has occurred, with local politics becoming more of a game played in local status systems than a field of genuine power transactions (Schulze, 1961; French, 1970).

The urbanization trend, at least as measured crudely with population data, appears to have changed in many parts of the country over the past decade (Fuguitt, 1971; Beale, 1975). Net migration rates have become greater for rural than for urban places since 1970, a reversal of a long-standing trend. Several factors likely are reflected in this change. One is that a larger proportion of urban residents than formerly now have the resources to allow them to live in nonmetropolitan settings. Public opinion polls over the past 30 years have indicated that a large proportion of metropolitan residents would prefer to live outside large cities (Zuiches and Fuguitt, 1972; De Jong and Bush, 1974). Another factor is that large cities in this country have experienced severe problems in recent decades in financing public services to provide adequate housing, law enforcement, air quality, and intergroup relations. These "push" factors probably have been accompanied by a number of "pull" factors, such as the increased availability of jobs, particularly in manufacturing, in nonmetropolitan areas and the general improvement of services and amenities in many smaller towns. The areas of greatest growth are counties adjacent to Standard Metropolitan Statistical Areas, indicating that to some extent ties to metropolitan centers are being retained (Beale, 1975). Parts of the rural hinterland are being rapidly incorporated into the urban system. On the other hand rural development, in terms of jobs, housing, and services, is occurring in outlying areas in some states more rapidly than ever before (Beale, 1974:27).

The changes that make up the "Great Change" are crescive. They reflect forces in the society at large, perhaps throughout western civilization, which are beyond the control of local residents or even of national policymakers. As institutional functions have shifted from locally based to extralocally based agencies, they have come to be organized on a regional and national basis. The economy-of-scale concept, for example, requires that many specialized services demanded in modern culture be provided on a regional rather than a local basis (Berry, 1970). The cost of meeting water quality standards through building tertiary sewage treatment plants can be met by few smaller localities and must be provided on a regional basis. Industrialization requires the agglomeration of labor supply and social infrastructure over a large area.

The general direction of social change at the local level now, as throughout history, continues to be toward increased differentiation of structures, services, and activities. Increased specialization and division of labor appear to be inevitable aspects of modernization (Young and Young, 1973). But the differentiation occurring in many localities is resulting in the transfer of functions from restricted areas to a larger regional area (Whiting, 1974:43-53). In smaller places, such as those studied by Bert Adams (1969) and W. F. Cottrell (1951) and in the former agricultural service centers across the Midwest, a loss of functions — something that might be called "de-differentiation" — has occurred as firms, facilities, patronage, and services have moved out, one by one, under competition from regional growth centers.

There is a question as to whether community can occur, as an interactional phenomenon, in the kind of expanded geographic area that seems to be necessary for efficient organization of social services and for economic viability. The research literature offers little evidence of the development of a strong sense of community on a regional basis, although it has been argued that such could be developed (Kaufman, 1975:26-34). A frequent observation is that leaders of formerly viable local communities tend first to resist, then to resign themselves to participation in regional development schemes. One line of research, dealing with community involvement, has noted a tendency for a gap to develop between the areas of behavioral and symbolic investment of individuals in local societies (Haga and Folse, 1971; Clemente, Rojek, and Beck, 1974). Behavior, for example in carrying out essential activities such as work, education, and shopping, tends to occur in a much larger region than does symbolic investment. In terms of the latter, people continue to relate symbolically to limited geographic settings. Insofar as community is based on sustained face-to-face interaction, the regional setting should seem unlikely to foster it.

OBSERVED CHANGES WITHIN THE RURAL COMMUNITY. Have such changes as noted above resulted in a loss of community or a shift from gemeinschaft (intimate, small, primary group life) to gesellschaft (formal, complex, secondary association)? The conclusion that gemeinschaft has given way to gesellschaft, potency to powerlessness, creativity and hope to drabness and malaise at the local level in response to changes in the larger society would require a misreading of history and an idealization of earlier conditions. Save among isolated ethnic and religious enclaves, a few intentional communitarians, and some of the Native American groups, the European tradition of gemeinschaft has never fitted American communities (Buck, 1963). The time since settlement has been too short and the structural conditions were there too briefly to support the kind of interpenetration of lives and generations and the development of sacred bases of solidarity apparently necessary for gemeinschaft. Rather, from the beginning of European migration, rural and urban life in America have been modeled on essentially the same patterns, the biggest difference being, as is true now, that rural Americans, except for a small, privileged elite, have had access to less of what urban Americans have sought, whether measured in dollars, years of schooling, political power, or opportunities for mobility (Johnson and Knop, 1970; Eberts, 1974). Despite apotheosizing images of the glories of backwoods poverty, rural culture in America has consisted in large part of the creative, and sometimes not so creative, adaptation to deprivation. With improved methods of data gathering we have discovered that material poverty is more widespread, overcrowding in housing more prevalent, suicide rates, rates of crime against property, morbidity and mortality rates higher, and services poorer in rural than in urban places (see, for example, the President's National Advisory Commission on Rural Poverty report, *The People Left Behind*, 1967).

What smaller places have had is a more manageable scale of social organization; and by and large it has been managed more rigidly, giving, in its control mechanisms and familial-religious ties, an appearance of gemeinschaft, but having rather more of the characteristics of symbiotic bondage. With the "Great Change" has come an increase in the quality of life, as measured popularly, and an undermining of the control mechanisms. This is not to argue that urban life, while freer, has been much better, but merely to deny the assumption that in the countryside utopia has been lost (see Veblen, 1969).

Major changes in community interaction noted in the research literature include the following:

1. The scale of local interaction (that is, in numbers of people, organizational mass, differentiation of functions and structures) necessary to retain a relatively complete community has been greatly increased. Relatively small places, unless they are located at great distance from larger centers, cannot, as they once could, provide most of the activities and services to meet local demands. Thus there are many instances of former local societies—some as small as a few hundred persons, others as large as 10,000 or more—that have become working-class residential suburbs of nearby centers (see Whiting, 1974).

2. Local institutions in small towns have come to depend heavily upon outside sources of goods and other resources for the meeting of local demands, thus restricting the autonomy of local decision-making processes (Warren, 1970:224).

3. The shift in economic power from local to regional and national agencies has created a vacuum in public affairs decision making in many localities (see Clelland and Form, 1964). Into that vacuum have moved highly specialized, and often highly motivated and competent, agents of the larger society. Much of the agenda of public action in many small towns is now set by employees of state and federal agencies. The result is a more vigorous assault on some public problems than formerly, but with an emphasis on public relations rather than on genuine citizen participation, and with very little coordination of efforts, resulting in interagency competition and discontinuities in projects.

4. The types of structural mechanisms discovered in some larger

places by which relatively autonomous "community decision organizations" are linked together into relatively well-coordinated action fields have apparently not developed in smaller places (Warren, 1972). Probably this is because the decision organizations themselves are products of scale and specialization, which are more likely to be found in larger places.

5. Collective action by local citizens, as through voluntary associations, has also become highly specialized and fragmented. In most localities, especially those near larger centers, it has also become more expressive (for example, of needs for fellowship) than task oriented (Smith, 1975). Where it is task oriented it has become more defensive in tone than formerly, with groups organized to resist some agency's development plan, or conversely to resist some agency's plan to prevent development, for example in a wilderness area. Indeed, it might be argued that such resistance is the last vestige of community in America.

In brief, these trends portray a decline or eclipse of community in America (Stein, 1960). Commentaries on the characteristics and consequences of this decline have appeared frequently over the past 30 years (for example, Brownell, 1950). Vidich and Bensman (1958) described social-psychological consequences of what they called "rural surrender to the mass society" in Springdale. Numerous studies have documented loss of power of indigenous leaders (see Walton, 1967; Schulze, 1961; French, 1970; Pellegrin and Coates, 1956). Roland Warren (1972) has argued that local citizens can best hope to adapt to crescive changes rather than seeking to direct them.

Relatively few documented instances of effective community action structures are reported in the literature. Evon Vogt and Thomas O'Dea (1953) described a number of successful action programs in Rimrock, a Mormon village in the Southwest. Kaufman and his associates have measured community action characteristics in several small centers in Mississippi and in India (Kaufman, Dasgupta, and Singh, 1975). The pattern suggested in these instances is one in which initiative is local, outside agencies are approached as resources to help with the implementation of local plans, projects are coordinated through one or more broadly focused voluntary organizations, and key actors play generalized, structure-building community roles. Very little is known about the conditions that give rise to such a pattern; nor for that matter has the hypothesis that such a pattern influences action outcomes been adequately tested.

COMMUNITY DEVELOPMENT. A central question for applied community research is whether such a pattern can be stimulated where it does not occur naturally. The assumption of a number of programs referred to as community development is that it can (see Brokensha and Hodge, 1969). Little evidence has appeared to support this assumption, owing in part to the limited amount of evaluation research associated with community development programs (for an exception see Voth, 1975).

The term community development has been applied to a variety of action processes and programs (see Sanders, 1970). Two broad types may be identified. One is a process through which outside groups have attempted to bring about changes in local societies, usually in limited, specialized sectors of local life, such as agricultural production or quality of health services, though occasionally on a more generalized, structural basis. The rhetoric of this process (reviewed in Etuk, 1973) usually emphasizes "felt needs" and "indigenous participation," but the practice of it, in the British colonial tradition out of which it grew, tends to be patronizing and co-optative; and such programs tend to be short-lived. A recent critique of this type of community development noted the lack of evidence of substantive accomplishment through it, identified the commitment to democratic values by its practitioners as a major limitation, and recommended a program of behavioral engineering based on operant conditioning principles as a more effective strategy for bringing about improvements in the lives of people (Speight, 1973).

A second type of community development is one in which the external agency serves mainly as a resource, with initiative for action coming, if at all, from within the local society (see Kaufman, 1975). The community developer, in this case, is the local actor. This might be called community development from the inside. Discussions of this process in the literature (for example, Wilkinson, 1972) posit the hypothesis that community as a structural phenomenon, in contrast to such artifacts as increased level of living or improved services, can only be achieved by local actors.

The term development itself is ambiguous and has been the subject of much debate as to its meaning and appropriate indicators. Suggestions of universally applicable objective criteria have generated little consensus, owing largely to the value relativity of the criteria proposed, but also to the arrogance of causal assumptions usually implied in the concept. One can never be sure that observed changes are in fact results of development efforts. A useful alternative approach is to define development as attempting to bring about certain changes rather than as achieving the goals pursued. Such a definition takes cognizance of the fact that no one controls the outcomes of interaction in a social field, that purposive actions encounter one another and other forces, with emergent reality resting as much on happenstance as on purpose.

Purposive attempts to create community should be distinguished from purposive attempts to bring about other changes in the local society. Both might be regarded as development, but only the former as community development. From this perspective, community development would consist of attempts to alter the interactional structure through which collective local action is undertaken. Research is needed to identify the conditions under which such attempts occur.

An extensive effort in community development programming in

American nonmetropolitan areas is carried out through colleges of agriculture in the land-grant universities. Extension work in Community Resource Development is an effort through which agents assigned to regions of a state meet with various local groups and agencies to discover areas of citizen interest and then work with state-level subject-matter specialists, and occasionally with researchers, to produce educational materials which county Extension staff can use in making presentations to local groups. Community leadership training programs are conducted by Extension sociologists in a number of states. Selected local leaders are given more or less intensive training in "group process skills" and in subject matter related to selected community problems. Rural Development is a new and in some ways creative program. Organized under the Rural Development Act of 1972, it is, in part, an attempt to combine research and Extension efforts on a "pilot basis" to attack limited development problems in each state. In many states a special community resource development agent has been assigned to work with local citizens and state agencies to accomplish the goals of the act: economic development, improved community services, elimination of poverty, and environmental protection. In general, the effects of these programs have not been adequately evaluated through research.

While interest has revived in recent years in community as a theoretical concept (Summers, Seiler, and Clark, 1970), community development has continued to be largely ignored in sociological theory and research. This is likely due to a number of factors. One is that the practical concerns of community development as a process are difficult to conceptualize in "value free" terms. The question of how things work continues to take precedence in sociology over that of how they might be made to work better. A second factor in the scientific neglect of community development is that from certain theoretical perspectives, notably that of human ecology, the purposive element of social action is regarded as of little consequence. A third factor might rest in the assumption, based on observation of the trends noted above, that community itself is of little empirical consequence in modern society, the total society being the relevant level for analysis of the principal conditions of social life.

If community as a purposive local phenomenon is assumed to be a vital aspect of social organization, the relative neglect of community development in sociological research must be viewed with great concern. As René König (1968:4-5) has observed, the community is the setting for the individual's contact with society. The level of integration of that setting should be of great consequence to individuals and to the larger society. In the broader sense of the term, as it is used by Nisbet (1953), for example, community can be assumed to exist along with its opposite, chaos or entropy, in every social event. If community is restricted in its expression by any force inside or outside the field of interaction, chaos in one of its forms tends to prevail. Community, thus conceived, is a central element, perhaps *the* central element of social organization. Efforts by people to foster it, whether successful or not, whether sincere or not, cannot be ignored if we would know the elemental conditions of social organization. There is, of course, a question as to whether community can be achieved through purposive action and another as to whether it can exist within the complex, vertically linked, fragmented form of local society which now seems to be the mode in nonmetropolitan America. The literature suggests that where it has occurred, it has resulted from the coalescence of many forces, only one of which, and perhaps an epiphenomenal one at that, has been the wills of actors (Wilkinson, 1970).

Research is greatly needed on community development. The topic has been eclipsed by other concerns in scientific literature, just as the topic of community was two decades ago. Along with the economic feasibility studies which now predominate in rural development research, attention needs to be given to the creation of methodology and the design of comparative studies to identify the characteristics of central community development phenomena. These phenomena would include actors — their characteristics, motives, and community roles; associations — their structure, scope, and interconnections; and activities — the phases, styles, and outcomes of action. Needed are refined methods for promoting the key processes, the structurally relevant interactions, which connect interests in the local society and provide community integration. Conceptually, we can assume that community integration is not a given characteristic of local social organization. The institutional structures of local life overlap and "free-wheel" (Hillery, 1968:8–9). Community is thus a variable. Once we learn to measure it, we can begin to uncover the conditions for it and its consequences.

FUTURE PROSPECTS FOR THE RURAL COMMUNITY. Small towns tend to persist and even flourish despite continued losses of population over many decades (Fuguitt, 1965). This ecological persistence stands against even drastic changes in social structure and functions, even in the smaller places. Larger places will likely persist for this and other reasons.

The more critical question is what will happen to the status of small towns as meaningful, effective interaction networks. It seems likely that the trend of metropolitan expansion will continue even despite the present slowdown of energy flow (Kasarda, 1972). Places within easy reach of the expanding metropolises should experience a decrease in local differentiation but increased differentiation of services and amenities available to their residents through access to the metropolitan area. More remote places are likely, through improved communications and the aggressive work of complex organizations, to become even more linked than now to the larger society. Distance and territoriality should cause at least a semblance of local distinctiveness in institutional functioning to be retained in these more remote places. An expansion trend for nonmetropolitan centers, that is, the development of relationships between hinterland communities, has been discerned in the demographic literature (Fuguitt, 1972). Such a trend should be more pronounced for centers that are being incorporated into a metropolitan field, but it also seems likely for the future in even more remote centers, the reasons being similar to those underlying metropolitan expansion. In brief, nonmetropolitan areas are likely to continue to be subject, directly or indirectly, to the same ecological and economic forces that are effecting changes in metropolitan areas.

What will be the role of the rural community in the future of society? Relationships similar to community, though much more restricted in scope and impact, are said to exist in metropolitan neighborhoods (Hunter, 1975). Given these and the formal mechanisms that link people through various organizations to the larger society, perhaps there will be little functional role for the rural community in the future. Former roles, such as supplying food and fiber, providing occupations, and sending in personnel for various urban activities, are taken care of elsewhere. One proposal being considered in decaying small towns along interstate highways within several hours' drive of New York City is to restore venerable old dwellings to attract corporate executives who no longer have to spend all of their time directly at headquarters. Another is the plan to use advanced communications technology to diffuse New York City culture and services into rural New England. Another is the new town concept, which appears to be more of an urban redevelopment than a rural community development strategy. Another is the back-to-the-land movement, which has received much attention in the press, but involves a very small proportion of the population. Other current strategies, such as the Walden Twos, the condominiums with shared common space, the group marriages, and the franchised communal living and self-realization centers on the West Coast, offer at best private, alternative life-styles for a very small number of people. The aggregate involvement in unusual living arrangements today in this country, though unmeasured in the literature, is probably no greater and perhaps is much less than it was a century ago. The changes in trend, if there are to be any, will have to relate to major features of the society at large—the polity, the corporate economy, the consumptive life-style, the energy budget, the class system.

The scenario I should like to promote is one which says that reason will prevail, that an expanded knowledge base, to which sociologists can contribute, will lead to mass realization of the human significance of what is being lost in the discarding of old-fashioned terms such as love and community; that the attractions of human scale in life settings, unlimited by the deprivations and bondages therewith connected in the past, will become widely known; that technology and formal organization will become tools for the good of people, making it possible for the profound as opposed to the extraneous benefits of modern life to be made available in all localities; that metropolitan expansion will in fact become decentralization; that Warren's famous criticism (1970) of the belief that one can have local autonomy, local viability, and widespread local participation in a complex society will be proven, on the future evidence, to be invalid (though it is apparently valid now); that lives of people in communities will interpenetrate as they deal together with the full range of human issues; that freedom and peace will be achieved. Mine is, of course, a value-based scenario. I place great value on community and see a rural setting as most likely for its realization.

8 Rural Government and Local Public Services

KENNETH D. RAINEY
KAREN G. RAINEY

THE availability of local government services once created a major distinction between rural and urban communities. The need and demand for services differed markedly from city to country. Today, rural and small-town communities are much closer to urban and suburban areas in their service needs and expectations. Like the more publicized urban crises, rural local governments and public service institutions face many difficulties in funding and providing quality public services.

WHERE ARE RURAL LOCAL GOVERNMENTS? Which among the more than 78,000 units of local government in the United States should be styled rural local governments? How many people live within their jurisdictional boundaries? Are enough people involved to make rural governmental problems a serious national concern?

Thirty percent of the U.S. population lived outside the Standard Metropolitan Statistical Areas in 1970. Eight percent (16 million) lived in nonmetropolitan municipalities of less than 10,000 people, while another 15 percent (31 million) lived in unincorporated parts of nonmetropolitan areas. Seven percent are in larger municipalities (over 10,000) outside SMSAs. Thus at least 1 American in 4 lives in a small, rural local government jurisdiction.

Of the 3,044 counties in the United States, more than 85 percent are

Kenneth D. Rainey is Vice-President for Program Management of the Academy for Contemporary Problems and Adjunct Professor of City and Regional Planning, Ohio State University. Karen G. Rainey is a Planner with the Mid-Ohio Regional Planning Commission and a Research Specialist in Local Government for the League of Women Voters, Columbus, Ohio.

nonmetropolitan. Of the nonmetropolitan counties, nearly 90 percent have less than 50,000 people and are rural in character.

Finally, looking at school district enrollments we find that 4 million pupils are enrolled in districts of less than 1,200 pupils. Of these, nearly 3 million (slightly over 6 percent of all pupils) are in nonmetropolitan school districts. This is a considerably smaller percentage than might be expected, considering the total nonmetropolitan figure (about 30 percent of the U.S. population), and apparently reflects the impact of school district consolidation and busing in rural areas.

Thus, while attention has focused on the metropolitanization of the American population and the problems of big city governments in providing public services, the problems of rural local governments are certainly worth attention.

THE DILEMMA OF RURAL LOCAL GOVERNMENT

The Pincers. Local governments all across the United States are finding themselves in a sort of pincers. The level of services provided by local government has risen steadily. In some cases this is the result of local demand, for example, for better police protection. In other instances it is a demand imposed by a higher level of government, such as a state requiring sanitary sewerage facilities to be installed.

The ability of local government to pay is not rising nearly so rapidly as service costs. Inflation influences local salaries and the price of equipment and supplies. Local governments have traditionally had a very restricted tax base, relying primarily on the property tax. This tax is minimally sensitive to economic shifts, and it is less lucrative than the graduated income tax. For these reasons, governments are caught in a pinch of rising service levels and costs and restricted ability to pay.

Rural local governments have a special financial difficulty. Because they usually comprise small towns or sparsely settled areas, they face problems of economies of scale. That is, it is much more expensive on a per capita basis to provide a service over a widely dispersed area for a few people than it is to provide that same service in a medium-sized town. School transportation costs are a good example; road maintenance costs are another. This creates a double bind — the need to overcome the cost problems of small scale, while overall costs are rising faster than tax revenues can keep pace.

Economies of Scale. Why is it more expensive to provide in rural areas the same kind of public services urban areas have? Public service costs are much like the costs of production (Richardson, 1973; Alonso, 1971; Real Estate Research Corporation, 1974). At very low levels of production, the costs are very high. If production levels are increased, the unit cost comes down until it reaches an optimum. Beyond this optimum level, congestion costs in the factory and the need for new equipment mean that unit costs again go upward. There is evidence that the same is true of some public services. To give a full array of public services to a small, isolated rural community would be impossibly expensive. On the other hand, very large cities also have extremely high public service costs. High density and congestion increase the pressure on public facilities; maintenance and replacement costs are high. Feasibility lies somewhere in between.

While the complexities of measuring costs and benefits (Alonso, 1971; Richardson, 1973) of local public services keep us from having a completely satisfactory model of how these costs vary with population, common-sense judgements and evidence on per capita costs give us some indication of the relationship between size and public service costs.

While analysts of public finance economies are not satisfied with per capita expenditures as a proxy for economies of scale (Richardson, 1973), these expenditures are among the few measures available to us through the U.S. Census of Governments. The following tables drawn from this source give us some actual distinctions between metropolitan and non-metropolitan governmental units to hold up against Richardson's judgements. Table 8.1 shows the distinctions between metropolitan and nonmetropolitan governments on a few basic measures of local government revenues and expenditures. It can be seen that nonmetropolitan values are generally lower except for hospital revenues and highway costs. Public welfare and police and fire expenditures are much lower on a per capita basis, reflecting lower service levels.

Figures 8.1, 8.2, and 8.3 show per capita expenditures by size class of the jurisdiction for municipalities, counties, and school districts respectively. They provide at least superficial validation of the proposition that costs first fall as size increases, then increase again for the larger jurisdictions. Again these no doubt primarily reflect differences in service levels.

The picture is less dramatic with school districts; Fig. 8.3 verifies that metropolitan and nonmetropolitan expenditures for local schools are much closer together than many of the other measures. These data reflect the general equalization that has been brought about through consolidation into larger districts of both rural and urban systems and the ever-larger role played by the state and federal governments in financing school systems. On the whole, however, settlement patterns are critical in determining the cost and extent of services. There are scale economies above minimum thresholds, but in very large cities scale diseconomies and higher service demands make their local governments more costly.

FINANCING LOCAL PUBLIC SERVICES

Financing Local Needs. The previous section focused on financing of services as a key concern. The subject merits additional attention for two

Table 8.1. Local government finance, in per capita dollars, inside and outside of Standard Metropolitan Statistical Areas.

	Metropolitan	Nonmetropolitan	Nonmetropolitan as Percent of Metropolitan
Total revenues	$622	$429	69
Intergovernmental revenues	207	167	81
From state govt.	180	156	87
From federal govt.	27	11	41
Revenue from own sources	414	262	63
Taxes	279	163	58
Property	229	147	64
School lunch sales	7	8	114
Hospitals	14	20	143
Total expenditures	646	434	67
Expenditures for personal services	309	214	69
By function			
Total direct general	577	397	69
Capital outlay	92	53	58
Education	249	217	87
Local schools	234	211	90
Highways	28	37	132
Public welfare	54	19	35
Hospitals	29	24	83
Health	9	4	44
Police	31	12	39
Fire	16	5	31
Sewer	19	8	42
Parks and recreation	15	4	27
Libraries	4	2	50

Source: U.S. Bureau of the Census, 1974a.

reasons. First, as earlier indicated, a substantial amount of evidence shows that rural areas have more difficulties than urban places of moderate size in paying for adequate levels of public services, although not so much difficulty as New York City. Second, real and imagined discontinuities exist between those who want and benefit from public services and those who pay for them.

There are three basic ways of paying for local services: taxes, user fees, and intergovernmental transfers. The principal subjects of taxation are property and income. The roles of taxes, fees, and intergovernmental payments have been shifting over time, as have the roles of taxes upon property and income.

The Structure of Local Government Finance. Historically, the backbone of local government finance has been the real property tax. Even with the growth of sales taxes, income taxes, and intergovernmental transfers of funds, in 1971 the property tax still accounted for 37 percent of

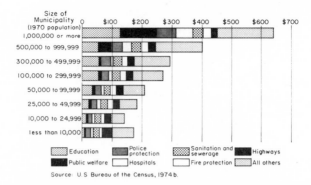

Fig. 8.1.   Per capita general expenditure, by function, for size groups of municipalities, 1971-72.

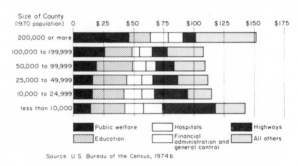

Fig. 8.2.   Per capita general expenditure, by function, for size groups of county governments, 1971-72.

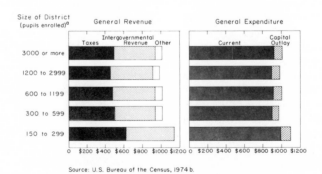

Fig. 8.3.   Per pupil amounts of general revenue and general expenditure for enrollment-size groups of school districts, 1971-72.

all local revenues. But the most significant growth in revenue has been in the role of intergovernmental transfer payments. These had grown to 40 billion dollars by 1972 (U.S. Bureau of the Census, 1974a). This shift reflects not just the growing role of federal grant-in-aid payments, but also state payments to localities, long a principal source of local funding.

The framework for local government finance as well as for its functions is established by state constitution and statute law. The amount of control or freedom that accompanies state grants to localities varies greatly from state to state. This may include detailed constitutional restrictions drawn in an earlier age, making it very difficult for a state to adapt to modern requirements for financing local services.

The role of state statute law or legislatively granted charters also varies greatly from state to state. Some states provide wide latitude or home rule powers; others have detailed legislatively established codes that control subjects and amounts of taxation, how taxes are assessed and collected, the amount and kind of debt a locality can undertake, and how accounts are to be kept.

The Property Tax. The property tax, no doubt as old as government, was well established in England and brought by settlers to this country. The real property tax was a convenient and relatively equitable way to pay for public goods and services in an agrarian society. Property, land, and buildings were the primary form in which wealth was held (as opposed to modern stocks and bonds). With less money in circulation, income was difficult to measure and less adequate as a measure of ability to pay taxes. The real property tax remains the primary local tax and may remain so for decades to come, although it is increasingly under attack. This tax raises many difficult questions.

What is a particular piece of property worth? The most usual method of assessment is to compare its value with one that has sold recently and fix an expected market value. This is far from an exact science. This method became inequitable in an era of rapidly rising land values and speculation. Farmers and ranchers charge that the speculative value of land is an index of neither its value for farm purposes nor of their ability to pay such rates. Many state legislatures are offering relief in the form of use value taxation or methods of transferring the right to develop the land to the state in return for lower assessments.

Questions have also been raised about the equity of the property tax and its utility as a revenue raising source for other reasons. Today, the ownership of real property does not necessarily imply affluence. Most people own property for personal use as a home, farm, or business. After decades of federal support to encourage low- and moderate-income people to buy homes, real property is a very poor index of ability to pay.

Moreover, property with little intrinsic worth may be assessed at or near full market value and still not yield enough in revenues to support government services. Small units of government, drawing taxes primarily from a small and poor area, will not be able to maintain a wide range of services.

Other Taxes. The many other kinds of local taxes range from theater admissions to the occupation tax to the local income tax. Some of these are more nuisances than revenue raisers. Local sales and income taxes are an important source of funds, but they are complex and costly for small units to collect. Countrywide and even statewide imposition and collection, with the revenues being returned to the locality, can overcome this difficulty, however.

Fees for Services. Fees have always been important in local finance, particularly at the county level. Many county officials have been compensated entirely from fees for services rendered. Fees for services have some obvious appeal. They are not suited for every local purpose, but they are likely to grow in importance for those services where it is possible to assess benefit, for example, trash collection: everyone pays according to the amount of trash collected.

Intergovernmental Transfers. The major growth area in local finance is use of funds from the state and federal government. Revenues from the state government long have been important sources of local funds. A typical example would be a state collected gasoline tax that is redistributed to the county or township governments to finance the maintenance of roads. As their local governments faced greater financial difficulties, many states began to impose sales taxes and later income taxes. The proceeds of these commonly were returned to the local school districts. By the time of the 1962 Census of Governments, 37 percent of school district revenues were derived from the state. In 1972, 47 percent were state funds.

Federal grants originally were almost entirely in the welfare field — aid to dependent children or aid to the blind. They reached the local level by being passed through the state government to the counties by a standard formula, or state established county offices served as the outlet.

The role of the federal government has grown tremendously in the past two decades, with federal grants-in-aid becoming not only a major source of local funds but also a major preoccupation of local officials. When someone asks, "Should we build a veebalafetzer?" the first question is not, "What is it?" but "Can we get a federal grant for it?" Grants-in-aid have warped local priorities and local activity. They tend to put local initiative in the background and make responding to federal grant programs a primary local function.

Revenue sharing, a program that has existed at the federal level for only a few years, adds a new dimension. It was intended to overcome some of the federal-dominance problems of grants-in-aid. Under the State and Local Assistance Act of 1972, $5.5 billion was to be distributed annually to state and local governments for a broad range of purposes. The amount each locality was to receive was fixed by formula, with the local government being freed from the paperwork required in grants-in-aid and having some discretion in use of funds. The act was renewed and expanded in 1976.

Revenue sharing presents some difficulties. The amounts are small, with some rural local governments receiving less than a thousand dollars. Still, revenue sharing is regarded as a boon by local governments. Funds can be used to purchase needed equipment or to upgrade programs beyond what the budget would ordinarily allow. However, inflationary pressures to stretch local tax dollars mean frequently that revenue-sharing funds offer local officials only a temporary respite from raising tax millage. No money is freed for major new initiatives. The result is an effort to continue grants-in-aid in addition to revenue sharing, rather than instead of it.

To summarize, two major fiscal issues need to be resolved for rural and small-town local government in the coming years. The first is the role of real property taxation, particularly as it relates to farmland. On the one hand, simply reducing the tax on farmland will increase the burden on other property, particularly on the owners of homes and small businesses. On the other hand, to tax land at its speculative value could force farmers to sell the land for real estate developments. Use-value assessments and transfers of development rights are possible ways out of the dilemma.

The other issue is the role of the state and federal government in local finance. Trends point toward state assumption of more of the financial burden of education, while welfare may become almost entirely a federally funded activity. Both of these changes would have a very significant impact in relieving the financial pressures on small governments.

ORGANIZING FOR LOCAL PUBLIC SERVICES

Outdated Boundaries. James Sundquist, in his Brookings Institution study *Making Federalism Work* (1969), put it this way, "Tiny jurisdictions lack expertise; their elected officials are part-time amateurs, and the communities lack the resources individually to employ professional personnel. . . . They are deficient in capacity to conceive, plan, design, and expedite projects. They lack the population base individually to support projects important to development — industrial parks, medical center, vocational schools, colleges, airports. . . ." (pp. 226-27).

In the decades from 1920 to 1960 the response to territorial inadequacy in the metropolitan areas was the politically inflammatory attempt to combine municipal and county governments into a metropolitan government. In many of the larger cities, studies that assessed the problems of providing local public services concluded that Balkanization of the metropolitan area into many small units of local government and special districts not only impeded the solution of problems, it wasted money. The studies generally recommended the redrawing of boundaries, consolidation of units, and the granting of more powers to the county level. Almost all of these attempts to rework the structure of local government failed at the polls. Only a few metropolitan forms of government were established: Miami–Dade County, Florida; Nashville–Davidson County, Tennessee; and Indianapolis–Marion County, Indiana are the most notable. The propositions to redraw boundaries and consolidate ·units failed in large measure because the people saw these as threats to "grass roots" control over local affairs.

Attempts to redraw boundaries in rural areas have not reached the same proportions as those in metropolitan areas, but the same factors of resistance are faced. "Grass roots" control is an important rural touchstone. People identify strongly with their county and resist becoming part of "District VII" or some new governmental amalgam.

In typical rural areas, services are administered by counties with some services also being provided by towns, special districts, and perhaps townships. Each provides certain services to a few people. In this situation, either boundary adjustment or governmental reorganization can help reduce service costs and increase service capabilities. A redrawing of boundary lines will not solve the scale problems, however. This can only be done by resettlement, new technology for small-scale local public services, or doing without. In some cases, reorganization may be a partial answer but experience tells us that such solutions are not easily achieved. The "grass roots" factor works against acceptance of change by local citizens and officials.

Planning and Development Districts. It is possible to overcome some of the scale problems of rural local government without doing major violence to the desire for grass roots control. One method is the creation of planning and development districts.

With the substantial growth of grant-in-aid programs in the early 1960s, many federal laws encouraged the creation of special county and community groups to implement the laws locally and to assure both expert and local citizen input. These ranged from the Technical Action Panels created by the Department of Agriculture to the Overall Economic Development Plan groups formed by the Area Redevelopment Administration. Comprehensive Area Manpower committees (CAMPs) were formed by the Labor Department. There were many other state and federal organizations.

While these groups were sometimes successful in generating local participation in the programs, they also created a great deal of confusion about overall local plans and objectives. A single village might be a part of six to ten special federal planning districts. Early efforts were largely confined to one county, which was not an effective planning unit. Furthermore, these tended to be direct federal-local programs with little state input, even where the state government had substantial program and policy interests.

These inadequacies led to a movement in the mid-1960s to create a network of state sponsored districts. Initially several states undertook this step in order to encourage federal agencies to take a more coordinated approach to local affairs. The Georgia General Assembly passed legislation as far back as 1960 to facilitate its area planning and development commissions (Georgia Regional Executive Directors Association, 1971).

Congressional studies of the problem of duplication and overlap in federally sponsored district programs were carried out. Procedures were developed by the Federal Bureau of the Budget (now the Office of Management and Budget) to encourage the states to establish these districts. If the states created such units, the federal agencies were required to clear all applications and local program plans through them.

All but four states had established multicounty districts by 1974. This number, however, masks a great variation in real progress. Some of the state districts represent little more than lines on a map while others are organized and staffed and are important actors in the local government structure. Some districts have been established by order of the governor, while others are based upon a new state statute.

These units can serve several functions that are especially valuable to rural localities, regardless of how they have evolved. First, they can provide areawide planning for public services, which cannot be done effectively by townships, villages, cities, and counties acting independently. Second, they can provide a forum where local officials in a multicounty area can meet to air and resolve differences. Third, they can hire professionals to assist communities and counties where those jurisdictions do not singly have the funds to afford them. Such arrangements to share professional managers (circuit riders) are used successfully by small communities in Maine (New England Municipal Center, 1975). Professional help has proven very valuable in applying for and administering federal and state programs, an increasing function of local government agencies.

The future of the multicounty development district as a mechanism of achieving territorial adequacy and economies of scale is one of the major developments to watch for in rural and small-town local government.

PROVIDING LOCAL PUBLIC SERVICES

Public Safety—Police and Fire Service.

Police. The popular image of a crime free rural America is not accurate. Partially it was based on poor statistics. The FBI's *Uniform Crime Reports* now have much better coverage of rural areas (81 percent of the total rural population). Current statistics indicate that rural crime is increasing at a faster rate than the national average or even the larger-city rate. However, rural rates are still much lower than urban ones, and a look at some of the details behind these statistics will help us put the increases into better perspective. As Table 8.2 shows, the overall reported rate of crime in rural areas in 1974 was slightly over 2,000 per 100,000 persons, an increase of 20.3 percent over the previous year. Large-city crime increased at a slower rate (12.2 percent), but it was over three times as frequent (7,498.8 per 100,000). Violent crime was a higher proportion of large-city crime (15 percent) than rural crime (8 percent).

The principal difficulty facing rural communities in the law enforcement field is that one-, two-, or ten-man forces are usually adequate for traffic work only. Modern law enforcement is a complicated business with the need for specialized training and expensive equipment. Few crime problems are confined to a single local government jurisdiction. When a bank robbery is committed in a small town, the thief can quickly travel through the jurisdictions of several different police forces casually tied together by radio contact and avoid apprehension. The effectiveness of rural law enforcement will require greater cooperation and coordination among local forces. Even better, a major improvement would be the establishment of a county or regional force, with state help in criminal investigation and communications. Grants from the Federal Law Enforcement Assistance Administration have helped some rural areas develop better communications networks and access to specialized equipment.

Fire Service. The volunteer fire department is the backbone of rural and small-town fire service. Such departments frequently involve most of

Table 8.2. Rural and urban crime, 1974.

	United States		Large Cities[a]		Rural Areas	
	Reporting population 187,688,000		Reporting population 42,261,000		Reporting population 25,120,000	
Type of Crime	Per 100,000 1974	Percent change 1973–74	Per 100,000 1974	Percent change 1973–74	Per 100,000 1974	Percent change 1973–74
All crime	5,169.9	+ 16.8	7,498.8	+ 12.2	2,011.4	+ 20.3
Violent crime	502.1	+ 11.0	1,107.9	+ 9.0	161.6	+ 6.1
Crime against property	4,667.8	+ 17.4	6,390.9	+ 12.8	1,849.8	+ 21.8
Specific types						
Murder, nonnegligent manslaughter	10.4	+ 5.1	21.5	+ 2.8	7.8	+ 1.0
Manslaughter by negligence	4.5	− 9.9	4.7	− 7.5	9.4	− 11.9
Forcible rape	28.4	+ 7.7	55.4	+ 7.0	13.1	. . .
Robbery	235.3	+ 14.5	648.4	+ 12.1	22.7	+ 21.8
Aggravated assault	228.0	+ 8.3	382.6	+ 4.7	118.0	+ 4.5
Burglary	1,519.4	+ 17.3	2,236.7	+ 12.7	791.6	+ 22.7
Larceny	2,647.6	+ 20.5	3,171.4	+ 18.1	955.8	+ 22.1
Motor vehicle theft	500.8	+ 3.8	982.8	− 1.7	102.5	+ 12.1

Source: Federal Bureau of Investigation, U.S. Department of Justice, 1975 (Tables 10 and 14).

[a]58 largest cities of over 250,000 population.

the town in fund-raising events and auxiliary groups, serving the town as a social organization as well as a public service organization. Volunteers are dedicated and able. Nonetheless, rural fire losses are relatively greater than urban losses, as reflected by the higher insurance rates that apply.

Because of personnel and equipment costs and the great distances that must be covered, it is hard to envision a situation where rural areas could have full-time professional fire fighters. At the same time, however, volunteer systems are becoming a weaker vehicle for fire fighting, as fewer people work in the communities where they live. This discontinuity between place of work and place of residence means simply that an adequate number of fire fighters may not be around during the day, or that the time needed to respond to an emergency is lengthened if the fire fighters must come from a distance.

Two steps can be taken to improve rural fire-fighting effectiveness. The first is a good police-fire communications network so that equipment can be directed to the places where it is needed and effectively shared. The second is training police to operate fire equipment and to serve as firemen when needed. Police vehicles equipped as emergency vehicles with fire extinguishers could also respond to many small fires. Police and fire fighters could be combined into a single public safety force.

Education. The dispersal of population creates the major distinction between rural and urban education systems. The dual problem of scale and distance must be conquered to provide quality education in rural areas. Many rural communities find it difficult to offer school programs comparable to those available in suburban school systems. Preschools are generally not available. Little adult or vocational education is provided, although the latter is being improved. The structure of public education has been changed dramatically, but most change has been resisted by rural people (National Academy of Sciences, 1971). To achieve the scale necessary to afford specialized teachers, libraries, gymnasiums, and the other expensive facilities of modern schools, rural communities must band together to form joint school districts or countywide systems.

A policy objective for rural education that has gained political acceptance is that rural children should have educational opportunities relatively equal to those available to urban and suburban children. Living in a rural area or a small town should not doom one to a lifelong disadvantage. If this premise is accepted, the first problem is obviously cost. As the previous section on public finance indicated, metropolitan and nonmetropolitan school expenditures are fairly equal. However, because personal income is lower in nonmetropolitan areas, rural people have more difficulty affording equivalent schools even without the problem of scale economies.

Furthermore, it is difficult to get local political support for rural school programs when the local people see their "investment in education" leaving the community, as frequently happens after high school graduation. Rural political leaders feel they are paying more than their fair share. One answer to equal access to educational opportunities is to have the state assume an even higher share of the cost of public education, perhaps even the total cost; this, of course, might also bring greater state control over standards, curriculum, and local finance.

A second problem is that rural communities also need specialized services, such as remedial reading programs and advanced teacher institutes. Technical training and college, or at least junior college education also should be available. Providing these in a rural school district is especially difficult. Special state and federally aided programs have been established to put junior colleges and technical-training schools within reach of most rural people. However, every state and area of the country does not yet have such a system.

An organization that has proven to be very useful in enriching the rural school program is the educational service district. This unit was originally established in the state of New York and later extended on an experimental basis by the Appalachian Regional Commission. The school districts of several rural counties band together to form an educational service district. It is a voluntary and cooperative arrangement. The district undertakes projects that all of the individual districts need but cannot singly afford. For example, they might hire a remedial reading teacher to be a circuit rider visiting each of the schools in the multicounty area. The service district might also be a vehicle for offering in-service training of teachers, or it might hire professional staff to assist the district in taking advantage of state and federal aid programs.

Other advances have been achieved through the use of telecommunications techniques — television, videotape, and transmittal to remote areas through communications satellites. An experimental program in the use of communications satellites by the Appalachian Regional Commission was conducted in 1975. It is expected that similar innovations will contribute to improvement in the overall quality of rural education.

Welfare. As *The People Left Behind,* the report of the President's Commission on Rural Poverty (1967), amply demonstrated, a high percentage of rural people are poor, disabled, aged, and otherwise in need of welfare and social service programs. (While it is ten years old, this report is still a valid statement of rural problems and their potential solutions.) The Bureau of the Census reports that less than 10 percent of the metropolitan population was below the poverty line in 1973 while 14 percent of the nonmetropolitan population was classed as poor (Bureau of the Census, 1975, p. 16).

Many welfare services are available to rural residents through state or federally established programs. Rural governments are sometimes unenthusiastic administrators of such programs, probably because many local officials have not possessed a social services orientation and would prefer not to pay the administrative costs involved. As a result, practical availability of benefits like food stamps may be considerably less than legal availability. There is also the problem of embarrassment to the recipient who must declare his poverty in order to participate in a welfare program; this is especially difficult for children receiving a free school breakfast or lunch. Ways need to be found for rural people to benefit from such programs without the feeling of inferiority which might accompany them.

One of the current political issues is whether welfare should be recast into a national and entirely federally financed system. Under such a system, entitlement and availability would not vary much between one community and another. A question that remains unanswered is whether such a system would substantially change the geographic distribution of those receiving assistance. It could make it feasible for some older people to stay in the small towns and not force them to move to the city. It might also attract more of the poor and disadvantaged from the big cities. Poverty may possibly be more manageable if the poor are more evenly dispersed, but the prospect of a movement of the poor to the small towns may be alarming and even inflammatory in some communities.

Water, Sewerage Systems, Waste Disposal. Providing water and sewerage systems presents a financial difficulty for rural and small-town governments. Historically, of course, farm and small-town families obtained their water through wells and cistern systems. Privies became a symbol of rurality. Even with indoor plumbing, rural areas generally use septic tanks and tile fields and not municipal sewerage systems.

Rural industries (hog lots, dairy barns, food processing, paper mills, coal washing) all create large amounts of waste. Some individual plants have attempted to take care of their own waste products, but most of the waste products of rural industries have found their way into streams, into the air, or have been just piled upon the land. Industrial and residential trash are an unfortunate feature of the rural landscape. The solid waste ranges from cannibalized and junked cars on front lawns to old iceboxes thrown into streams, from the culm banks of mining towns to the large bark and sawdust piles in logging and mill towns. Under the Appalachian Regional Development Program and other federal grant programs some progress has been made with programs to collect solid wastes, notably automobiles, and to recycle them or dispose of them in an acceptable manner.

Rural pollution is no longer acceptable. Rural industry and rural local governments are being forced to take steps to provide sewage collection and treatment and water systems. Rural communities also recognize that water and sewerage systems are necessary to attract industry. This is one reason that federal economic development programs have invested heavily and indiscriminately in small-town sewerage systems. At one time four separate federal aid programs existed for construction of sewerage systems in small towns. They were besieged with applicants. The Area Redevelopment Administration was criticized because it put so much of its money into sewerage systems that economic development became merely a euphemism for building sewers. The pressures for making sewerage systems investments were very real: small towns and rural communities were being ordered by state sanitary water authorities to install systems to reduce pollution levels, and local officials also knew they had to have water and sewerage systems to attract industry. The problem was that there was just not enough money in the federal treasury to build sewers for all the small towns in America. Furthermore, having a sewage treatment plant was no guarantee of industrial prosperity.

Providing sewers and water in small towns is especially costly. Until recently little technology was directly applicable to small-town needs. Architectural and engineering firms engaged by the towns designed cutdown versions of big-city systems which were too high in cost to serve a small community economically. Federal officials saw grant applications where the cost of the sewerage system exceeded the market value of real estate in the town.

While some progress has been made in the development of small-scale systems, technological breakthroughs are still needed to put comprehensive water supply and sewage collection and treatment within reach of most small communities.

Rural Transportation. Rural America has a generally well developed road network. These highways are essential for access to markets, to employment, to medical care, to consolidated schools, to shopping areas, and to specialized services. At the same time, rural America is almost totally dependent on the private vehicle — public transportation is almost nonexistent. Although the incidence of car ownership is higher among the poor in rural areas than in urban areas, the poor drive older, less reliable cars. Their problem is compounded by the effects of inflation and the energy crisis.

While few economical alternatives to the private vehicle exist in sparsely settled areas, some innovations have been tried. These include the use of school buses for public transit, simplified access to intercity buses, demand responsive service using vans or school buses in off-hours, and the use of postal vehicles for passenger transport.

Private transit companies in small towns have been going under at an alarming rate, caught in the vicious cycle of rising costs, service cutbacks, and reduced revenues. Few will be able to survive without public subsidy. Fixed-route operations in particular cannot make it financially in areas of minimal population density. In their place, various types of demand responsive service are being tested.

The Office of Economic Opportunity has funded several demonstration projects to develop and improve public transportation in rural areas. Typically, these provide van or small bus transportation to health facilities, technical education facilities, social service agencies, and, less frequently, to places of employment, either through fixed-route or demand responsive service. While survival rates for the programs are uncertain, they generally hold promise of giving mobility to those too old, too young, or too poor to drive.

Most of rural America is already criss-crossed by a public transit network—but one that serves only students. Some communities are beginning to use school buses for nonwork trips, and some states are changing regulations that have prohibited such use. Many school buses have capacity in excess of student needs and are also free much of the day. The cost of utilizing them is less than maintaining a separate bus system. Summer use of school buses is also possible.

In Great Britain and some other European countries, mail and people are transported together. In the U.S., where rural carriers operate their own vehicles under contract, it is possible for them to also provide passenger transport. This arrangement requires no investment in capital equipment or additional salaries. A demonstration project in West Virginia is under way to determine feasibility and costs.

In many rural areas, taxis are the only available means of public transit, and they are often priced out of reach for many who need them. In some jurisdictions passengers are prohibited from sharing a taxi unless traveling together to the same destination. In these areas, changes in regulations to permit multiple occupancy would help to lower costs for passengers.

To overcome severe isolation problems, the use of communications tools—the telephone, radio, and television—may come into greater use as a substitute for actual presence on the job or in the classroom (Goldmark, 1972).

Health Care. The disparity between urban and rural health care has grown in recent years. No active nonfederal physician was available in 132 counties in 1970, an increase of 34 over 1963 (American Medical Association, 1972).

Another area open for substantial improvement in rural areas is preventive medicine. Regions of physician shortage may be serviced by mobile units from the closest population center for diagnosis and immunizations. Where lack of transportation prevents good rural health care, school buses can be used to bring the patients to the medical personnel. Group practice and prepaid group health plans, two widely touted means of improving health care, will work only where transportation is available.

While rural areas have a disproportionate share of elderly people and low-income families with greater health needs than average, they also have poorer access to services.

According to the American Medical Association report on rural health care:

We find that rural people in the more sparsely populated areas have only about one-half the access to physicians, nurses, dentists, hospital beds, and other health resources when compared with the rest of the Nation. The health problems of rural areas are further compounded by environmental hazards, an aging population, and a high degree of poverty (1972: p. 5).

Rural communities fortunate enough to have a physician are often lacking in facilities for specialized care. Rural hospitals are often small and inefficiently operated. Under the impetus of new federal legislation, the nation is in the process of being divided into 200 health service areas, each with an agency responsible for developing and implementing health plans, approving or disapproving applications for federal health funds, and recommending hospital construction or remodeling. The legislation is a new attempt to coordinate facilities and program planning for an area large enough to make a difference in achieving greater utilization of facilities, thus preventing costly duplication. The same legislation encourages medical group practices, physician assistants, and activities to improve health care and disease prevention.

All of these federally legislated measures are being tried with some success. The training of volunteer firemen and emergency squad personnel as paramedics to cope with accidents and cardiac arrests, for example, is being done through cooperation with teaching hospitals in metropolitan areas. Improved communications systems and hookups with hospitals are also being used to improve emergency treatment. Much of this must be done on a regional basis, and initially with sizeable amounts of federal money.

CONCLUSION. One's view of the major problems likely to face rural and small-town America over the next 20 years is, of course, largely shaped by what one expects the nation's demography and economy to be like. Factors including settlement patterns, available occupations and their vulnerability to national economic shifts, and the public measures taken to guarantee the well-being of all individuals will determine how·non-metropolitan areas fare in relation to the nation as a whole.

Programs to assist areas with economic problems depend upon the nation's overall economic performance. One can forecast a set of likely policies to deal with the problems of lagging rural areas in a national economy that is otherwise largely healthy, and a quite different set if the nation as a whole is suffering profound economic dislocations. This is precisely the distinction between the industrial location assistance programs of the 1960s and the WPA, CCC, and NYA projects of the Great Depression. Industrial relocation is of little help to rural communities when there is little or no industrial growth. Some economists, notably Schumacher (1973), forecast severe economic dislocations that may mean a return to subsistence and barter economies. Others say we are only beginning to understand the shifts in production, consumption, and demography that are likely to be dictated by the changes in the supply and cost of energy.

Given the coming changes in energy supply and cost, the most reasonable view is that dispersed settlement patterns and remote economic activity will become more expensive. Survival and progress in non-metropolitan areas will depend upon an approach to public services that has never been popular — more planning and more frank discussion of difficult public choices. Good public services — even minimally adequate ones — may demand tighter development controls and more compact settlements.

Under these assumptions, the major public policy issues for rural communities are these:

1. *Land use controls.* The control of land use has been primarily the province of local government. Rural local governments have traditionally adopted the most minimal controls, and these are not sufficient. State and federal interest in land utilization is increasing and likely to become more dominant in determining certain controls, particularly to protect unique or valuable areas, such as prime agricultural or energy resource lands, from being used for short-run and less productive purposes; to control the location of power plants; and to protect fragile environments. Although land use management has not been popular in rural communities, land use controls to discourage sprawl and to encourage more compact settlement patterns may prove to be one of the most effective ways of improving rural public services.

2. *Public service districts and planning districts.* Another major decision will be whether to advance the utilization of multicounty planning districts so they become more effective planning vehicles and even, perhaps, provide public services directly. In many areas, the choice seems to be whether communities are willing to do without certain services or are able to get together in using these new institutions.

3. *Local finance.* The real property tax seems to have reached its economic or political limits in many parts of the country. It will be unrealistic to rely on this traditional source to maintain quality public services or to expand into new areas of service. Other taxing systems — sales taxes or income taxes — while lucrative, are not easy for local areas to levy and administer. Such taxes generally require state permission to levy the tax and a centralized collection agency to make administrative costs feasible.

A revamped system of local taxation requires answers to the major questions of what proportion of local service costs for education, welfare, and other public services will be paid for with local funds and what proportion will be financed by intergovernmental transfer of funds. On the federal level, continuation of the revenue-sharing program will give local governments some flexibility in funding local services.

4. *Education.* Consolidation of rural school districts is largely completed. Larger districts seem impossible unless children are to spend unrealistic amounts of time on buses. Affording relatively equal educational quality to rural and small-town people, therefore, seems to

depend upon three things: the state paying more of the cost of local education programs; technological advances in the use of telecommunications systems; and the use of special-service districts to share the cost of specialized services and equipment.

5. *Health care.* Here again difficult choices have to be faced. Improving rural health care will require deliberate planning, control by state or federal government (especially in facility location and construction), and the development of integrated health care systems. Current federal programs provide incentives to physicians to serve rural areas, but greater involvement of the local community is called for in providing the supportive services necessary to attract and hold competent medical personnel.

6. *Transportation.* If energy costs increase substantially or if supply is constricted, the impact on nonmetropolitan areas will be profound. Gasoline prices of a dollar or more per gallon are threatening; the rural poor cannot afford to drive their typically large, old, and inefficient automobiles down the road at a dollar a gallon. Rural residents must have an alternative to the private automobile, and that alternative is almost certain to be publicly funded.

All of the above suggest a much more important role for rural local government. These issues point to the need for the providers of public services to take an active role in preparing for the future. Small local government has usually meant part-time local government with once-a-week officials responding to the most immediate problems. This approach frequently has not prepared rural localities to anticipate and prepare for major changes such as a sudden decline or a sudden rise in population. Urban and rural local governments both face a cost-services crisis with rising service demands and inadequate revenue sources. The future requires both rural local government officials and citizens not only to accept but to actively utilize planning and innovation in meeting public service needs.

9 Rural Ethnic Minorities: Adaptive Response to Inequality

THOMAS J. DURANT, JR.
CLARK S. KNOWLTON

THE three largest ethnic minorities in rural America—blacks, Mexican-Americans, and Native- or Indian-Americans—share a common position of relative deprivation and inequality, but they do not represent a monolithic or homogeneous entity of rural society. Each minority group has experienced a unique historical development from which its current status has evolved. In addition, the responses of the three groups to minority status and inequality have been both strategically and contextually different, and they have experienced varying degrees of success in improving their status and in getting the rest of the society to recognize and respond to their needs.

THE RURAL BLACK MINORITY. From a historical viewpoint, the current status of rural blacks in the United States evolved from the biracial caste system established by slavery. Like most traditional American institutions, slavery was born and nurtured in a rural environment. In fact, rural areas have been the initial location and have provided the original sociocultural context for most racial and ethnic groups, and the rural South has served as such for most blacks.

Blacks became a true minority, in the contemporary use of the term, following emancipation, which awarded them the legal recognition of nonslaves but did not drastically change their low position in the rural

Thomas J. Durant, Jr. is Associate Professor of Sociology, Louisiana State University. Clark S. Knowlton is Professor, Department of Sociology and American West Center, University of Utah.

social system. Moreover, it did not radically alter their dependence on agriculture (Beale, 1966). Although emancipation created the potential for social mobility and status competition, this occurred mainly on an intraracial or subcultural basis. The post–Civil War years were a crucial period in the social evolution of America, for it was then that it became definite that the basis for inequality would be color or ethnic origin in conjunction with social class.

Rural Black Population Changes: 1910–70. The Great Migration of blacks began around 1910. This population movement was marked by a moderate decline in the rural black population up to 1930. The decline slowed during the next decade, that of the Great Depression, but accelerated rapidly after 1940. By 1970 only 18.7 percent of the total black population resided in rural areas, compared to 72.6 percent in 1910.

The large majority of the rural black population historically has resided in the South. Therefore, the rural black population trends in the South largely reflect the population redistribution trends of blacks as a whole. In the 15 southern states, the rural-farm black population has declined considerably over the past 50 years. Proportionately the urban black population has increased rapidly since 1950, while the rural-nonfarm black population experienced a slight increase over the same period (Table 9.1).

These trends in the redistribution of the black population serve as evidence that blacks have become a less significant part of rural America, especially in the rural-farm sector. While the heavy exodus of blacks from farms is evidence of their dissatisfaction with their status, recent figures suggest dissatisfaction also among blacks residing in rural-nonfarm areas. Between 1960 and 1970 (for the first time since 1940), the rural-nonfarm black population declined as a proportion of the total black population (Table 9.1).

It is highly unlikely that population redistribution policy is the answer

Table 9.1. Percentage distribution of the black population of the United States and of 15 southern states, by residence, 1920–70.

	1920[a]	1930[a]	1940[b]	1950[b]	1960[b]	1970[a]
United States	100.0	100.0	100.0	100.0	100.0	100.0
Urban	34.0	43.7	48.0	61.6	72.4	81.3
Rural-nonfarm	17.2	16.9	16.7	17.2	19.8	15.7
Rural-farm	48.8	39.4	35.3	21.2	7.8	3.0
15 southern states[c]	100.0	100.0	100.0	100.0	100.0	100.0
Urban	25.3	31.8	36.4	47.6	57.8	67.2
Rural-nonfarm	17.8	18.5	18.3	21.6	29.0	29.2
Rural-farm	56.9	49.7	45.3	30.8	13.2	3.6

[a]Source: U.S. Bureau of the Census, 1920, 1930, 1970a, 1970b, and 1970c.
[b]Source: Price, 1968:13–14.
[c]The 15 southern states are Alabama, Arkansas, Florida, Georgia, Kentucky, Louisiana, Maryland, Mississippi, Missouri, North Carolina, Oklahoma, South Carolina, Tennessee, Texas, and Virginia.

to producing a more uniform rural-urban distribution of the now urban-skewed black population. However, the implementation of socioeconomic development policy and the provision of opportunities for blacks to improve their status and life chances can make rural America a more attractive place for blacks to live. It was not an accident that prompted the majority of blacks to abandon farming. For the most part, the movement represented a deliberate and conscious action to escape a castelike system of inequality in which the large majority were sharecroppers and tenant farmers of the lowest rank in the class hierarchy of rural society. Sharecropping and farm tenancy among blacks reached their peak in 1920, declined slightly during the Great Depression of the 1930s, and thereafter declined sharply under the impact of mechanization. The decline of blacks in farming continued from World War II to 1950, as increased mechanization displaced thousands of black sharecroppers, tenant farmers, and farm laborers. In its wake, this extensive population movement has left behind a small group of older black farmers of the lower economic class, mostly working subsistence and poverty level farms.

Changes in the Social and Economic Status of Rural Blacks: 1960–70. Current literature reveals an improvement in the social and economic conditions of blacks in the United States. A recent report by the U.S. Bureau of the Census (1974a) indicated that blacks have shown continued progress on the educational and political fronts, a trend consistent with earlier reports in this series (U.S. Bureau of the Census, 1971, 1972, and 1973). The 1973 report indicated, however, that although the overall income ratio between black and white families has declined, "the picture is particularly mixed with significant regional and family status variations" (p. 1). This finding raises several questions regarding the status of blacks relative to that of whites—namely, whether the inequality gap between blacks and whites has narrowed or widened, and the relative versus the absolute improvement in social and economic conditions of (1) rural blacks and rural whites, (2) rural blacks and urban blacks or urban whites, and (3) rural-nonfarm blacks and rural-farm blacks. Whereas in the past it has been common to compare the rural with the urban, interest has shifted recently to metropolitan-nonmetropolitan differences and black-white comparisons.

The overall educational level has improved for both rural-nonfarm and rural-farm blacks. Relative to whites, however, the educational level of rural-nonfarm and rural-farm blacks ranks substantially lower. Between 1960 and 1970, median years of school completed by the population aged 25 and over increased from 6.4 to 7.6 years for rural-nonfarm blacks and from 5.7 to 7.0 years for rural-farm blacks. For the same period, the median years of school completed increased from 9.9 to 11.5 years for rural-nonfarm whites, and from 8.9 to 11.0 years for rural-farm whites. While rural-nonfarm blacks hold a slight edge over rural-farm blacks with regard to educational level, both groups lag behind urban blacks. In addition, rural-nonfarm and rural-farm blacks showed smaller increases in median years of school completed than did urban blacks between 1960 and 1970.

The rate of increase in median years of school completed was slightly greater for blacks than for whites in both rural-farm and rural-nonfarm areas between 1960 and 1970. Perhaps of greater importance is the fact that educational inequality, as measured by median years of school completed, actually widened between blacks and whites of both areas. The difference in median years of school completed for rural-nonfarm blacks and whites was 3.5 years in 1960 and 3.9 years in 1970, and for rural-farm blacks and whites 3.2 years in 1960 and 4.0 years in 1970. For the same years the differences between urban blacks and whites in median school years completed declined slightly from 2.8 years to 2.0 years.

The unemployment gap between rural-farm blacks and whites widened between 1960 and 1970 (Table 9.2). In 1960, 2.8 percent of the rural-farm white civilian labor force was unemployed as compared with 3.4 percent for rural-farm blacks. In 1970, 2.0 percent of the rural-farm white civilian labor force was unemployed compared with 4.7 percent for rural-farm blacks. In fact, the percent unemployed among rural-farm blacks increased between 1960 and 1970 compared with a decrease for rural-farm whites during the same period. The percent unemployed among both urban and rural-nonfarm blacks was also higher than that for whites of the same areas in 1960 and in 1970 (Table 9.2).

These unemployment trends raise crucial questions: whether rural industrial and economic development has widened or reduced economic status differences between blacks and whites, and whether they have offset outmigration of the most highly educated, occupationally skilled, young black adults. There is some evidence that outmigration of blacks from the rural-farm population has led to an increasingly aging or dependent rural-farm population and a decrease in young working-age adults (Tucker, 1974).

When compared to whites, a disproportionately small percentage of blacks were found in 1960 and 1970 in the higher status white-collar occupations (the first four occupational categories of Table 9.2, including professionals, managers, sales, and clerical). This was true in all three residence groups. In spite of the fact that blacks in all areas made significant absolute gains, greater proportions of blacks than whites were found in the lower status occupations in 1960 and 1970. Blacks in the rural-nonfarm and rural-farm categories made only minor gains in the higher occupational categories. As might be expected, the proportions in the upper categories were highest for urban blacks and lowest for rural-farm blacks. Furthermore, within the rural-farm group a higher percentage of whites were farmers and farm managers, while a higher percentage of blacks were farm laborers and foremen. The gap between the proportions of rural-farm blacks and whites who were farm owners or managers actually widened between 1960 and 1970. The percentage of

Table 9.2. Employment and income of blacks and whites in the United States, by residence, 1960 and 1970.

| | Black | | | | | | White | | | | | |
| | Urban | | Rural-nonfarm | | Rural-farm | | Urban | | Rural-nonfarm | | Rural-farm | |
	1960b	1970	1960b	1970	1960b	1970	1960	1970	1960	1970	1960	1970
Percent unemployed[a]	9.3	6.6	8.6	5.6	3.4	4.7	4.6	3.6	5.9	4.1	2.8	2.0
Occupational distribution	100.0	100.0	100.0	100.0	100.0	100.0	100.0	100.0	100.0	100.0	100.0	100.0
Professional and technical	6.5	8.9	4.1	5.2	1.8	4.6	13.9	17.0	10.0	11.8	4.2	6.5
Managers, officials, and proprietors	2.3	2.5	1.3	1.5	0.4	1.2	10.4	9.4	9.0	8.3	2.9	3.8
Sales	2.0	2.5	0.8	1.0	0.4	0.6	9.2	8.4	6.6	5.7	2.7	3.1
Clerical	8.6	15.5	1.7	4.1	0.5	2.8	18.5	20.3	10.8	13.2	5.0	8.2
Craftsmen and foremen	7.6	9.1	5.9	9.1	2.1	5.7	15.2	13.6	17.7	18.0	6.3	9.0
Operatives	22.5	23.2	19.2	27.3	8.3	20.0	18.5	15.3	24.3	22.9	11.7	13.9
Laborers, except farm	12.9	8.7	17.3	13.5	6.5	8.4	3.8	3.6	6.1	5.2	2.9	3.2
Farmers and farm managers	0.4	0.2	4.4	1.2	32.3	17.4	0.3	0.2	2.8	1.4	46.3	37.0
Farm laborers and foremen	1.1	0.7	17.0	10.2	35.4	21.6	0.4	0.3	3.2	2.3	13.6	8.5
Service workers	20.8	21.0	10.6	15.1	3.2	9.8	8.4	10.5	7.7	10.2	3.2	6.1
Private household	15.3	7.7	17.7	11.8	9.1	7.9	1.4	1.4	1.8	1.0	1.2	0.8
Median Family Income	$3,711	$6,581	$1,917	$4,027	$1,263	$3,197	$6,433	$10,629	$4,981	$8,528	$3,472	$7,288

Source: U.S. Bureau of the Census, 1960 and 1970a.

[a] Male civilian labor force, 14 years of age and over.

[b] Only the nonwhite population category was used by the 1960 Census; blacks compose approximately 95 percent of the nonwhite population. Blacks were a separate category in the 1970 census.

farm laborers declined for both blacks and whites between 1960 and 1970, but the ratio of black farm laborers to white farm laborers remained 2½ to 1 (Table 9.2).

Family income in rural areas falls far below that in urban areas for blacks as well as whites. Median family income in both 1960 and 1970 was lowest among rural-farm blacks and highest among urban blacks, while rural-nonfarm blacks ranked in between. Comparing rural-farm with rural-nonfarm incomes, the percent increase was greater in the rural-farm category, but the absolute value was higher in the rural-nonfarm. Whereas this may suggest a narrowing of the income gap between the three groups of blacks, the differences in absolute income values do not suggest any radical change in this direction (Table 9.2).

The income inequality gap between blacks and whites of the rural-farm group definitely widened between 1960 and 1970, as shown in Table 9.2. The median income of rural-farm black families in 1970 was only 44 percent of that for rural-farm white families, while the median income of rural-nonfarm black families was 47 percent of that for their white counterparts. Only in urban areas did the black median family income rise to more than half (62 percent) of that for whites.

Rural-Urban Migration as Adaptive Response to Inequality. The massive exodus of blacks from the South may be viewed as an adaptive response to minority status and inequality. This nonviolent action was one of the most phenomenal population movements in the history of America. Most of the forces contributing to black migration from the South during the early 1900s were "push" factors as contrasted with "pull" factors. A traditional push factor was the desire to avoid a biracial caste system of inequality supported by prejudice, discrimination, and regional traditionalism. A related push factor was the desire to escape the "plantation syndrome," the semicaste system of sharecropping and tenant farming which blacks viewed as menial, cruel, status degrading, and oppressive.

After the Great Depression, including the post–World War II years and up to the 1950s, another push factor impacted heavily upon rural blacks. This was the increase in farm mechanization and the application of advanced technology to farming, which reduced the farm labor force and displaced sharecroppers, tenant farmers, and farm laborers, many of whom were black (Beale, 1966 and 1970).

The greater abundance of employment opportunities in the North emerged more recently, in the 1950s, as a prominent pull factor. This triggered the social force of family solidarity, manifested in the reconvening and reuniting of black families in urban areas of the North and West.

Black Return Migration to the South. A recent focus of interest has been a counterstream of black migrants from the urban North and West to the South. (Counterstream is a term used by E. S. Lee to define counter-migration trends. Another phrase commonly used is return migration [Campbell, Johnson, and Stangler, 1974].) According to Campbell and his colleagues, this counterstream has been increasing since 1940, but a complete reversal of the black migration stream from the South to the North and West is not likely. Factors that have facilitated return migration of blacks include the development of a communication network and transportation system (Everett Lee, 1966), increased economic opportunities in the South, a decrease in racial discrimination in employment, and a snowballing effect of the countermigration trend (Campbell, Johnson, and Stangler, 1974).

The main interregional migration counterstream flows from the metropolitan North to the metropolitan South. Campbell and his colleagues found that only a fourth of the returnees of their sample moved to rural areas. In addition, they discovered that most return migrants are likely to be young adults with small families, with at least a high school education, and with a higher income level than their nonmigrant counterparts. Although the economic motive prevails in the literature as the main incentive, the explanation of return migration is still unclear. Personal and family factors have been considered more important by a few authors (Shryock, 1964; Johnson, 1971). While a definite conclusion cannot be reached, it seems apparent that blacks of the metropolitan North and West are taking a new look at the South, the present attitudes of the white South, the success of the civil rights movement, opportunities in human rights areas such as voting and holding public or political positions, and the desegregation of public schools and public facilities. However, discrimination in housing and employment remains an obstacle, and the overall social and economic conditions and opportunities of blacks still lag behind those of whites.

The Poor People's Movement: An Adaptive Means of Survival for Rural Blacks. Rural blacks have been depicted as a vanishing population (Jones and Lee, 1974). The black farmer is becoming extinct (Wadley and Lee, 1974), and the urbanization of the black population is largely a reality (Reid, 1974). These trends raise serious questions concerning whether or not the remaining rural blacks can survive in their present locations and what factors may influence regional variation in survival rates. Certainly, the answer to the survival of blacks in rural areas must involve the eradication of poverty. In 1967, the President's National Advisory Commission on Rural Poverty made over 200 recommendations which spelled out what its members believed should be done to "eliminate" rural proverty. The implementation and effect of these recommendations, however, have yet to be fully realized.

The poor people's cooperative movement has represented an attempt by blacks to adapt to a changing rural society. Stimulated by the War on Poverty, almost 100 rural cooperatives have emerged in the last 10 to 15 years. The majority have been farming cooperatives consisting largely of poor black farmers, principally in the South. These cooperatives have actually represented experimental strategies for the survival of blacks in rural areas. One assumption of the cooperative movement is that effective remedies for poverty among rural blacks are not likely unless the poor have organizations that can exert pressure for change (Marshall and Godwin, 1971). But the future of these cooperatives is just as uncertain as the future of blacks in rural areas.

While it is not clear that the survival of these cooperatives means the survival of the rural black population, the potential does exist for improvement of their social and economic conditions. Public policy in agriculture and in economic and human resource development will determine much of the success of the cooperatives as well as the success of black farmers. However, there are those who see economic factors, the mobilization of local community resources, and the elimination of the problem of federal sponsorship as paramount in determining the duration of the cooperative movement of the rural poor (Finney, 1973). Others see the elimination of discrimination by agencies of the federal government (Howze, 1970) and strong government commitment to rural reconstruction in the poor areas (Weintraub, 1970) as important. Some hold at least a little optimism for black survival in rural areas (Beale, 1966) while others claim there is little evidence that the future of blacks in agriculture will be significantly improved by existing federal policies (Marshall and Godwin, 1971). Finally, others have shown the need for policies relating to service needs created by population redistribution (Lee and Bowles, 1974).

MEXICAN-AMERICANS

A Heterogeneous Minority. Mexican-Americans, although sharing many cultural values, are one of the most heterogeneous minorities in the United States. The various Mexican-American subgroupings differ somewhat from each other in historical experience in the United States, length of residence in the country, rural-urban residence, dialect, amount of Spanish and English spoken, degree of cultural isolation from American and from Mexican cultures, differential integration into Anglo-American society, degree of socioeconomic deprivation, and perceived identity. This heterogeneity is reflected in the fact that no single group-identity term has yet been acceptable to a majority of the Mexican-American people. The many names in existence such as Mexican, Spanish-American, Latin-American, and Chicano reflect not only cultural differences among subgroupings but also changes in Mexican-American self-definition and identity (Grebler, Moore, and Guzman, 1970).

The Establishment of Dominance and Minority Status. The Mexican residents of the Southwest at the time of the American conquest, when they became American citizens against their will, were a largely rural people living in frontier settlements of California, New Mexico, and Texas. Poorly articulated into the political, economic, military, and cultural life of Mexico, these frontier settlements lacked the social, educational, and economic amenities found in more settled areas in both Mexico and the United States. They were, however, free of the social pathology of crime, violence, and alcoholism that marked the Anglo-American frontier. Social control among the frontier Mexican-American population was maintained by the large, rural, extended family, the influence of religion, and the cultural values of a closely knit ranch and village population (McWilliams, 1968).

The first major Anglo-American intrusion into the Southwest occurred in Texas. From 1819 to 1834, Anglo-American immigrants, taking advantage of the liberal land policies of the Spanish and Mexican governments, had come to outnumber the Mexican inhabitants. What began as a joint Anglo-American and Mexican-American uprising against a centralizing Mexican regime in 1835 ended as an Anglo-American drive for independence and dominance in Texas. Events such as the Battle of the Alamo generated deeply rooted prejudices against the Mexicans and Mexican-Americans that were carried by Anglo-Texans throughout the West (Day et al., 1968; Weems, 1971; Richardson, Wallace, and Anderson, 1970). In many Texas counties, the entire Mexican-American population was driven out. In others, the landowners lost their land but the Anglo-Americans hired Mexican-Americans to perform the necessary labor. As Meinig states, by 1880 "the Anglos had gotten control by fair means or foul of nearly every ranch worth having north of the Nueces River" (Meinig, 1971:54). Only in south Texas and along the Mexican border were the Mexican-Americans able to preserve their landholdings and to maintain a political presence.

The thriving, vigorous, and self-confident Mexican-American society of California fell to Anglo dominance during the gold rush of the late 1840s and early 1850s. Within a few years, the Mexican-American residents of California were reduced to an insignificant minority, losing their land, social status, and political power. They managed to survive as an unskilled and semiskilled group, living on the margins of Anglo-American society (Pitt, 1970; Cleland, 1959).

It was only in New Mexico that the Mexican-American population managed to retain a strong socioeconomic and political position in the dominant Anglo-American society. New Mexico did not receive many Anglo-American immigrants until the 1870s, and Anglo-Americans did not come to outnumber the Mexican or Spanish-American (as they prefer to be called) population of New Mexico until the 1940s. Many wealthy Spanish-American families early sent sons to be educated in American schools and universities. Members of these families showed no hesitation in entering politics, business, finance, or the professions. The large Spanish-American rural village population was and is most resistant to Anglo-American dominance. Although the Anglo-Americans did eventually

establish dominance, their political and economic groupings had to include Spanish-American leaders.

**The Curious Ways of the United States Bureau of the Census with
Mexican-Americans.** From 1930 to 1970, the United States Bureau of the
Census tried without conspicuous success to develop census techniques
refined enough to count the Mexican-American population accurately.
Aware of the deficiencies, the Bureau in 1970 modified past procedures
and concepts. However, as the U.S. Civil Rights Commission stated in
1974, "The Bureau's technique for measuring the number of persons of
Spanish-speaking background in 1970 was a compromise and not the result
of its customary careful scientific planning. It is no wonder that the 1970
Census, more than any previous census, was criticized for its measure of
this group" (U.S. Civil Rights Commission, 1974:8).

Based on the current population reports, the Bureau of the Census
estimated 9.2 million persons of Spanish origin in 1970. Of this number,
55 percent, or 5,073,000, were estimated to be of Mexican-American
origin. Virtually everyone familiar with the Mexican-Americans felt that
this was a gross undercount, but it was still larger than the 4.5 million
persons of Mexican-American origin enumerated in the 1970 census.

For a discussion of the terminology used and limitations of the data
for Persons of Spanish Origin and Subgroupings, see page ix of the Introduction to U.S. Bureau of the Census, 1970a.

The Bureau of the Census seems to have agreed with criticisms of its
procedures for counting ethnic minorities; with the inclusion of additional
categories in its March, 1973 *Current Population Reports,* it came up with
an estimate of Mexican-American or Mexican population numbering
6,293,000, an increase of 38.8 percent over the 1970 count (U.S. Bureau of
the Census, 1973). Many observers feel that this estimate is still in error, as
it does not include either those Mexican-Americans who refused to accept
the categories offered them as an identity or the very large number of
illegal immigrants. A reasonable estimate of the number of Mexican-
Americans in the United States falls between 7 and 8 million.

Rural-Urban Distribution of the Mexican-Americans. In 1970,
85.5 percent of the official total of 4,532,435 Mexican-American people in
the United States resided in urban areas. (U.S. Bureau of the Census,
1970a:2). Among persons of Spanish origin, Mexican-Americans are the
most rural. In analyzing the data on rural-urban distribution by state for
the Mexican-Americans, it is important to keep in mind that the data are
influenced by the following factors: (1) many illegal Mexican urban and
rural workers, in numbers large enough to influence census findings for
many states, avoid contact with any local, state, or federal agency, including the Census Bureau, and therefore, are not counted; (2) in urban
barrios, or Mexican-American neighborhoods, many families and
especially young adult males are quite mobile and difficult to locate; (3)

large numbers of rural Mexican-American migrant workers live during the winter in the Southwest, leaving in the early spring and returning quite late in the fall. Their location at the time of the census might well determine whether they were defined as urban, rural-nonfarm, or rural-farm.

The present rural-urban distribution of Mexican-Americans is the product of a complex set of cultural, economic, and social forces. Among the more important factors were the recruitment of Mexican-American workers by western and midwestern railroads early in the century to build and repair tracks, the recruitment of Mexican-Americans into urban centers in periods of labor shortage, their recruitment as strikebreakers in the 1920s, and the employment of Mexican-Americans as defense workers during World War II.

As commercial growing of fruits, vegetables, sugar beets, and other crops that require large numbers of workers during one or more phases of the crop cycle developed, large numbers of Mexican-American migrant workers began to move in a vast eddy, leaving their home communities in the early spring and returning in the late fall after swinging through the West and Midwest. Mexican-American migrant workers constantly settled out of the migrant stream in small villages, medium-sized towns, and large metropolitan centers. Gradually, new Mexican-American settlements sprang up and old ones expanded from the 1920s to the 1960s, with brief interruptions during periods of depression. As Mexican-Americans migrated, usually in family groups, the extended family structure facilitated urbanization. Once families settled down in a reasonably secure economic situation, they were joined by friends and relatives whom they assisted to secure employment and housing. Substantial Mexican-American urban settlements sprang up throughout the Midwest, the Rocky Mountains, and the Pacific Coast, drawing migrants directly from the Southwest and from Mexico during and after World War II.

Since World War II, Mexican-Americans have migrated east in two types of movement. The first was the more traditional movement of agricultural migrant workers. Mexican-Americans and Mexicans, both legal and illegal immigrants, have moved into southern agriculture as migrant agricultural and resident farm workers. They are now moving north in the eastern migrant stream. They are also settling out wherever opportunities present themselves. Many of these farm workers by now have settled in southern urban areas, often working in the surrounding countryside. The second movement east has been made by industrial and urban workers seeking jobs in industries and cities in the Northeast and the Middle Atlantic states.

The Current Social and Economic Status of Rural Mexican-Americans. In 1969, the median family income for all families in the United States was $9,586, compared with $6,962 for families of Mexican origin. In the urban population, median income for families of Mexican

origin was $7,256, compared with $5,229 in rural-nonfarm areas and
$5,020 for Mexican-origin families on farms (Table 9.3). The median
incomes for all rural-nonfarm and rural-farm families of the U.S. were
$8,231 and $7,082, respectively.

In states having 100,000 or more residents of Spanish origin, the
highest median family incomes for Mexican-Americans were found in the
large Mexican-American communities located in the midwestern states of
Michigan, Illinois, and Indiana. The lowest median family incomes were
in Colorado, New Mexico, Texas, and Florida, (Table 9.3).

The highest median income for the Mexican-American rural-
nonfarm population in 1969 was $10,600 reported by the Census Bureau
for Indiana, an extraordinarily high figure which may be a census error.
Rural-nonfarm Mexican-American residents in Illinois came in second
with a median family income of $9,312, followed by the states of
Michigan, Ohio, Arizona, and California. The states of Colorado, New
Mexico, Florida, and Texas occupied the lowest positions. Rather surprising is the relatively low median family income in Florida, where the
Mexican-American rural population is apparently increasing.

The highest rural-farm family median income among Mexican-
Americans was found in California, with Arizona close behind, followed by
New Mexico and Colorado. The lowest median family income for rural-
farm Mexican-Americans was found in the state of Texas. With these
statistics, it is understandable that the Mexican-Americans are moving out
of rural-farm employment, and that they are leaving the Southwest for the
Midwest and other regions with higher income levels.

In 1970 Mexican-Americans had the lowest median school years
completed of all the racial and ethnic minorities for which specific data
were available. The poor educational showing of the Mexican-American is
partly caused by the consistent migration to the United States of large

Table 9.3. Median income of families with head of Mexican origin in
United States and in states with 100,000 or more persons of
Spanish origin, by residence, 1969.

States	Total	Urban	Rural-Nonfarm	Rural-Farm
U.S.	$6,962	$7,256	$5,229	$5,020
Arizona	7,082	7,156	6,855	6,161
California	8,050	8,228	6,291	6,577
Colorado	6,518	6,813	5,365	5,043
Florida	5,078	5,689	4,512	. . .
Illinois	9,301	9,300	9,312	. . .
Indiana	9,299	9,255	10,600	. . .
Michigan	9,391	9,642	8,548	. . .
New Jersey	9,109	8,683	. . .	. . .
New Mexico	5,582	5,965	4,765	5,671
New York	9,093	9,016	. . .	. . .
Ohio	8,778	9,160	7,709	. . .
Pennsylvania	8,217	8,379	. . .	. . .
Texas	5,430	5,708	4,192	4,066

Source: U.S. Bureau of the Census, 1970a:121–34.

numbers of legal and illegal Mexican immigrants with little school attendance. If the data on native-born Mexican-Americans could be separated from that on Mexican immigrants, the median school years completed by urban Mexican-Americans might well be ahead of that for other minority groups. The median years of school completed among rural-nonfarm and rural-farm Mexican-Americans was 6.2 and 5.4 years respectively and lagged far behind that of other minority groups.

Employment and Occupation Level. Disproportionately large numbers of Mexican-Americans are employed in the relatively low-paying, low prestige occupations, as may be seen in Table 9.4. Less than 10 percent of the employed Mexican-Americans were found in the better-paying, more prestigious occupations of managers, administrators, and kindred workers, and professional, technical, and kindred workers in 1970. A mere 0.5 percent were classified as farmers and farm managers, but the number tabulated as farm laborers and foremen was also quite low (7.5 percent), thus destroying the myth that the majority of Mexican-Americans are migrant farmworkers. This enumeration may have been too low, however, as it excluded large numbers of Mexican illegal workers employed in agriculture.

Poverty. In 1969, almost a fourth of the Mexican-American families in the United States received incomes below the poverty level. A slightly lower percentage (22.4) of urban Mexican-American families lived below the poverty level compared with 38.5 percent of rural-nonfarm families and 32.7 percent of the rural-farm families. The percentages of Mexican-American families living in poverty in 1969 were much larger in the southwestern states of Arizona, California, Colorado, New Mexico, and Texas, and in Florida, than in other states with substantial numbers of

Table 9.4. Occupational distribution of employed persons of Mexican origin and of total United States population 16 years of age and over, by sex, 1970.

Occupational Groups	Persons of Mexican Origin						Total U.S.
	Male		Female		Total		
		(%)		(%)		(%)	(%)
Professional and technical	47,246	5.3	28,120	6.6	75,366	5.7	14.8
Managers and administrators, except farm	35,853	4.0	8,388	2.0	44,241	3.3	8.3
Sales	29,080	3.2	25,142	5.9	54,222	4.1	7.1
Clerical	51,589	5.8	103,718	24.2	155,307	11.7	17.9
Craftsmen and foremen	188,682	21.0	10,074	2.3	198,756	15.0	13.9
Operatives	242,234	27.0	113,419	26.4	355,652	26.8	17.6
Laborers, except farm	120,007	13.4	7,677	1.8	127,684	9.6	4.5
Farmers and farm managers	5,592	0.6	465	0.1	6,057	0.5	1.9
Farm laborers and foremen	82,372	9.2	17,187	4.0	99,559	7.5	1.2
Service workers	93,589	10.4	90,487	21.1	184,076	13.9	11.3
Private household	836	0.1	24,061	5.6	24,897	1.9	1.5
Total	897,080	100.0	428,738	100.0	1,325,818	100.0	100.0

Source: U.S. Bureau of the Census, 1970a:95.

Mexican-origin people (Table 9.5). Spanish-surname persons compose 23 percent of the total poor in the Southwest (Moore, 1970) and are two to three times as heavily represented as Anglos in the poverty category (Stoddard, 1973).

In the rural-nonfarm category, the lowest percentages of Mexican-American families living below the poverty level were found in the midwestern states of Indiana, Michigan, Illinois, and Ohio. The percentages of rural-nonfarm families living in poverty were quite high for the southwestern states. The Mexican-American village populations of New Mexico and probably of southern Colorado had high percentages of families living below the poverty level in 1969, as did the Mexican-American migrant labor population home based in Texas.

Social Trends. At the present time, the Mexican-Americans are one of the faster-growing minorities in the United States. They are growing both from a high fertility rate and from the very large number of legal and illegal Mexican immigrants entering the United States. Mexican-Americans are also in the process of becoming a national rather than a regional minority. Although the largest numbers are still found in the Southwest, important major concentrations now exist in the midwestern and Great Plains states. Mexican-Americans have found their way through the Rocky Mountain states into the Northwest. From Texas they are moving into the South, and a few have discovered the Middle Atlantic and northeastern states. Although they are one of the more rural minorities, the majority of Mexican-Americans are now city dwellers.

Table 9.5.   Total United States families below the poverty level and Mexican-origin families below the poverty level in the United States and in states with 100,000 or more persons of Spanish origin, by residence, 1969.

	Total	Urban	Rural-Nonfarm	Rural-Farm
		(%)		
Total, U.S.	11.6	9.8	16.2	17.9
Mexican Origin				
U.S.	24.4	22.4	38.5	32.7
Arizona	23.9	23.5	25.2	32.8
California	17.5	16.7	27.3	14.7
Colorado	23.9	21.3	35.8	26.9
Florida	35.0	32.4	41.2	. . .
Illinois	10.2	10.0	12.5	. . .
Indiana	8.6	8.5	7.0	. . .
Michigan	11.4	11.3	11.7	. . .
New Jersey	8.2	9.1	. . .	. . .
New Mexico	33.0	27.6	44.0	33.1
New York	9.9	10.6	. . .	. . .
Ohio	12.9	11.7	15.8	. . .
Pennsylvania	13.6	12.7	. . .	. . .
Texas	35.6	32.7	53.0	44.8

Source: U.S. Bureau of the Census, 1970a:122 and 1970b:962–74.

Cycles of protest have waxed and waned among rural Mexican-Americans in the Southwest over loss of land and over social and economic position in an Anglo-American world. One cannot say that the struggles of migrant Mexican-American workers or of the Spanish-American village people of northern New Mexico have ended. They have not; and further protest activities can be predicted. Protest has now spread into the Mexican-American urban neighborhoods. Riots in Los Angeles, Denver, and elsewhere are evidence that Mexican-Americans have been disturbed by discrimination, poverty, and feelings of powerlessness in urban areas as well as in rural areas. No longer a silent minority, if in reality they ever were, both the rural and the urban Mexican-American groupings will be heard from in the future as they struggle to improve their situation in American society.

INDIAN-AMERICANS

The Evolution of Minority Status. In 1976, many Americans celebrated the bicentenary of their country, commemorating an era of freedom as an independent and organized nation state. But for many Native Americans the bicentenary meant 200 years as subjects of political, social, economic, and cultural domination and subordination. During these 200 years, a dynamic and complex sequence of events helped to shape the minority status that Indians share today. Among these events were war and intermittent conflict between Indians and whites, which served to reduce the size and vigor of the Indian population (Johnson, 1969). Reservation communities were established for Indians, depriving them of land and natural resources and the freedom to practice their culture in an open and uninhibited manner. These reservations soon became the Indian ghettos of America, characterized by high infant mortality, ill health, low education, low income, and poor housing. The alternative to reservation life was forced assimilation, which obliterated the very foundation of Indian life, their culture. Today most Indians hold a subordinate socioeconomic and power position within the larger society.

Indians consider themselves an ethnic or cultural minority as opposed to a racial one, in that their identity is derived from "association in culturally and socially distinct Indian groups" (Lurie, 1966:1). Indian-Americans have been in a continuous struggle to maintain their cultural identity and to reduce inequality, using both dynamic and passive means.

Changes in Total Population. Indians as a minority group are quite difficult to define with any degree of precision. Racial characteristics are no longer an adequate measure. Some Indian tribes are now composed of many racially mixed individuals while in others racial intermixture is limited. In addition, tribes and pueblos can be placed on a continuum from those that still retain native languages, cultures, and social systems to those that have almost been acculturated if not assimilated by Anglo-Americans. Reservation residence is not an adequate criterion either, as the majority of the current Indian people do not live on reservations. Many Indian tribes have developed tribal rolls listing the names of those considered to be eligible for tribal benefits. On many of those lists, persons having only one-third Indian "blood" are enrolled. According to the 1970 Census, the category "American-Indian" included persons who indicated their race as "Indian (American)" as well as persons not classifying themselves in one of the specific race categories but who reported the name of an Indian tribe (U.S. Bureau of the Census, 1970:ix).

The Indian population began to decline in what is now the United States from the time of white contact, and the decline did not stop until after the first quarter of the present century. After this period, population growth began gradually and then accelerated between 1950 and 1970. The Indian-American population totaled 244,437 in 1920; 343,352 in 1930; 345,252 in 1940; 357,499 in 1950; and 523,591 in 1960. The great increase in the Indian-American population between 1950 and 1960 was to a large degree the result of a change in census enumeration procedures. Beginning in 1960, the self-identification method was adopted. Prior to 1960, Indians were placed into a racial category derived by the Bureau of the Census and were most likely underreported. In 1970, the total Indian-American population was listed at 792,730. The total Indian population increased by 46.5 percent between 1950 and 1960 and by 51.4 percent between 1960 and 1970. Indian-Americans are now one of the fastest growing elements of the American population.

Rural-Urban Population Distribution. States with large Indian reservation populations tend to be among the most rural states in the country (Table 9.6). These states contain fewer industrial and metropolitan centers toward which Indians might migrate. Among the ten states with the largest Indian populations, the following had relatively low percentages of their Indian population in 1970 living in urban areas: North Dakota, North Carolina, Arizona, New Mexico, Montana, and South Dakota. The majority of the Indian inhabitants of these states lived in the rural-nonfarm sector. If urban growth takes place near Indian reservations and pueblos, many rural-nonfarm Indians will commute to urban jobs in the cities. This is happening around Albuquerque, Santa Fe, and Los Alamos in New Mexico, and around Phoenix, Tucson, and other Arizona communities.

A significant number of states contain both rural Indian populations, living often in semi-isolated reservations, and growing numbers of urban Indians, often coming from out of state. The most urbanized Indian-American populations tend to be located in states with major metropolitan and industrial centers. These centers attract Indian rural migrants from many different regions and have few native rural Indians.

The rural-farm category among the Indian-Americans is a bit dif-

Table 9.6. Distribution of Indian population by state and residence, 1970 (states listed in order of Indian population size).

State	Total Indian Population	Urban Percent of state total	Rural-Nonfarm Percent of state total	Rural-Farm Percent of state total
U.S.	763,594	44.6	49.2	6.2
Oklahoma	96,803	49.2	45.5	5.3
Arizona	94,310	17.4	75.1	7.5
California	88,263	76.1	22.6	1.3
New Mexico	71,582	18.7	71.9	9.4
North Carolina	44,195	14.0	65.1	20.9
South Dakota	31,043	29.4	59.9	10.7
Washington	30,824	52.3	43.9	2.8
Montana	26,385	19.2	69.0	11.8
New York	25,560	67.1	32.0	0.9
Minnesota	22,322	52.4	43.9	3.7
Wisconsin	18,776	39.6	58.4	2.0
Texas	16,921	86.0	12.6	1.4
Alaska	16,080	29.2	70.8	0.0
Michigan	16,012	65.8	32.4	1.8
North Dakota	13,565	13.3	78.5	8.2
Oregon	13,210	52.8	43.2	4.0
Utah	10,551	35.0	53.1	11.9
Illinois	10,304	92.6	6.7	0.7
Kansas	8,261	74.2	22.0	3.8
Colorado	8,002	67.8	27.4	4.8
Nevada	7,476	37.9	52.7	9.4
Nebraska	6,671	48.5	45.2	6.3
Idaho	6,646	29.9	52.7	17.4
Florida	6,392	66.9	30.7	2.4
Ohio	6,181	82.2	15.8	2.0
Pennsylvania	5,543	79.6	19.9	0.5
Missouri	4,890	74.0	23.0	3.0
Virginia	4,862	62.8	33.8	3.4
Wyoming	4,717	22.0	62.3	15.7
Louisiana	4,519	34.1	60.1	5.8
New Jersey	4,255	88.8	10.7	0.5
Massachusetts	4,237	79.0	20.9	0.1
Maryland	3,886	84.4	15.3	0.3
Mississippi	3,791	15.2	77.4	7.4
Indiana	3,305	70.7	26.4	2.9
Iowa	2,924	70.2	26.8	3.0
Connecticut	2,322	80.1	19.5	0.4
Georgia	2,271	69.5	28.1	2.4
Alabama	2,163	55.9	37.5	6.6
South Carolina	2,091	41.0	57.1	1.9
Arkansas	2,088	58.7	36.0	5.3
Maine	1,872	45.7	53.5	0.8
Tennessee	1,432	76.5	22.6	0.9
Rhode Island	1,417	86.4	13.3	0.3
Hawaii	1,168	88.5	11.5	0.0
Kentucky	1,322	70.7	27.5	1.8
District of Columbia	673	100.0	0.0	0.0
West Virginia	518	37.3	61.8	0.9
Delaware	479	37.6	59.5	2.9
New Hampshire	310	51.3	47.1	1.6
Vermont	204	7.4	81.4	11.2

Source: U.S. Bureau of the Census, 1970: 1–2, 15–17.

ficult to assess. Many Indians in the Southwest and in Oklahoma have found employment as migrant agricultural workers and, therefore, earn their living in agriculture but are not defined as rural-farm. Other large numbers of Indians who are defined as rural-nonfarm are part-time farmers working small landholdings while holding down urban jobs. The only states with significant percentages of their Indian population classified as rural-farm are North Carolina, 20.9 percent; Montana, 11.8 percent; Utah, 11.9 percent; Idaho, 17.4 percent; Wyoming, 15.7 percent; and Vermont, 11.2 percent. A significant percentage of the Navajo population of Arizona and New Mexico earn their living from herding sheep. There are also Apaches in Arizona who are cattle ranchers. They may not always be defined as rural-farm by the Bureau of the Census, but they are certainly dependent upon agriculture.

Current Social and Economic Status of Indian-Americans. The more education members of a minority group possess, the better they are able to move out of poverty or increase their social mobility. Despite the neglect of Indian education, Indian-Americans have made great educational progress during recent years. In 1970, the highest educational levels among Indian-Americans were found in the urban Indian population and in those states with the largest urban Indian population. The urban Indian population of Utah was the best educated (median of 12.0 years) of all states with 10,000 or more Indian population. The rural Indian population of Utah, however, had a mere 4.0 median years of school, the lowest level among the states for which data were available. Twelve of the 16 states with 10,000 or more Indians had a median educational attainment for the rural population of less than 10 years.

The extremely low levels of education among rural Indian-American groups are an indictment of the American educational system, which is failing to prepare large numbers of Indian children for full participation in the economic, political, and cultural systems. The statistics do not reflect the quality of education offered the Indian-Americans, which is often quite low. Many Indian leaders have complained that the public schools attended by Indian children do not recognize the existence of Indian languages and cultures, a complaint similar to those of other ethnic minority groups.

Unemployment rates of Indian-Americans at the time the census was taken in 1970 were extremely high, with male unemployment rates of more than 20 percent in several states. They undoubtedly climbed considerably higher with the recession in 1973. Male unemployment rates in the majority of the states were higher than female unemployment rates, and the rates varied sharply by state.

Unemployment rates of Indian-Americans are higher in rural areas than in urban areas, although they are extremely high in both areas. Almost every government of a major industrialized nation would consider the rates of unemployment common to Indian-Americans as unac-

Table 9.7. Median school years completed by Indians in states with 10,000 or more Indians, by residence, 1970.

State	Total	Urban	Rural
Alaska	8.8	10.5	8.3
Arizona	7.6	9.6	6.9
California	11.4	11.8	10.1
Illinois	11.0	11.0	10.3
Michigan	10.0	10.2	9.5
Minnesota	10.1	11.1	9.0
Montana	9.7	10.3	9.6
New Mexico	8.1	11.5	6.8
New York	10.4	10.7	10.0
North Carolina	8.3	8.9	8.2
North Dakota	8.9	10.3	8.8
Oklahoma	10.3	11.6	9.0
Oregon	10.8	11.4	10.1
South Dakota	9.4	10.6	8.9
Texas	11.2	11.5	10.2
Utah	7.8	12.0	4.0
Washington	10.7	11.2	10.1
Wisconsin	9.9	10.4	9.5

Source: U.S. Bureau of the Census, 1970:20–26.

ceptable. The excessive unemployment rate for Indian-Americans is a cause of the poverty that exists among them, and evidence of their social isolation from the industrialized economy of the United States and their exclusion from the main currents of American life.

The occupational distribution of Indian-Americans shows that in 1960 and 1970 most urban Indians were found in the categories of operatives, service workers, and craftsmen (Table 9.8). Between 1960 and 1970 sizeable increases occurred in the clerical and professional and technical occupations, while decreases occurred among laborers and farm laborers and foremen. Employment in white-collar occupations increased from 24 percent to 36 percent among urban Indians. Most rural-nonfarm Indians were employed as operatives, laborers (except farm), service workers, farm laborers, and craftsmen. The proportion employed in white-collar occupations increased from 16 percent to 24 percent between 1960 and 1970. Among rural-farm Indians, between 1960 and 1970, white-collar occupations increased from 6 percent to 18 percent. Sharp decreases occurred in the occupations of farm laborer, farmer, and farm manager, while sizeable increases were experienced in the craftsman, operative, and service worker categories. Other sources also have reported a decline in the number of Indians engaged as migrant farm workers (Johnson, 1975).

Another measure of status and resources is family income. Median annual family incomes for Indians by state and residence are shown in Table 9.9. It should be kept in mind that these figures reflect cash income only. Indian tribes with low relative income but living where land is available for use, or where natural resources may be utilized, may be better off than Indians totally dependent upon a cash income. In any case,

Table 9.8.   Occupational distribution of employed Indians 14 years of age and over, by residence, 1960 and 1970.

Occupational Category	Urban		Rural-Nonfarm		Rural-Farm	
	1960a	1970	1960a	1970	1960a	1970
Professional and technical	8.0	11.6	6.1	7.9	2.5	6.8
Managers, officials, proprietors	3.0	4.3	2.8	3.5	1.1	3.0
Sales	3.0	4.0	1.8	2.1	1.0	2.1
Clerical	10.4	15.9	5.2	10.3	1.8	6.7
Craftsmen and foremen	14.8	14.4	11.0	14.5	4.0	10.1
Operatives	24.7	21.8	20.1	22.4	8.7	16.2
Laborers, except farm	11.4	6.9	19.3	11.2	8.9	7.7
Farmers and farm managers	0.5	0.2	4.5	1.4	31.4	17.6
Farm laborers and foremen	2.2	1.3	12.1	6.5	34.7	16.9
Service workers	15.0	16.6	12.2	17.5	3.9	11.4
Private household	7.0	3.0	4.9	2.7	2.0	1.5
Total	100.0	100.0	100.0	100.0	100.0	100.0

Source: U.S. Bureau of the Census, 1960:104 and 1970:87–89.
aEmployed persons who did not report an occupation were excluded.

median annual family incomes of rural Indians were lower than those of urban Indians in the vast majority of the states with 10,000 or more Indians.

Poverty.   A third of all Indian families had incomes below the poverty level in 1969. Two-fifths of rural Indian families fell in the poverty category compared with one-fifth of urban Indian families. States having the highest percentages of Indian rural families with earnings below the poverty line in 1969 were the more rural states with large Indian populations. Indians of these states lived mostly in the Southwest, the Rocky Mountains, and the Great Plains. The better-off rural Indian

Table 9.9.   Median family income of Indian population in states with 10,000 or more Indians, by residence, 1969.

State	Total	Urban	Rural
Alaska	$3,317	$4,250	$1,845
Arizona	2,221	3,205	1,953
California	3,932	4,211	3,202
Illinois	4,067	4,067	. . .
Michigan	3,707	3,703	3,717
Minnesota	3,279	3,266	3,311
Montana	2,783	2,410	2,922
New Mexico	2,541	3,977	2,248
New York	3,933	4,037	3,300
North Carolina	2,805	3,417	2,633
North Dakota	3,039	. . .	2,985
Oklahoma	3,283	3,629	2,977
Oregon	3,520	3,575	3,318
South Dakota	3,215	3,693	2,912
Texas	3,514	3,426	. . .
Utah	3,267	3,267	2,386
Washington	3,492	3,838	3,054
Wisconsin	3,293	3,417	3,190
United States	3,198	3,695	2,435

Source: U.S. Bureau of the Census, 1970:122–128.

families lived in the states of Illinois, California, Michigan, Texas, and New York. The states of Utah, Arizona, South Dakota, New Mexico, and North Dakota had the highest percentages of rural families earning below the poverty level. Johnson has found that rural Indians not only have lower incomes, but also larger families on the average than the United States rural population (Johnson, 1975:6).

Social Trends and Rise of Unrest. Perhaps the three most significant trends affecting Indian-Americans today are an important shift in governmental and public attitudes toward the Indian-American; Indians' growing interest in tribal cultures, languages, and identity as well as the development of an ethnic identity rising above tribal differences; and a new surge toward ending the economic and political paralysis created by decades of powerlessness and dependency upon the federal government. Indians are forming many diverse movements to achieve desired social and political goals and to protect Indian rights. These range from militants willing to resort to radical means to those working within the framework of the American political system.

Current Indian movements were preceded by a long history of conflicting Indian-white relations. White settlement and land distribution and allocation policy resulted in the removal of Indians from more desirable lands to less desirable lands (Tyler, 1974:54–69). Indians resisted policies that led to the breakup of tribal landholdings and to incorporation of Indians into American society as citizens and individual landowners and farmers. As few Indians actually farmed their allotment of land, the government allowed the leasing of Indian allotments to non-Indians. As a result of this policy, Indian landholding diminished from 155,632,312 acres in 1881 to 77,865,373 acres in 1900 (Tyler, 1974:125–49; Wise and Deloria, 1971:357–62). The Indian Reorganization Act of 1936 sought to make amends for some of the injustices by permitting Indians to organize tribal government bodies and to make contracts directly with the federal government and private agencies. Although some improvements were made in Indian housing, health, and education (Tyler, 1974:151–88; Wax and Buchanan, 1975:78–98), full implementation of this plan was not possible, due to World War II.

The end of World War II brought economic prosperity, and more and more Indians moved from the reservations and rural areas to metropolitan and industrial areas. Gradually, pressure grew upon Congress to adopt a new Indian program that would terminate the reservation system and end any unique relationships between Indians and the federal government. In 1953, the U.S. Congress passed House Concurrent Resolution 108, formally adopting a termination program designed to put an end to all Indian reservations. Termination proceedings began to wind their way through Congress for Indian tribes believed ready for termination (Tyler, 1974:169–253). Several tribes were terminated, but as states and Indian organizations began to assess the implications of termination, resistance spread. Termination proceedings slowed down and eventually were terminated themselves.

Urban relocation programs were developed to foster and expedite job replacement and training in urban areas. Under most antipoverty programs, Indian communities and reservations have been included among areas eligible for participation. The development of the natural resources of the Indian reservations and their industrialization have been encouraged. A wide variety of other programs designed to improve conditions of Indian life in both rural and urban areas have been implemented. The official government philosophy for the moment seems to be one of self-determination for the Indians, assistance to Indians who desire to relocate in urban areas, and development of the natural resources of the reservations for the benefit of the Indian population (Wise and Deloria, 1971:375; Levine and Lurie, 1968:106).

American Indians are now forming a wide variety of organizations — tribal, regional, and national. More and more Indian groupings of diverse ideologies and tendencies are finding a voice. It is true that conflict between organizations and factionalism within organizations continue to exist. Some large tribes, such as the Navajo, tend to remain aloof from regional and national Indian organizations. Such organizations also tend to have a fluctuating membership. But all of them express an ever-stronger Indian-American drive toward the control of their own destiny, the preservation of their cultures and languages, the elimination of poverty and discrimination, and the support of a system of cultural pluralism within the United States.

SUMMARY. The preceding sections have given an account of the status of the three largest ethnic minority groups of rural America — blacks, Mexican-Americans, and Indian-Americans. Three aspects of these minority groups were seen as important in assessing their status in rural America: the historical processes that influenced their current status; their present status vis-à-vis the larger white majority; and prospects for enhancing their status in rural areas in the future.

The statuses of all three ethnic minorities are rooted in a complex of historical events and processes; for blacks, this included subjection to slavery and a system of inequality based on race, ethnicity, and caste; for Mexican-Americans, it involved their regional and territorial concentration in the Southwest and their relegation to the lowest stratum of the status hierarchy; and for Indian-Americans, it included their loss of land and natural resources, the infliction of war and violence, and the uprooting of their cultural foundations.

While all three ethnic minorities have made economic gains in rural areas over the past several decades, their statuses continue to rank well below that of whites of the same areas. In addition, the economic conditions of rural minorities are worse than those of urban people, majority or minority. With reference to education and income, the status gap between rural blacks and rural whites has, in fact, widened, especially among the rural-farm population. Furthermore, poverty affects an abnormally higher proportion of blacks than whites.

A crucial concern which must eventually be confronted is the future of blacks in rural areas. It seems apparent that rural society must afford blacks opportunities for improving their socioeconomic condition and life chances if the syndrome of economic caste is to be obliterated.

Rural Mexican-Americans make up one of the most economically disadvantaged minorities. In the Southwest, they hold the lowest position on the socioeconomic status hierarchy. Economically, Mexican-American migratory agricultural workers suffer more severely than the stable Mexican-American population. Their situation is not likely to improve much unless steps are taken to adopt and implement policies and programs aimed at improving their economic conditions.

Rural Indian-Americans have sought to protect and preserve their land and their culture, but they have watched both diminish considerably over the years. Indian reservations which previously served as the Indian ghettos of America may now become the last legacy of Indian wealth and power as the demand for land has increased more and more, making reservation land and its natural resources more valuable.

At present, however, rural Indians are a severely deprived group, worse off economically than either blacks or Mexican-Americans. More and more, Indians are making an active effort to reduce the inequality which has plagued them and to improve their socioeconomic lot. They have aroused a greater interest in and public concern for Indian-Americans; they have attempted to revive their traditional culture and to establish their identity within the American society; and they are trying to preserve their remaining land and natural resources. As in the case of the other minority groups, their future in rural America rests on positive societal responses to minority needs and demands.

10 Discarding the Distaff: New Roles for Rural Women

CORNELIA B. FLORA
SUE JOHNSON

THE resurgence of the women's movement has caught the national eye and increased our awareness of the complexities and changes in women's roles and the power and status derived from them. The roles of rural women have always exhibited greater diversity in content than have those of urban women; those roles include some tasks heretofore defined in the urban context as men's work. Some changes in urban America today may simply be the result of urban women demanding to do what rural women have expected to do. Nevertheless, the roles of rural women also are changing, and we can be sure that the changes are evolutionary in the same way that changes in the roles and identities of urban and suburban women have developed.

BASIC FUNCTIONS OF THE RURAL WOMAN'S ROLE

Sexuality. The expression of female sexuality has been problematic and controversial in American society since its inception. Traditional societies tend to sweep sexuality under the rug and concentrate on the reproductive function instead, and that has been true in rural American society until very recently. Even now, the evidence indicates that the so-called sexual revolution has made only tiny inroads, and mostly in rural-nonfarm areas rather than in rural-farm areas.

By and large, the sexuality of rural women has been expressed

Cornelia B. Flora is Associate Professor of Sociology, Kansas State University. Sue Johnson is Research Coordinator, Center for Developmental Change, University of Kentucky. This chapter is contribution No. 45-B, Department of Sociology and Anthropology, Kansas Agricultural Experiment Station, Kansas State University.

traditionally through the institution of marriage. Normative forces against premarital and extramarital sex had their grounding in fundamentalist Christianity and were swift and severe in retribution, especially for women. Country music today still draws a strong distinction between good women and bad. The good women marry, have children, and are warm and supportive of their husbands.

Like her sisters of yesteryear, the single woman in rural society today finds herself surrounded by many marriageable men; because rural life's occupational opportunities are largely for men. The rural normative order typically not only stresses the primary importance of marriage and family for her but also strongly warns about sexual transgressions on the wrong side of the marital fence. Generally speaking, the rural woman who eschews migration to towns and cities marries earlier, spends a greater portion of her life in a married state, and suffers fewer marital breakdowns than does her urban sister (U.S. Bureau of the Census, 1970a, 1960, and 1950). A "stable" marriage configuration is more typical than not of rural life, though its normative hold on the sexes is less strong in rural-nonfarm areas. The small-town woman marries earlier than her rural-farm counterpart; however, her marriage is more likely to end in divorce or widowhood, and she is somewhat less likely to marry at all. In contrast, almost all farm women marry (well over ninety percent of those who remain on the farm), though some marry late, and they remain in stabler marriages of longer duration than do rural-nonfarm women (U.S. Bureau of the Census, 1970a, 1960a, and 1950a).

Although the stable marriage configuration typical of rural women provides a well-structured and long-lasting role, it is not without its costs. It is, first of all, restrictive in being the only "acceptable role for decent women . . . housewife and mother" (Nietzke, 1975:66). Second, the double standard, judging from popular country music, is still alive and thriving in rural areas. "Stand by Your Man," so far, the best-selling country single sung by a woman, stresses loyalty to one's mate above all else. Many other songs forgive him, no matter how profligate his behavior with other women or how patronizingly he treats his wife. Country music provides a rationale for the double standard, which boils down to the assumption that "men have to be 'the way they are' "—full of human frailty; "while women have to be what their men want them to be"—each to suffer silently through her man's transgressions and to take care of the house and kids while patiently awaiting the errant's return (Nietzke, 1975:66–68).

It is not surprising that lower levels of marital and personal satisfaction are found among farm than among rural-nonfarm families: given that farm families conform to traditional norms to a greater degree (Blood and Wolfe, 1960; Burchinal, 1964), it is likely that farm women are socialized not to place a high premium on personal values such as sexual satisfaction, stressing instead more holistic values such as the farm enterprise, economic security, and the family unit. And we should not forget the force of fundamentalist Christianity, with its emphasis on reproduction and maternal values rather than on sensual ones.

The complexities of male-female relationships expressed in country music are, by and large, not happy ones; in fact, one of the distinguishing characteristics of country music is its lugubriousness. Sex-role rigidities are at least partly at fault here: the decent woman's life and her primary source of power and identity are to come from her man; the more "human" (that is, reprehensible) man has his work, his friends, his woman, and other women from which to draw an identity. More importantly, the identification of a woman's life with that of her man is an abdication of her ability to wield a great deal of power save through interpersonal manipulation, often through inducement of guilt.

Some relaxation of traditional sex norms is occurring for contemporary rural women, however, even for decent women, if popular music is at all faithful in mirroring the sentiments of its listeners:

The happiest songs narrated by married men . . . are those in which the conflict [between good, non-sexy wives and bad, sexy women] is resolved for them by a wife who can be sexy at appropriate times. The best known example of these is probably Charlie Rich's "Behind Closed Doors," in which his woman is always a "lady" until he gets her behind closed doors where no one sees what goes on, where she lets her hair hang down and makes him glad he's a man. Jerry Wallace brags of a similar ideal setup in "I've Got So Many Wives at Home," for his wife, too, is both lady and satisfying lover, and "If I need a devil, as all men sometimes do/You got just enough to make me love the devil out of you." (Nietzke, 1975:67).

Further evidence that sexual expression among good women is becoming more acceptable, at least with their husbands, and also that the double standard is weakening, can be found in Loretta Lynn's musical manifesto "The Pill," popular in 1974: the woman, tired of staying home having babies while her husband runs around on her, announces her liberation from forced childbearing, but more importantly, also announces her intention to run around a little herself if he does not straighten up.

The rural woman of today, like her urban and suburban sisters, is beginning to insist on her sexual rights and on similar standards for male and female sexual behavior. In conjunction with the decline in rural fertility and time spent in rearing children, women have more time to pay attention to themselves, and their sexual and emotional needs are likely to be presently in the forefront of their concerns. The normative climate regarding female sexual expression is slowly liberalizing, and the sanctity of the family is being challenged by a rising divorce rate. (U.S. Bureau of Census, 1970a, 1960a, and 1950a).

This is not to say that the sexual revolution will overturn rural life. Rather, it seems likely that most rural women will continue to marry as they have in the past (though the trend is toward later marriage) and that for most of them sexual activity will be confined within marriage; however, the quality of their sex life will probably improve. They will also probably feel freer to leave an unsatisfactory marriage, and because of the rural traditionalism about marriage, the percentage of those marrying again will probably be greater than that of their urban sisters.

Reproduction. Traditionally, the many pregnancies sustained by most rural wives served not only the symbolic function of realized fecundity and virility, but also the important economic one of providing needed future laborers for the family farm or business. Maternity, though highly valued, was a somewhat perilous undertaking in the early part of the century. Of the many children born, many died in infancy, and the gravestones of some adjoin those of the women who bore them. The injunction "to be fruitful and multiply" ensured that a reasonable number of children would survive to carry their share of the load. High fertility was probably a major source of feminine identity and self-worth, for the reproduction function was a crucial one in rural society.

As the economic necessity for large families decreased in importance and improvements in health care increased children's chances of surviving to adulthood, rural people began having fewer children, though their family size continues to be larger than that of urban folks. However, if we compare recent rates of fertility decline, rural women have decreased their fertility to a greater extent than have urban women (Rice and Beegle, 1972:8). Current evidence indicates that rural women still plan to have more children, and to have them earlier, than do their urban sisters (U.S. Bureau of the Census, 1975:20).

The largest current difference in fertility between rural and urban areas is among young women. This fact suggests that the life-cycle patterns for women in the two areas differ greatly and that some contradictory trends about fertility are currently impinging on the consciousness of rural women. Lingering values support the desirability of large families and the rationale that the country, where large families are less problematic than in the city, is a great place to rear children (National Geographic Society, 1974:56). Nonetheless, rural women having responded relatively quickly to a lessening of the economic necessity to have large families, as if relieved at the prospect of not having quite so many children as their forebears had. The decline in rural fertility of course also has been helped by other trends frequently discussed by demographers: increasing education and urbanization with associated changes in values, rising incomes, readier access to contraception, and higher age at marriage (Rice and Beegle, 1972:32). But those factors are important for fertility only insofar as they affect one's personal behavior and the motivation to limit fertility.

These trends suggest that the normative and physical environment of rural areas is generally selective of and supportive of maternally and domestically oriented women. Moreover, in scattered locales conditions still are such that large families contribute to the economic well-being of the family. Women originating in rural areas and not wishing to conform to rural fertility norms probably have migrated elsewhere, leaving a residue of women still preferring a family oriented life and reinforcing the normative atmosphere supporting relatively high fertility.

Socialization of Children. Maternal values, along with time and energy devoted to rearing children, are likely to continue to affect the lives of rural women significantly. The total portion of a rural woman's life dedicated to child rearing, however, is likely to continue to decrease.

The rural woman of yesteryear, with large numbers of children and minimal schooling of them, found socialization to be an everyday task, spanning decades, and one which she integrated with all other facets of her busy, hardworking life. The socializing process was shared, however, by older siblings and by the father, whose occupation tended to keep him near his children. The father often took his sons with him on his daily rounds, while the girls helped their mother. This kind of integrated familial socialization, which uses children's labor potential while providing them an education in rural occupational skills, is still found in some rural areas (National Geographic Society, 1974:92-109, 174-91).

Nonetheless, the rural woman of today more often than not is likely to find herself at home alone with her small children, though for comparatively fewer years than yesterday's rural women. The overall burden of child rearing has decreased in absolute amount of time and energy expended, but it has changed qualitatively in that almost total responsibility for early child rearing has shifted to the woman.

That shift implies a change in role identification for rural women, with socialization beginning to stand apart as a separate function rather than being integrated into the entire familial enterprise. And it suggests that the rural woman's feelings of maternal responsibility may have increased, along with potential culpability if something goes awry in the process. The rural mother, like the urban mother, may have extra responsibility for the fate of her sons, with father, the role model, usually absent except on evenings and weekends. On the other hand, her children are going to school for a longer time, so the overall responsibility for how they turn out is diffused. Recent returnees to rural American communities, as well as long-term rural residents, continue to insist that rural areas are great places to rear kids — in part because of the familiarity engendered by rural and small-town life, which makes the socialization task easier and more publicly shared, and in part simply because of the greater space in rural than in urban areas (National Geographic Society, 1974:56).

As a source of pride, identity, and lifework for rural women, socialization is a declining function; yet it is still quite important for the majority of women, at least during their reproductive and early child-rearing days. Even school-age children are a burden for the middle-class rural mother, who provides the cultural and associational benefits of urban life for her children by chauffeuring them long distances to 4-H,

Little League, ballet lessons, and scouting. We expect the function of socialization to continue to decline in importance for rural women, but not to urban levels in the near future, because rural life still more strongly supports and places a greater value on maternal endeavors.

The evidence suggests that the lives of many rural women will continue to mirror the familistic inheritance of their forebears, although some countervailing trends are present. The recent reversal of the migratory flow may foreshadow greater influence of urban norms on rural family life — norms more "liberal" in the array of options a woman has in her life. The increasing acceptability of abortion and other less drastic forms of birth control has made it feasible to separate sexuality and reproduction, quite likely with greater emphasis on the former. Other influences likely to affect the rural woman's fertility and consequent child rearing are her increasing education and resulting potential employability, her tendency not to marry at a young age, and the growing affluence of rural life, along with her desire to attain and maximize that affluence.

Production. The Calvinist belief in the virtues and necessity of hard work which pervades rural life is not a sexist one. Women were and are fully expected to contribute their labor not only to necessary household maintenance tasks and child rearing but also to other tasks, as needed, to hold together the family economic enterprise. Work burdens shouldered by rural women have varied by residence (farm, ranch, small town), by the economic status of the household, and by whether or not their labor has been rewarded with wages. Because the majority of rural women have never been a formal part of the labor force, we shall first describe their typical production functions as unpaid family workers.

Previous generations of farm women tended their gardens and preserved the gardens' output as an important household food source; they took care of the assorted barnyard animals, also a source of food; they produced many of the household necessities such as soap, quilts, and brooms; and they did all the cooking, sewing, and cleaning as well as a lion's share of child rearing, including in some circumstances educating the children. They also worked in the fields as needed (Smuts, 1959:7-10).

Undoubtedly today some rural women, quite a few of them poor, still perform many such tasks, particularly on family farms and ranches in remote reaches of the country; many, however, do have modern appliances which make the tasks easier. Today, for example, some dedicated Nebraska farm women work 12 hours a day, six days a week, with their husbands on modest farms and may be found, as often as not, doing "men's work." Their contribution of unpaid labor commonly means the difference between a farm's success or failure (*New Land Review*, 1975:1, 11).

Women who share almost all facets of their husbands' lives appear to be relatively satisfied with themselves, their families, and the variety of skills and knowledge they can contribute to the overall well-being of the farm or ranch enterprises. Furthermore, they believe that such labor falls within the boundaries of the traditional female role of helpmate, undoubtedly partly because they thus essentially meet masculine expectations of performance in a male dominated occupation and partly because of their closeness with their husbands and their sharing in the decision-making process. If life on the Nebraska farm is typical, the only part of the division of labor that is sex based is that encompassing housework, cooking, and child rearing, which remain largely the woman's province (*New Land Review,* 1975:1, 11).

Relatively affluent women (whose husbands run large-scale farming enterprises) as well as those of more modest circumstances (but whose farms are highly mechanized or highly specialized) probably lead lives more similar to those of middle-class suburban housewives and mothers than to the lives of low-income farm wives and mothers. Most rural-nonfarm housewives, too, have roles similar to those of their suburban counterparts. Suburban housewifery, with its emphasis on household maintenance and consumption functions, is familiar enough not to be elaborated here.

Poor women (both farm and nonfarm) who do not work outside the home, many of whom are southern blacks, are not likely to have the advantages of work-saving appliances, though some are able to rely on nearby kin to meet the difficult demands of their daily lives. Rural women of any class have greater flexibility in their lives if there are kin to help, especially with sex-determined functions such as child care or even gardening. Rural residence is more likely to be kin based than is urban life, meaning that not all rural women need face sex-determined tasks alone.

Women who work for wages outside the home are a distinct minority among farm residents, making up only one-third of the potential female labor force. They form, however, from 40 to 50 percent of the female nonfarm population of working age and are a growing force as more and more rural women enter the labor market (U.S. Bureau of the Census, 1970b:684). Rural women who work are most likely to be between 20 and 24 years old or between 40 and 55, since many leave the labor force during the childbearing and child-rearing years. Reproduction and socialization functions cut a wider swath in the working lives of farm than of rural-nonfarm women, largely because of higher fertility, greater normative constraints on working mothers, fewer occupational opportunities, and the lack, perhaps, of extrafamilial child care services (U.S. Bureau of Census, 1970b:684).

Many women who work, and especially those with children, probably do so because they have to. Generally speaking, about two-thirds of the rural women in the labor force work full time; the one-third that work part time are likely to be between 25 and 40 years old. Wages generally are not high among rural working women, but they may often make the difference between marginal middle-class life and near-poverty. That is true for both farm and nonfarm households containing working women.

The proportion of women employed in agriculture has declined sharply during the past 30 years: more than 25 percent of employed farm women worked as farm laborers and foremen in 1940, but only 6 percent did so in 1970; female farmers and farm managers declined from 13.5 percent in 1940 to 6 percent in 1970 (Table 10.1). The decline in feminine participation in farming enterprises is largely in response to the technological changes in farming that have lessened useful roles for women.

Many not-well-off employed farm women today are likely to be found in low level service occupations or working as operatives where there is industry (Table 10.2). A recent book, *Hillbilly Women* (Kahn, 1973), describes the work of some of these strong, resilient women who share lives of economic hardship with their husbands and numerous children in remote rural areas. Their men work as miners, laborers, or construction workers, or in factories, holding jobs prone to layoffs and low wages even when work is available. These women have struck along side their miner-husbands, picketed the coal companies, struck and picketed the textile mills and other industries they work for, all in an effort to raise their standard of living and ensure a better future for their children. Many possess qualities reminiscent of frontier women; hardwork and economic privation are no strangers to their households. The helpmate role gives them broad alternatives within acceptable female behavioral norms.

Many poor black women working in rural areas suffer similar fates, their employment options being similar to those of the women described above except that almost a quarter of black farm women and almost 30 percent of rural-nonfarm black women work in private households as maids, cooks, and babysitters — not exactly well-paying jobs (Table 10.2).

The most common occupation of all rural women is clerical, accounting for about a fourth of rural women in the labor force, though the percentage of black rural women in that category is minimal (6 percent). These middle status jobs do not always pay well; however, it seems plausible that many rural women who work in the jobs are, by and large, supplementary wage earners contributing to or making possible the middle-class status of their households. It also seems likely, given rural definitions of the proper roles for women, that they are largely responsible for care of the household and children as well.

Relatively high prestige occupations (professional, managerial, administrative positions) offer opportunities for better educated rural women, both black and white (Table 10.2). Interestingly enough, when age and education are controlled, rural-nonfarm black women between the ages of 25 and 44 with four years or more of college outearn their white peers, as do rural-farm black women with a college education (U.S. Bureau of the Census, 1970c:860-72). However, slightly smaller proportions of rural black women than rural white women have professional jobs. Eleven percent of black rural-farm women and 8 percent of black rural-nonfarm women work in professional positions, compared

Table 10.1. Occupational distribution of employed women in the United States, by residence, 1970, 1960, 1950, and 1940.

	United States				Rural-Farm				Rural-Nonfarm				Urban			
	1970a	1960	1950	1940	1970a	1960	1950	1940	1970a	1960	1950	1940	1970a	1960	1950	1940
Professional, technical, and kindred workers	15.7	13.0	12.3	13.4	15.1	12.0	10.0	12.8	13.6	12.4	13.3	16.1	16.3	13.2	12.4	12.6
Farmers and farm managers	0.2	0.6	0.7	1.4	6.0	9.5	8.5	13.5	0.2	0.4	0.4	0.2	.005	0.1	0.1	0.0
Managers, officials, and proprietors, except farm	3.6	3.7	4.3	3.5	2.9	2.1	2.0	1.7	3.8	4.2	5.7	5.8	3.6	3.7	4.2	3.7
Clerical and kindred workers and sales workers	42.3	37.5	35.8	28.5	28.6	21.0	14.8	8.6	33.2	29.9	28.0	20.7	45.0	40.3	39.2	32.5
Craftsmen, foremen, and kindred workers	1.8	1.2	1.5	1.1	1.9	0.8	0.7	0.3	2.2	1.1	1.3	0.7	1.7	1.2	1.5	1.1
Operatives and kindred workers	14.1	15.4	19.2	18.1	18.1	15.1	13.2	8.8	21.1	19.4	20.5	18.2	12.7	14.5	19.5	19.6
Private household workers	3.9	7.9	8.5	17.7	3.9	8.7	7.0	20.0	4.8	9.7	10.3	22.4	3.6	7.4	8.3	16.4
Service workers, except private household	16.6	13.4	12.2	11.0	16.2	10.2	5.9	4.6	18.7	15.7	14.4	12.0	16.1	13.1	12.3	12.1
Farm laborers and farm foremen	0.5	1.1	2.9	2.9	6.1	15.5	32.1	26.9	1.1	1.7	2.5	1.2	0.2	0.2	0.2	0.1
Laborers, except farm and mine	1.0	0.5	0.8	0.9	1.3	0.5	0.7	0.8	1.4	0.7	1.1	1.2	0.9	0.5	0.8	0.8
Occupations not reported	n.d.	5.7	1.8	11.6	n.d.	4.6	5.1	2.1	n.d.	4.7	2.5	1.6	n.d.	5.9	1.4	1.0

Source: U.S. Bureau of the Census, 1970b (Table 91); 1960b (Table 53); 1950b (Table 53); and 1940 (Table 19).
a 1970 Census figures are for women age 16 and over; preceding Censuses are for women age 14 and over.

Table 10.2.   Occupations of employed females over age 16, by race and residence, 1970.

Occupational Category	Urban	Rural-Nonfarm			Rural Farm			Total
		White	Black	Total	White	Black	Total	
				(%)				
Professional, technical and kindred	16.3	14.0	8.4	13.6	15.3	11.4	15.1	15.7
Managers and administrators, except farm	3.6	4.0	1.0	3.8	3.0	1.3	2.9	3.6
Sales	7.7	6.8	1.3	6.3	5.8	1.2	5.5	7.4
Clerical and kindred	37.3	28.6	6.1	26.9	24.1	5.7	23.1	34.9
Craftspersons, forepersons and kindred	1.7	2.3	1.4	2.2	2.0	1.9	1.9	1.8
Operatives, except transport	12.2	20.1	23.0	20.3	16.8	21.7	17.0	13.9
Transport equipment operators	.4	.8	.7	.8	1.1	.9	1.1	.5
Laborers, except farm	.9	1.4	2.0	1.4	1.2	1.6	1.3	1.0
Farmers and farm managers	.005	.2	.3	.2	6.0	3.5	6.0	.2
Farm laborers and forepersons	.2	.8	4.4	1.1	5.9	8.8	6.1	1.0
Service workers, except private household	16.1	18.3	22.5	18.7	16.1	18.2	16.2	16.6
Private household workers	3.6	2.8	28.9	4.8	2.9	24.8	3.9	3.9
White collar[a]	64.9	53.4	16.8		48.2	19.6		61.6
Blue collar[a]	35.1	46.7	83.2		52.0	80.4		38.4

Source: Adapted from U.S. Bureau of the Census, 1976.

[a] White collar is defined as professional, technical, managers, administrators, and sales. Blue collar refers to the remaining census categories.

with 15 and 14 percent, respectively, of their white peers. Apparently, women in rural areas have relatively limited opportunities to follow a professional career; nonetheless, those who do are likely candidates for being role models of fairly egalitarian marriages in rural areas, because of their higher education and relatively higher earning power.

Though black women receive mean earnings that are generally much lower than those of white women, reflecting the lower status occupations they tend to be found in, they are also more likely than white women to work full time, even if they have small children. That trend reflects not only economic need, but also normative expectations: Kuvlevsky and Obordo (1972) found that among women with similar fertility expectations, black women planned on working after bearing children far more often than did white women.

Few rural women, black or white, have jobs that, alone, are sufficiently well paying to support a household, suggesting that the role of contributory wage earner is by far more common than that of wage earner. That undoubtedly is partly due to the lack of good occupational opportunities for rural women in general and farm women in particular. Even the supplementary wage earner production function is circumscribed by the other functior.s of reproduction and socialization, which seemingly have primacy for most rural women. Trends toward supplementary wage earning are less prevalent among black than rural white women (although their wages are lower), because black women are more likely to head families for which they are the chief if not sole wage earner.

Generally speaking, rural-nonfarm women, a relatively heterogeneous group representing some unincorporated suburbs as well as
small rural communities, form a middle ground between patterns
characteristic of rural-farm women and urban women. We have suggested
that rural-nonfarm women, even those who work, continue to reflect traditional norms in terms of sex-defined functions—for example,
reproduction, socialization, and care of the household, though we have no
hard data on which to base that generalization. It would be somewhat
surprising, on the other hand, to find rural-nonfarm women leaders in
such "liberated" behavior as equal sharing of household responsibilities,
equal division of child care, and an equal voice in decision making, when
their married urban sisters are not succeeding in such endeavors all that
well, except in households where both spouses are equally highly educated
and earning approximately the same amount (usually quite a bit) of
money.

The recent feminist movement has had great impact in three areas—
freeing women to express more openly their sexuality; giving them effective
control of fertility; and granting them the freedom to work if they choose
to do so, regardless of age, marital status, or reproductive history. The
movement has been less successful in obtaining equal pay for equal work,
in liberating women from sex-typed occupations, or in getting men to take
over an equal share of traditionally feminine tasks. If this surmise concerning the feminist movement is correct, the impact on the roles and
functions of rural women is likely to follow the same course generally
outlined for changes in the four major female functions (sexuality,
reproduction, socialization of children, and production): farm women
following slowly in the steps of rural-nonfarm women, who, in turn, are
following their more liberated urban sisters.

If rural women are to change their roles and self-definitions, there
must be changes in all four functions, changes that continue to uphold the
integrity of the traditional feminine pursuits while simultaneously
providing new options. Without changes in the production function (that
is, in the availability of work for decent wages), it is unlikely that the
relative importance of the time-consuming functions of reproduction and
socialization of children, as well as the production function of household
care and maintenance, will change much in the lives of rural women.
Underlying all that, woman's self-images—her sources of identity, status,
and power—are crucial, for they are the motivating factors for any kind of
psychological or behavioral change. To this we next turn our attention.

SOURCES OF POWER AND STATUS. The God of fundamentalist Christianity created woman to be the "helpmate" of the more
powerful male, and in so doing placed the primary sources of power and
status outside the women herself by casting her in a dependent and
secondary role. As with every other stereotype, variations are great in the

ways women have adapted to the cultural exigencies that surround them from birth to death. Women in rural society have, until quite recently, had fewer adaptive models to follow than have their urban sisters. So it is not surprising that our analysis of rural woman's estate has revealed that the majority of rural women still conform to traditional norms concerning woman's proper place: in the home, with the children, and supportive of her spouse's endeavors.

A recent survey provides empirical evidence that rural women are holding rather tenaciously to traditional values, more of them than urban women agreeing that "women should take care of running their homes and leave running the country up to the men" (Roper, 1974, authors' analysis). Stokes and Willits (1974) found that women of rural origin are neither traditional nor modern in their sex-role attitudes, but instead show considerable ambiguity: they feel on the one hand that the home is woman's responsibility, but on the other that they should get equal pay for equal work, regardless of family status.

The rural woman who works, whether by her husband's side or in paid employment, is likely to be more powerful than one who does not, both in access to resources and in the exercise of influence. If she does share the farm work, then she is likely to have a greater say in basic decisions on the farm (Wilkening, 1958), putting her on a more egalitarian footing with her husband, while she handles household matters as well. The woman who works outside the home has access to financial resources, though how that increases her power will depend in part on how much she earns and how great a contribution she makes proportionately to the economics of the household. As more and more rural women enter the labor force, even if in ill-paying jobs, the distribution of power will tend to change, because that labor is a resource the woman has independent of her husband. However, there is some evidence that rural women in low-status jobs are more traditional in their thinking than are their urban counterparts; that is not true of women in high-status jobs, regardless of residence (Roper, 1974, authors' analysis). Rural women probably do not regard being a supplementary wage earner as an important source of status or power but instead as a matter of economic necessity and an extension of the helpmate role. For the farm woman, work can be an alternative source of status, though perhaps not the primary one, especially if she continues to fulfill her household and socialization responsibilities.

As rural women begin to act upon alternative sources of status and power, through control of their functions, we should begin to see a subtle shift of both real and perceived power to women. However, this shift is likely to be in the arena of the female functions we have described here and the shift will pose little threat to the citadel of male superiority. The assault on male dominance by urban and suburban women has just begun to dent the armor of society, and it seems likely that rural areas will be the last to change in that regard. Moreover, we have argued that in some ways rural life is selective of women with traditional viewpoints. It may be simply that they are not socialized to think of themselves in any other way. However, those who wish to lead another kind of life seemingly elect to leave rural society, and it is possible that the new rural inmigration brings to rural areas those who prefer the more traditional roles and relationships.

THE RURAL WOMAN'S FUTURE. The rural landscape is increasingly becoming dotted with suburban-style homes, replacing the drafty farmhouses of yesteryear. Farming, more often than not, is a highly technical enterprise calling for heavy machinery and men with specialized skills. Next to the ubiquitous pickup is "mother's car," an American-made sedan or station wagon, which links her to the nearest larger community. Women shopping in small towns are virtually indistinguishable in appearance from their suburban cohorts, and many of their domestic concerns are identical.

The women who work side by side with their husbands smooth their overalls with roughened hands. Simultaneously, they point with pride to the "men's work" they have done and declare that they are not women's liberationists — women who want to "be the same as men, take over their roles," instead of "accepting the role God intended them to fulfill" (*New Land Review*, 1975:11). An operative in a factory looks up from her work and tells you that she's only working 'til Billy gets his job back in the mines and then she's going to go home and take care of him and the kids. A poor black woman in the South tells you about her work as a maid in a nearby town, and how the eldest daughter looks after the kids while she works, since her man was killed in a farm accident. A school teacher tells you how much she loves her work, and yet how important it was that she stay home for ten years while her children were little because "that is a woman's most important role."

Proud of her rather large family; of being emotional bulwark for her man; of her roles as housekeeper, wife, and mother; of giving a willing hand when needed — these ingredients for a stereotype of the rural woman today are not radically unlike those of past decades. And like all stereotypes, there is some basis in reality for it.

The stereotypical image of rural women cannot be relied on too heavily, however, for the growing diversity of rural women will eventually shatter it. Rural women who are nurses and teachers may become administrators; women who work in the fields with their spouses may move to doing paperwork as the farm grows prosperous; wives of agribusiness farmers may pursue careers or be community leaders; and housewives who never considered working before may enter the labor force for the first time. In short, we expect to see in the next few decades rural women beginning to take advantage of or to create more varied options in their lives.

As women's sexuality emerges as a more potent force in rural society, we expect that the reactions will range, as they have in the larger society, from horror at the thought to a warm welcome. Nonetheless, we expect the modal response to be increasing freedom of sexual expression within the institution of marriage.

Women's ability to control their fertility probably means there will be not only smaller families, but more husband-wife discussion concerning this basic function and greater agreement on family size. With fertility decline comes less time spent in the rearing of children and more freedom for women to pursue other interests. Nonetheless, the mothering role will remain a visible and valued source of status for many rural women.

We do not see much sign as yet of men's willingness to share with women the traditionally feminine tasks; thus, like many of her urban counterparts, the rural woman who chooses to work will have two jobs. Nor do we see much decline in the traditional view of the male as the superior sex, with most women's lives revolving around their men. And insofar as the economic production function continues to be constricted for most rural women, that function will not be a powerful force for change.

Nonetheless, the fact that women are beginning to have a greater say in the outcome of their interrelated functions of sexuality, reproduction, and socialization means that the dialogue between men and women about new roles, sources of identity, and relative power and status is probably just beginning.

11 Rural Poverty

BRUCE A. CHADWICK
HOWARD M. BAHR

ALTHOUGH poverty has been a feature of life in rural America from the nation's beginning, its identification as a national problem is of more recent vintage. Not until the Great Depression was poverty recognized as a national concern (Starnes, 1976:56). American society has enjoyed general prosperity since the Great Depression, although there have been periodic economic recessions of modest scale. Yet in the context of widespread prosperity during the 1960s, poverty emerged as a national problem. In terms of absolute deprivation, rural life was much better than it had been during the dust bowl years and even the 1950s. Certainly there is no evidence that things were worse in the early 1960s, when Michael Harrington's manifesto (1962) helped to marshal opinion in favor of a "War on Poverty," a war defined from the outset, like the Viet Nam war, in a way that precluded winning.

Harrington's *The Other America* contained a chapter on the rural poor, and from time to time the War on Poverty directed forays into Appalachia or to Indian reservations. Rural poverty was recognized, and a few rural antipoverty programs were initiated; but in the struggle against poverty the major engagements were in the cities, and most of the resources were spent in urban areas. On balance, the rural poor were relatively neglected, perhaps because there were few riots or demonstrations among the countryfolk.

President Johnson recognized this neglect and created the National Advisory Commission on Rural Poverty, which was charged to make a comprehensive study of rural poverty, to evaluate means of eliminating such conditions, and to develop recommendations to local, state, and federal governments and private groups about how to accomplish this

Bruce A. Chadwick and Howard M. Bahr are Professors of Sociology, Brigham Young University.

goal. True to tradition, the Commission's final report (1967) had little impact in directing public attention to the plight of the rural poor or in diverting program funds from urban to rural programs. From the present vantage point, it appears that the War on Poverty was even less successful in rural America than it was in the cities.

HOW MANY POOR? Poverty, like beauty and virtue, lies in the eye of the beholder. But government programs require standards, and researchers in the Social Security Administration (Orshansky, 1969) developed the "poverty line," based on income, which was adopted as a standard to assess the progress of the War on Poverty. Poverty level was defined as the amount of income needed by a family to provide itself with a basic diet meeting recommended nutritional goals. Families not having enough income to do this were designated "poor."

This original standard was subsequently modified by a Federal Interagency Committee to take into account family size, sex of family head, number of children under 18, and farm versus nonfarm residence. The poverty threshholds for 1969, utilized in the analysis of the 1970 Census, range from $1,475 for a woman aged 65 or more living alone on a farm to $6,116 for a nonfarm family of seven or more with a male head.

There are other ways of measuring poverty. According to a psychological definition of poverty, a person contrasts himself to his significant others and evaluates his relative position. If he perceives himself as having less than the others who serve as reference points, then he is experiencing poverty. If poverty is a state of mind, absolute levels of income or life-style are irrelevant to feelings of deprivation and alienation.

Some definitions of poverty are based on stereotypes about the social correlates of poverty. Some social scientists have argued that the distinguishing characteristics of the poor are their unique values, beliefs, and behavioral patterns — their "culture of poverty" — which maintain and perpetuate their conditions of deprivation. The debate over whether a "culture of poverty" exists continues (see, for example, Lewis, 1968; Vallentine, 1968; Gans, 1969; Rainwater, 1969; and Leacock, 1971) and we will not discuss its details here.

Poverty is relative, and different definitions yield different levels of poverty. More importantly, different definitions of poverty suggest different solutions, both preventive and remedial. "Objective" definitions focused upon low income or material deprivation suggest monetary transfers or food distributions. Psychological definitions suggest educational programs aimed at changing reference groups and at reducing feelings of deprivation. Sociological definitions are apt to lead to attempts by the dominant groups in society to speed up the assimilation of the culturally deprived (which often translates in practice to the "culturally different"), perhaps through remedial education programs. Because most empirical studies of poverty have used level-of-income definitions, discussions of the extent of rural poverty necessarily reflect the standard income levels of poverty accepted by governmental agencies.

Most data on rural poverty have been derived from the Census, which utilizes a definition of "rural" that is widely misunderstood. "Rural" is a residual category including everyone not defined as urban. The problem with this definition is that 30 percent of the "rural" persons who live in communities with populations under 2,500 also reside within a metropolitan area. Thus, they have the services and opportunities of an urban center readily available.

The median incomes of families and unrelated individuals, by race and by rural-urban location, as reported in the 1970 census, are presented in Table 11.1. White, black, and Spanish-surname families all demonstrate the same trend with respect to rurality and income: urban families have the highest median income, followed by rural-nonfarm families, and then rural-farm families. For all three racial groups, the rural-nonfarm median family income ranged from 61 percent to 80 percent of the corresponding urban median income, and the rural-farm median family income varied from 52 to 72 percent of the urban. The same trend holds for unrelated individuals except that rural-nonfarm individuals experience the greatest deprivation.

The number and percentage of persons, unrelated individuals, and families having incomes below the poverty level during 1969 for urban, rural-nonfarm, and rural-farm populations are given in Table 11.2. In all, nearly 10 million persons residing in rural areas were living in poverty in 1969. Approximately 1 out of every 6 rural white persons or white families was poor, compared to 1 out of every 2 blacks and 1 out of every 3 persons of Spanish origin. As expected, the rural rates of poverty are considerably higher than the urban rates. The rural rates for white and black families are twice as high as for their urban counterparts, and for Spanish families about one and a half times as high.

A more sophisticated method of examining rural-urban differences works from a ten-point continuum of county sizes ranging from core

Table 11.1.   Median income by race, family status, and residence, 1969.

	Urban	Rural-Nonfarm	Rural-Nonfarm Percent of Urban	Rural-Farm	Rural-Farm Percent of Urban
White population					
Family	$10,629	$8,542	80	$7,534	71
Unrelated individuals	2,725	1,885	69	2,082	76
Black population					
Family	6,581	4,035	61	3,445	52
Unrelated individuals	2,125	1,088	51	1,128	53
Spanish heritage population					
Family	7,717	6,119	79	5,630	72
Unrelated individuals	2,470	1,682	68	2,233	90

Source: Adapted from U.S. Bureau of the Census, 1973a.

Table 11.2.   Populations in poverty by race, family status, and residence, 1969.

	Urban	Rural-Nonfarm	Rural-Farm
White population			
Total persons	11,754,972	5,636,009	1,543,841
Percent	9.4	14.7	15.7
Unrelated individuals	3,725,123	1,056,645	152,150
Percent	32.8	48.8	40.8
Families	2,283,228	1,268,205	370,081
Percent	6.9	12.5	14.0
Black population			
Total persons	5,643,921	1,859,102	366,082
Percent	30.6	54.8	54.4
Unrelated individuals	755,167	143,627	17,881
Percent	44.5	72.3	66.9
Families	1,050,248	680,290	133,787
Percent	25.9	49.2	49.0
Spanish heritage population			
Total persons	1,772,498	325,899	55,437
Percent	22.0	34.9	31.5
Unrelated individuals	142,014	16,715	3,572
Percent	38.6	55.0	39.6
Families	346,911	58,465	9,736
Percent	19.2	30.3	27.3

Source: Adapted from U.S. Bureau of the Census, 1973a.

counties of greater metropolitan areas to totally rural counties not contiguous to Standard Metropolitan Statistical Areas. Hines, Brown, and Zimmer (1975) sorted counties into the ten categories and contrasted their social and economic characteristics. The median 1969 family income in the ten types of counties reveals a direct linear relationship between population of community and median family income. Family incomes in greater metropolitan areas are nearly double those in the totally rural counties. The inverse relationship between community size and the incidence of poverty was also apparent in contrasts between metropolitan and nonmetropolitan counties in incidence of low income. The lowest rate of white (6.5 percent) and nonwhite (21.9 percent) poverty appears on the fringes of the greater metropolitan areas and increases consistently to a high of 27.4 percent (whites) and 59.2 percent (nonwhites) in totally rural counties not adjacent to an SMSA.

Paradoxically, the higher incidence of poverty in rural areas is accompanied by lower quality of public assistance available. There are several reasons for the limitations of rural public assistance programs. Rural communities generally do not have a tax base sufficient to support a well-developed system of public assistance. Also, residents of rural communities tend to be politically conservative, public sentiment is often opposed to "liberal welfare," and many of the needy in rural areas refuse to accept aid even when it is available.

Table 11.3 shows that the percentage of unrelated individuals and families with income below the poverty level who reported receiving public assistance was significantly higher in urban areas than in rural communities, and the difference is even more pronounced between urban and rural-farm areas. In the case of unrelated individuals the rural-nonfarm population fares a little better than the urban, and, as usual, the rural-farm population comes in last. Welfare critics frequently have alleged that this urban-rural differential in the availability of public assistance has been one of the factors drawing indigent rural people to the city.

A slightly different picture emerges when public assistance support is compared across the urban-rural continuum of counties developed by Hines, Brown, and Zimmer (1975). The urban-rural difference is not as sharp as that between the metropolitan areas and the smaller urban communities. In fact, the less urbanized and totally rural areas have higher rates of assistance than the smaller urban communities.

DETERMINANTS OF RURAL POVERTY. Several socioeconomic conditions have been identified as correlates of rural poverty, and sometimes they are treated as causal factors. These include the low educational attainment of many rural people, the limited employment opportunities in many rural settings, selective outmigration which has left rural areas with a high dependency ratio, and family characteristics such as high fertility.

Education. The 1970 Census revealed that the incidence of poverty varies inversely with the education of the family head; in 1969, 19 percent of family heads with only an elementary school education had incomes below the poverty line, as compared to 12 percent for high school

Table 11.3. Recipients of public assistance by race, family status, and residence, 1969.

	Urban	Rural-Nonfarm	Rural-Farm
	(%)		
White population			
Families	18.1	16.2	6.5
Unrelated individuals	9.4	14.0	7.7
Black population			
Families	37.1	29.7	24.5
Spanish heritage population			
Families	32.4	20.8	13.2
Unrelated individuals	17.7	19.7	8.1

Source: Adapted from U.S. Bureau of the Census, 1973a.

dropouts, 6 percent for high school graduates, 5 percent for college dropouts, and only 2 percent for college graduates (Schiller, 1973:99).

The educational deprivation of rural communities is apparent when the median education across the metro-nonmetro county continuum for whites and nonwhites is studied. A small but consistent decrease in median years of education appears as we move from greater metropolitan counties to the totally rural counties. When the differing age distributions of residents in these settings is taken into account, the differences are reduced only slightly.

Education is not the only determinant of income; race, age, inherited wealth, geographical location, ethnic discrimination, and general economic conditions all influence income opportunities. Duncan and his associates (Blau and Duncan, 1967; Duncan, Featherman, and Duncan, 1972) found that after controlling for other factors, education had only a moderate effect on the incomes of a national sample of white men. The causal link between education and income is even more tenuous for blacks, Mexican-Americans, and other minority populations. For example, several studies have assessed the utility of education in terms of increments in income that accrue for each additional year of school and have discovered that education has significantly less impact on the incomes of blacks than it does on whites (Miller, 1960; Borland and Yett, 1967; Fogel, 1966).

These recent findings have led some to challenge the assumption that education, particularly postsecondary education, is the solution to income inequality and poverty. According to Jencks, mass postsecondary education for the poor does not make economic sense:

Rate-of-return estimates do tell us that efforts to keep everyone in school longer make little economic sense. The average rate of return for post-secondary education is quite low. For the kinds of students who are not now in college, it is even lower. For working class whites, Blacks and women, dropping out seems in many cases to be the most economically rational decision. Efforts to get everyone to finish high school and attend college must, therefore, be justified primarily on noneconomic grounds. Otherwise, they probably cannot be justified at all (1972:224).

The same conclusion is reached by Schiller, who argues that education does not determine the availability of jobs, but does influence who gets the jobs that are available. He illustrates this with a hypothetical case of a high school dropout seeking the job of sales clerk:

If he had a high school diploma, his competitive position would undoubtedly be stronger, but would his graduation, by itself, contribute to an increase in the number of such jobs available? Clearly not. His graduation may enable him to compete successfully for the available job, but his success will leave someone else unemployed. If there is only one job and four applicants, no amount of educational improvement or redistribution will succeed in leaving fewer than three persons unemployed. Education may influence who gets the available jobs, but the demand for labor will determine how many jobs there are (1973:104).

If Jencks and Schiller are even partially correct, the failure of many educational antipoverty programs is more easily understood.

Employment Opportunities. The ability to find and maintain employment is a major deterrent to poverty. When jobs become scarce there is generally an increase in poverty. The past 50 years have witnessed a drastic reduction in farm related employment opportunities in rural areas. Industrial development in rural communities has offset some of the loss of agricultural employment but has not been sufficient to support a growing population. Many rural areas have been handicapped in attracting industrial development because they have an inadequate and undertrained local labor force, because they are too remote from the source of materials, or because they are too distant from markets for the finished product.

The 1970 labor force participation of the rural and urban population is summarized in Table 11.4. Some small but consistent rural-urban patterns appear. Among males, labor force participation is lowest in rural-nonfarm areas. For females, labor force participation steadily decreases from urban to rural-nonfarm to rural-farm areas. This same gradual decline in the percent of the population in the labor force was also found in comparing the metro-nonmetro county groups. Generally, as rurality increased, labor force participation decreased.

These relatively small differences in labor force participation are not responsible for the much larger urban-rural differences in poverty. We anticipated that workers in rural areas would experience greater seasonal variation in the availability of jobs than urban workers, and that this might

Table 11.4.   Labor force participation by race, sex, and residence, 1970.

	Males 16 and Over			Females 16 and Over		
	Urban	Rural-nonfarm	Rural-farm	Urban	Rural-nonfarm	Rural-farm
			(%)			
Total population	100	100	100	100	100	100
In labor force	78	73	77	43	37	30
Unemployed	4	4	2	5	6	5
Not in labor force	22	27	23	57	63	70
Black population	100	100	100	100	100	100
In labor force	72	61	63	49	39	30
Unemployed	7	6	5	7	10	11
Not in labor force	28	39	37	51	61	70
Spanish heritage population	100	100	100	100	100	100
In labor force	79	72	80	39	31	25
Unemployed	6	6	3	8	10	9
Not in labor force	21	28	20	61	69	75

Source: Adapted from U.S. Bureau of the Census, 1973b.

account for the higher poverty rate. However, census figures on the number of weeks worked in 1969 show that the differences between the urban and rural communities were neither large nor consistent.

Another possible explanation for the greater poverty of rural people is that more members of a family are employed in the urban areas. If two or more members of a family are employed the family income is likely to be much higher. Rural-urban comparative data on the employment of family members indicates that very little of the income differences between urban and rural people stems from the higher percentage of wives or other members of the family working in urban areas. In families with both husband and wife present, the husband was the only employed member in 41 percent of the urban families, 42 percent of the rural-nonfarm families and 46 percent of the farm families. Rural families headed by a female were more likely than comparable urban families to have two or more family members in the labor force.

Schiller (1973) rejects the hypothesis that unemployment is largely responsible for poverty. He contrasts those who are poor with those who are unemployed and concludes that "unemployment appears to account for only a small fraction of poverty at best" (Schiller, 1973:37). He adds,

What is perhaps more noteworthy is the observation that the poor are integral members of the labor force and are constantly shifting from one labor force status to another. Therefore, we may conclude that millions of individuals are poor, not because they never work, but because they do not work as much or as often as others.

The work loss of the poor takes many forms. They may, at any given time, be out of the labor force, unemployed, or under-employed. These conditions are not independent but instead are related, in the marketplace, by the forces of aggregate demand. Together they constitute a condition of subemployment and may be costing the poor as much as $2 billion a year in lost income. Hence, subemployment appears to be a major cause of American poverty.

Finally, we have seen that the subemployment of the poor is not the consequence of their failure to seek employment. On the contrary, it appears that their subemployment is determined in large part by the decisions society makes regarding the utilization of economic resources. Where a nonzero level of aggregate unemployment becomes a part of society's goal structure, some individuals are simply prevented from working their way out of poverty (1973:46).

Our observations about the labor force participation of rural populations are consistent with Schiller's conclusions. The rural poor are not poor because they don't work; they are poor because they work at low wage rates, because they are underemployed, or because they suffer frequent changes of labor force status.

Dependency Ratio. The young and the aged are dependent segments of the population. They have a low level of labor force participation and require supportive assistance in the form of education, health care, retirement assistance, and custodial care. In view of the greater dependency needs of such persons, economists have created an indicator of the degree to which they are represented in a population. The "dependency ratio" is calculated by dividing the dependent population, including all under 18 and over 65 years of age, by the economically active population, defined as persons between the ages of 18 and 65. Dependency ratios for the ten-category continuum of counties for 1970 show that for both the white and nonwhite population a fairly strong linear relationship exists between rurality of county and degree of dependency. For the general population the dependency ratios range from 74 for core sections of greater metropolitan areas to 96 for rural areas, and for nonwhites the corresponding range is from 85 to 131. Apparently the migration out of rural areas has been selective in that the young adults have left to seek educational and occupational opportunities in the city, leaving behind a population distribution with disproportionate numbers of the very young and the very old. The higher fertility rates in rural areas also contribute to the high dependency ratio.

A certain amount of community stagnation is the probable result of the migration of young adults, which is often associated with a high dependency ratio. The high dependency ratio means that resources needed for community development must be expended for the delivery of social services. Too high a proportionate outlay in delivery of maintenance services leads to further deterioration, which in turn forces more young, productive individuals and families to leave.

Family Structure.   One-parent families, especially female-headed families, have received considerable attention as being particularly prone to poverty. The increasing number of female-headed black families (11 percent in 1960, 27 percent in 1970, and 35 percent in 1975) has been viewed as an important influence perpetuating black poverty. To determine whether family instability contributes to rural poverty the percent of female-headed families in rural and urban areas was compared. In 1970, 12 percent of urban families had a female head, compared to only 8 percent for rural-nonfarm and 5 percent for rural-farm families (U.S. Bureau of the Census, 1973). Thus family instability does not explain rural poverty; if anything, rural families are better off than urban families in this regard.

A second family characteristic associated with poverty is family size. Children strain the family budget in at least two ways. First, there are the direct costs in feeding, clothing, and caring for children. Then there are the costs in income foregone because both parents are not in the labor force. The more children a woman has, the fewer opportunities she has for participation in the labor force. The 1970 Census revealed a strong relationship between number of children and family poverty. For example, nearly 30 percent of all poor families had at least four children, but only 13 percent of the nonpoor had that many children (Schiller, 1973:76).

If family size is a determinant of poverty, it may account for much of the poverty in rural areas, and may explain some of the urban-rural differentials in the incidence of poverty.

While a causal link between family size and poverty appears to exist, the direction is not always easy to determine. True, children cost money, but the financial responsibilities of a large family also pressure parents to work overtime or to moonlight at a second job. After careful consideration Schiller concludes that "excessive family size is not an important cause of poverty on the basis of . . . [the] observation that large poor families were, by and large, once small poor families rather than smaller nonpoor families" (1973:78). Thus high fertility may perpetuate poverty and prevent rural families from climbing out of poverty, but it does not appear to be a significant initial cause.

ALLEVIATING RURAL POVERTY. Attempts to diminish or do away with poverty have generally used one or more of three basic strategies. First, some programs ignore the cause or causes and simply try to reduce deprivation and suffering. The various public assistance programs, such as old age assistance, aid to dependent children, food stamps, and aid to the blind and disabled are examples of this strategy. Second, rehabilitative programs may focus on the community as well as the individual, and are directed to a wide range of community objectives. Such programs have provided needed community services such as provision of adequate water supply, electrical power, housing renewal, or sewage disposal. Some have even been organized to attract industry into a rural area.

The third strategy is the prevention of poverty. Minimum-wage laws are preventive measures intended to insure that wages in most occupations provide an adequate standard of living. The Social Security program, which forces employees and employers to provide retirement income for the individual and his family, is another example of a preventive program.

Some of these programs are directed by agencies of the federal government, but most are administered by state and local governments, and there is considerable regional variation. There are indications that rural residents have access to fewer programs and receive fewer benefits than people in urban areas.

Improving Human Resources. One tactic to combat rural poverty has been to try to improve the quality of the human resources in rural areas. This involves both rehabilitative and preventive activity. The objective is to provide people with experiences and attitudes that will facilitate their participation in the labor force.

According to a recent review of federal rural antipoverty activity (Morrison et al., 1974), the Neighborhood Youth Corps and Operation Mainstream, two programs that emphasized work experience rather than formal job training, were the most popular programs in rural areas. Two major limitations on the involvement of rural people in the more direct training programs such as Manpower Training are the facts that large agribusiness groups have little need for skilled labor and thus give little cooperation or promise of employment for graduates, and that most manpower training programs have been designed for the urban population and often are irrelevant to the vocational training needs of rural populations. As a consequence, the participation of rural people in manpower training programs is significantly lower than that of urbanites (Marshall, 1973).

Not only are manpower training programs notably ineffective in reaching the rural poor, but little is known about whether those who participate have been able to find employment related to their training. It may very well be that the major consequence of the programs of human resource development has been the creation of a population of unemployed skilled workers as compared to unemployed unskilled workers. The Comprehensive Education and Training Act, passed by Congress in late 1973, has greatly reduced federal direction of manpower programs by shifting grants to states and local governments, to be used in accordance with local needs and plans. It is too early to tell whether this switch from federal to state supervision will make the human resource development programs more responsive to occupational opportunities.

Improving Employment Opportunities. A second approach has been to increase employment opportunities by attracting industry to rural areas or by relocating the rural population to nonrural areas where there is a labor shortage. The now defunct Office of Economic Opportunity (OEO), which was created in 1964, developed several types of programs for rural areas. OEO provided funds to stimulate local industrial development and community resource development. However, there are some questions as to the effectiveness of these programs in reducing rural poverty.

The Public Works and Development Act of 1965 created the Economic Development Administration (EDA), which distributed funds for public works and business loans. The EDA was generous in assisting small communities and received considerable criticism for concentrating too many of its resources in rural areas which have less potential for development than more populous areas.

A new approach was initiated in 1972 with the passage of the Rural Development Act. This legislation gave the Department of Agriculture the responsibility for overall coordination of rural poverty programs. Moreover, the definition of "rural" was expanded to include communities of up to 50,000 population. The consequences of the Rural Development Act are not yet apparent, as funding for 1973 and 1974 was limited.

Although the attraction of new industry is often viewed as a good thing for rural people, there is serious question about industrial development as the answer to rural poverty (Morrison et al., 1974). Many of the jobs created by such development are not filled by local residents but rather by migrants into the community. Other reasons that rural industry often fails to have the desired economic impact are discussed by Bertrand in Chapter 5.

Some attempts to relocate the rural poor in areas of greater economic opportunity have been moderately successful. A long-range relocation program was instituted by the Bureau of Indian Affairs (BIA) in 1956. Since this time 100,000 Indian Americans have been relocated. A recent review of the BIA relocation program has shown that employment, income, and housing all greatly improved following relocation (Clinton, Chadwick, and Bahr, 1975). Moreover, the relocatees themselves said that relocation had improved their quality of life.

A fairly high rate of success is also reported for the Manpower Development and Training Act, which relocated over 14,000 individuals and their families between 1965 and 1969. As with the BIA program, many of the relocatees report that the migration was "economically rewarding" and "personally satisfying" (Morrison et al., 1974).

The Future. In his State of the Union message in 1970 Richard Nixon called for a new kind of assistance to create a new rural environment:

What rural America needs most is a new kind of assistance. It needs to be dealt with not as a separate nation, but as part of an overall growth policy for America. We must create a new rural environment which will not only stem the migration to urban centers, but reverse it. (Office of the Federal Register, 1971)

The war on rural poverty was little more than a holding action, and even that may be an overgenerous assessment. New strategies are needed to improve the quality of life of rural people, and there is no dearth of recommendations as to what should be done. In its final report, *The People Left Behind* (1967), the prestigious President's National Advisory Commission on Rural Poverty made 158 recommendations for action. The recommendations fall in three general strategies: to alter conditions and provide better employment opportunities, to improve people's skills so that they can take advantage of improved opportunities, and to create conditions insuring a basic standard of living for those who are unable to respond to the improved conditions.

These strategies are not new or unique. What is new is the length to which the Commission recommended the government go in carrying out the proposed strategies. Rather than recommend programs designed to attract industrial development to rural areas, the Commission recommended that the government *guarantee and if necessary provide* employment at national minimum wage rates to every person willing and able to work. Congress has not yet been willing to accept this position. Some economists argue that "full" employment will bring with it rapid inflation, and many advisors argue that unemployment rates of 5 to 10 percent are a necessary evil if inflation is to be controlled.

Also, many economists (see Schiller, 1973; McPherson, 1968) assert that while full employment may drastically reduce rural poverty, it certainly will not entirely disappear. Employment opportunities will not aid those unable and/or unwilling to take advantage of them.

Some of the Commission's recommendations about retraining rural workers have been initiated. As noted above, substantial resources have been spent in vocational training, on-the-job training, and basic education. But successful training is only part of the picture. Without an increase in opportunities for rural employment, the only alternative to continued unemployment is migration, and that frequently has negative consequences for the rural community.

The recommendations aimed at insuring a quality standard of living for rural people have met a mixed fate. A few have been enacted. Others have been rejected, and most have been ignored. The extension of unemployment insurance, minimum wages, and workmen's compensation to agricultural workers was recommended, and this remains to be done on a national basis. The Occupational Safety and Health Act of 1970 may have an effect in extending workmen's compensation to farm workers, who frequently must endure hazardous exposure to herbicides, pesticides, and other injurious chemicals.

One topic noticeably absent from the Commission's report was the problem of people unwilling to be retrained, to migrate, or even to work. The only recommendation was that such persons be "counseled." Mc-Pherson (1968) reports that in West Virginia only 640 of 8,000 unemployed were interested in retraining, even though subsistence pay was offered during the retraining period. Most replied that they were not interested, were too old to start again, or expected to return to work soon. Research is needed to identify how many rural people are unwilling to work or to be retrained and to find ways to encourage them to participate in antipoverty programs.

We do not believe that full employment programs will appear in the near future. Agricultural jobs will continue to diminish. But given the nation's commitment to energy independence, it is anticipated that employment opportunities are going to increase considerably in rural areas. Rural poverty will not necessarily disappear: not all rural areas have energy resources, and many will remain economically depressed. Also, migration of urban dwellers will increase to fill jobs in energy-related industries. But energy development does present an opportunity to reduce rural poverty. Programs and policies are needed to maximize the participation of rural people in the expected boom. Preferences ought to be given to local residents in hiring and training, and professional counsel should be available to help landowners maximize their returns from the selling of lands or mineral rights. Rural social institutions should be strengthened by the energy industry, which should provide funds for the necessary community planning and increased provision of services before the industrial development destroys the rural community. Adequate housing, medical facilities, schools, and shopping facilities should be planned and provided before a crisis condition appears. In cases where resources are exported to other communities, local taxation should be sufficient to strengthen the local community. In brief, conscious attention ought to be given to insuring that the rural poor benefit from energy development. Rural America is on the edge of a new era, in some regions a revolutionary era, which has the potential to improve greatly the quality of life for the people left behind.

Part 7
THE FUTURE

12 Public Policy and Rural Social Change

W. NEILL SCHALLER

HOW have public policies influenced social change in rural America? What role has rural change played in shaping public policy? The answers will not only help us understand why rural society is what it is today, but also what it may be like in the future.

"Rural policy" has two possible definitions—policy to benefit rural people, and policy concerned with rural areas. The difference in these two meanings was once quite insignificant. For most of the nation's history, rural policy meant agricultural or farm policy. Farm policy was designed to help farms and farmers, and most rural people lived on farms.

The situation is changing. Nonfarm people are becoming more important as the intended beneficiaries of farm policy. And what is now popularly known as rural development policy is often geared more to the interests of urban and rural-nonfarm people than to those of farmers. In turn, the well-being of both farm and nonfarm rural people is influenced more and more by policies other than those traditionally labeled rural.

FARM POLICY

Intended Beneficiaries, Ends, and Means. The historical justification for public policy to benefit farmers took several forms. Foremost was the fact that farmers were not sharing equitably in the nation's economic prosperity. But the support for farm policies also came from nonagricultural quarters. The belief that a plentiful supply of reasonably priced food should be provided everyone, as well as the importance of agriculture to the nation's economy, further justified policies to benefit

W. Neill Schaller is Acting Deputy Director for Extension, U.S. Department of Agriculture, Science and Education Administration, Washington, D.C. He was Associate Managing Director of the Farm Foundation, Oak Brook, Illinois, when this chapter was written.

farmers. Additional support traced to our national scheme of values. Agriculture, and the family farm in particular, were considered to be components of American life well worth protecting.

Indeed, two major farm policy ends survived the test of time. One was concerned with the general welfare of the nation, with emphasis on the adequate *production* of goods and services. Thus, the well-being of farmers was also an intermediate end, or means, to the well-being of society. The other major end was concerned with the just *distribution* of well-being within the total society. Schickele (1954:38) speaks of two major distribution principles that have consistently shaped public policy. One he calls the *subsistence* principle, which says that everyone should have access to a decent minimum standard of living. The other is called the *contributive* principle. It says that beyond some minimum level of subsistence, the individual should be rewarded according to his contribution to society. Both principles have undergirded farm policy.

Historically, farm policy has concentrated on the economic well-being of farmers. There were reasons other than that the farmer's problem was basically an economic problem. One was the long-held assumption that if a person had an adequate income, he could afford not only more goods and services but also other components of well-being. Higher income simply meant a higher quality of life. Another reason for the economic emphasis is that it has always been easier to measure the economic than other components of well-being.

The dramatic shift in the early 1970s from a long period of excess agricultural production to one of tight supplies seemed to bring about a sudden change in farm policy ends. The Agriculture and Consumer Protection Act of 1973 was reported out of the U.S. Senate Committee on Agriculture and Forestry with this revealing preface:

> The country appears to be moving toward a period of shorter supplies of food and fiber with consequent higher prices to consumers. The purpose of this bill is to assure the production of adequate supplies at reasonable prices to consumers by insuring producers against losses if their expanded production results in prices below the target prices (U.S., Congress, 1973:1).

Significantly, concern for the well-being of farmers appeared at the end of the statement, not at the beginning, and as a means rather than an end.

Two different kinds of policy means have been used to benefit farmers. Introduced first were public programs to provide farmers with resources and farming skills, in order to increase efficiency and lower costs per unit of farm output. The list of programs is long and varied: a pioneering national land policy of dispersed ownership, launched by the first Congress of the United States in 1789; establishment of a farm credit system; cost-sharing soil conservation programs; the development of a system of railroads to ensure the distribution of farm products; the establishment of land-grant colleges of agriculture with agricultural experiment stations and, later, an extension education system; programs to provide farmers with irrigation water and to allow them to graze livestock on public lands.

The second and newer set of policy means dealt more directly with the prices and incomes received by farmers for their products. The need for price and income support traced in part to the success of the earlier policy means, which lowered costs and increased total production, thereby putting a downward pressure on market prices. Also included were steps to improve the farmer's bargaining position in the marketplace. Antitrust legislation, though not strictly an agricultural policy, was influenced by monopolies in the meat-packing industry. Passage of the Capper-Volstead Marketing Act of 1922 gave farmers the right to organize marketing cooperatives, free from antitrust restraint.

Numerous other measures, from school lunch programs to foreign aid, were added over time to expand the demand for farm products at home and abroad, or to reduce price-depressing supplies. More familiar, however, are the price support and production control programs initiated with passage of the Agricultural Adjustment Act of 1933. Though amended many times, the act remained the basic price and income legislation for decades. (Two excellent, up-to-date historical reviews of this policy are Rasmussen, 1976 and U.S. Congressional Budget Office, 1976).

The purpose of the Agricultural Adjustment Act was to restore the farmer's purchasing power to the level that prevailed in a more favorable earlier period, 1910–14. Thus, "parity" became the perennial policy yardstick. Initially, farmers were paid to plow up surplus crops and to dispose of surplus livestock. Soon, various price support measures were put into effect to raise the prices of individual commodities in the marketplace. Acreage allotments or production quotas followed, simply because the increased production stimulated by higher prices tended to wipe out the intended gains in farm income.

As a result of recent food shortages, price supports and acreage controls are not now in effect. The Agriculture and Consumer Protection Act of 1973 substituted target prices for support prices. Nevertheless, authority to restrict acreage was retained, should surpluses return.

The Consequences. Volumes have been written about farm price and income programs and their results. Kaldor concluded:

Mainly as a result of large market removals and land retirement, these programs induced a substantial increase in farm prices. . . . The programs, however, did not solve the low-returns problem for the large majority of small, less well-organized units because the problem of low returns on these farms involved more than just low prices. In general, they sold a smaller volume of output, which was produced at higher per unit costs (1975:144).

Whether these programs actually worsened the lot of smaller farmers has been debated for years.

Gradually, and at times reluctantly, came the discovery that *farm* policies were in fact *commercial farm* policies. Some observers felt that these programs were never intended to solve the problems of the smaller farmer or the rural poor. Others argued that the shortcomings of farm policy were due largely to the choice of policy means. Schnittker wrote:

It is not essential that farmers benefit in direct proportion to their production, but that was a plausible way to begin 35 years ago when agricultural production was less concentrated than it is today. . . .

In the early years of modern farm policy, there was an element of truth to the rhetoric which insisted that farm programs were needed to help, or even to save the small family farmer. This meant most farmers in the 1930's, when there were nearly 7 million farms and deep economic depression. It is different today. The United States has 3 million farms but only 1 million of them are serious producers and major beneficiaries of farm programs (1970:97).

Commercial farm policies, by benefiting larger farm operators, seem to have hastened the decline in the number of farms and the steady increase in farm size (Heady 1970:viii). Higher support prices typically translate into higher land values. This not only defeats the purpose of income support but puts small and would-be farmers at a distinct disadvantage. The integration of farms with other agribusiness firms, absentee ownership of farms, and the use of hired managers are now important parts of the agricultural scene. The increasing size and specialization of farms has also been accompanied by a substitution of hired workers for family labor. The unionization of farm labor, now well along in California, is an inevitable consequence.

Changes in the structure of agriculture were a major force in the now-legendary migration of labor from agriculture to urban areas. The resulting efficiency has been both a bane and a blessing to society. National economic growth was made possible by the release of labor from agriculture, but the migration also contributed substantially to urban problems of congestion, crime, and pollution. Equally troublesome were the effects of outmigration on rural communities. It was mainly the young who moved. The depopulation of towns caused public services to deteriorate. Local firms serving agriculture were increasingly bypassed by the centralization of agribusiness.

The changing structure of agriculture has led to various modifications of farm policy. In the 1950s, special provisions for smaller farmers, such as exemption from acreage allotments, were included in the basic price and income legislation. During the 1960s, after much debate, an upper limit on the government payment any one farmer could receive was added to the legislation, and some eight states have now passed laws with the intent of banning large corporation farms, aside from family farm corporations.

The Policy Process. From the 1930s until only a few years ago, the farm policy making process was straightforward and unchanging. The major actors included the U.S. Department of Agriculture, the agriculture committees in Congress, and the farm organizations. Although different interests were represented in the agriculture power cluster, internal compromises were reached in a fairly predictable manner.

The Supreme Court in 1936 declared the production control provisions of the Agriculture Adjustment Act unconstitutional, but that hurdle was crossed with passage in the same year of the Soil Conservation and Domestic Allotment Act, which tied acreage reduction to the more socially acceptable goal of soil conservation. In later years, fear that unchecked surpluses could only mean higher taxes undoubtedly lowered public resistance to acreage controls.

Society also accepted the supporting of farm prices in the market. As long as consumers were not complaining about high food prices, farm interests had the power to readily uphold the farmer's strong preference for price supports over direct payments. More recently, however, direct government payments (for the difference between market prices and a "fair" price) have become a prevalent mode of support, another indication of the changing farm policy setting.

The farm policy process is now undergoing a transition triggered by the world food "crisis" of 1972. New actors are becoming involved. People now talk of *food* policy, instead of *farm* policy.

Don Paarlberg, the USDA's former director of agricultural economics, explained this development in terms of the issues on the "farm policy agenda" and who put them there (1976:95–96): higher food prices — placed on the agenda by consumers; food distribution programs — by the so-called hunger lobby; ecological questions — by environmentalists; land use issues — by those who question the farmer's first claim on the use of land; civil rights — by those who challenge the white male tradition of agriculture; and collective bargaining — by organized labor.

Indeed, it is no longer obvious who will control the farm policy agenda committee. California economist Wood offers one view:

Most, if not all, future food and farm policy is going to be developed outside the traditional agricultural establishment. Most food policy will be initiated by the Department of State and other agencies that are concerned with the use of food as a political tool or those agencies and institutions that are concerned with food for humanitarian purposes. Farm policy, on the other hand, is going to be determined substantially by such agencies as the Environmental Protection Agency, which in terms of administering and enforcing various rules and regulations has a much more effective way of making supply management a reality in the agricultural production sector (1976:112).

Regardless, confusion grows as to who is and who should be a member of the agricultural power cluster. Spitze (1976:8) points out that 92 special interest groups and 60 other interested individuals testified in congressional hearings on farm price and income policy in early 1975. The vying for recognition raises the visibility of real and imagined conflicts between different policy ends, which then increases the difficulty of resolving conflicts within the power cluster (Ogden, 1972). When resolutions to conflicts are not hammered out before an issue is turned over to Congress, considerable time may be required to achieve a policy compromise.

An inevitable part of this new policy environment is the questioning of the rationale for a U.S. Department of Agriculture as constituted in the past. Some feel that the Department has been a spokesman for large farmers. Former President Nixon proposed that many of the Department's responsibilities be shifted to the Department of Commerce, and other responsibilities to new departments of Community Development and Natural Resources. The change was successfully resisted by existing power clusters. In early 1976, Senators McGovern and Humphrey introduced a bill to rename the USDA the "Department of Food, Agriculture, and Rural Affairs."

Implications for Rural Society. Some interpret the apparent shift from traditional agricultural policy as a fad which will quickly pass when food supplies again outrun market demand. Others see no major policy change, but simply an adjustment to new conditions.

It is my judgment, however, that the recent world food shortage was only the catalyst for a significant change, already under way, in both the content and process of farm policy. Whether it is called food policy or farm policy is not the important issue. Henceforth, the justification for farm policy will emphasize the well-being of consumers and society as a whole more than the economic well-being of farmers.

Most of the historical reasons for commercial farm policy have all but disappeared. The larger commercial farm hardly resembles the family farm society once sought to protect, and even if new spurts in production or sluggish demand cause a decline in farm prices, growing pressure to contain the federal budget will all but rule out the option of boosting price supports.

Ironically, the agricultural community itself has contributed to the declining support for farm policy. Many farmers who once viewed farming as both a way of life and a way of living now think more like their industry counterparts. A policy to support feed grain prices will be favored by grain producers but opposed by livestock feeders. Fewer grain producers are also livestock feeders.

The outcome for rural society is far from clear. Although nonrural interests will undoubtedly play a larger role in the farm policy process, they are apt to take conflicting stands with regard to different issues on the policy agenda. Consumers may line up with farmers in opposition to the alleged control of the food system by so-called middlemen, but take an opposite position on issues such as export embargoes or government intervention in the market. Lower income people will be especially concerned about food prices, while suburban or other interests may qualify their stands. Certain interest groups could oppose greater concentration of agriculture on philosophic grounds or because of growing concern about bigness.

Food and the family farm, once viewed as parts of the same policy issue, will be treated more and more as two very different issues. Interest groups concerned about one may be quite unconcerned about the other. Separate policies to benefit smaller farmers, supported by both rural and nonrural interests, are already replacing the past practice of adding small farm benefits to commercial farm policies. Examples include state laws restricting corporation farming and the increasing reference to small farms in legislation such as the Rural Development Act of 1972.

At the same time, it is also possible that the pursuit of different policy ends will erupt in open conflict between opposing interests. Two underlying forces could be responsible. One is the recognition that as energy, land, and other resources become more scarce, the traditional way to solve disputes over their use — more for everybody — is no longer realistic. Instead of increasing the size of the "pie," the issue will be how to divvy up a pie of constant or even declining size. It matters little if the resource base is far from exhausted. If people think that it is, or soon will be, competition for those resources will intensify.

Another force likely to increase policy conflicts is the difficulty of knowing what in fact is in one's self interest. Those who seek to control the food or farm policy agenda seem more certain of what they do *not* want than what they do want. In such a setting, the time and appetite for rationally examining the alternatives diminishes. Moreover, it is not at all obvious how different interests would be affected by different policies.

A North Central Regional Extension 1972 publication, Who Will Control U.S. Agriculture?, is an excellent study of future policy alternatives and consequences.

RURAL DEVELOPMENT POLICY

Intended Beneficiaries, Ends, and Means. Current rural development policy, in contrast to farm policy, is almost too young to analyze. For decades, rural development was virtually synonymous with agricultural development — which made sense when most rural people were farmers. But economist Earl Heady introduced a 1969 conference with these words:

It is simply true that a very large proportion of the rural population is passed over by our current economic and social policies. We have a fairly effective set of income supplementing policies for the most commercial of our farmers. We are rapidly developing a major set of policies to cope with the most urgent economic and social problems of our cities. But in between these two poles of national policy, programs and aids effective for much of our rural population are notable for their absence (1970:viii).

Just as farm policy was seen as ultimately benefiting consumers, so rural development was promoted as a benefit to the entire nation. The well-being of rural people was perceived not as the final end, but as an intermediate step.

Former President Nixon's Rural Development Task Force made this clear:

The fact that the immediate concern of rural development focuses on the 65 million people who live in nonmetropolitan America — and that the urgent challenge is to improve the opportunities for these people . . . does not alter the fact that the real goal is to benefit simultaneously the 140 million people who now live in metropolitan areas, and the millions more who will live there by the end of this century (President's Task Force on Rural Development, 1970:2-3).

The selling point for rural development was not what new economic and social gains it would offer society so much as the extent to which it could help solve the problems of congestion, crime, and pollution in metropolitan America.

A general statement of rural development policy ends appears in Title IX of the 1970 Agriculture Act: "The Congress commits itself to a sound balance between rural and urban America. The Congress considers this balance so essential to the peace, prosperity, and welfare of all our citizens that the highest priority must be given to the revitalization and development of rural areas" (1975:1).

The idea of revitalizing rural areas through other than strictly agricultural policies was officially endorsed, if not initiated, during the Eisenhower administration with the establishment of a pilot Rural Development program. In 1961, Congress passed the Area Redevelopment Act to aid rural and other areas suffering from underdevelopment. During that period, the Farmers Home Administration was given increased authority to provide rural areas with financial assistance in housing, water distribution, and sewage disposal. Regional development committees were formed at the county level under the Department of Agriculture. Throughout the 1960s, public leaders continually deplored the irrational piling up of people in cities. Terms like "balanced growth policy" and "population distribution policy" were coined.

In 1972, rural development achieved greater national visibility when then-President Nixon transmitted to the Congress a series of proposals to improve the quality of rural life (U.S., Congress, 1972:1). Later in 1972, Congress passed the Rural Development Act, which attempted to expand and pull together into one piece of legislation many rural development related efforts. It expanded the authority of the Farmers Home administration to make loans and grants to stimulate rural industrialization and to improve community facilities.

The term rural development went far toward defining the choice of policy means. Clearly, the focus was on the development of *places* rather than *people*. The reasoning was simple. Rural and urban people were expected to benefit from making rural America a better place to live and work.

Although the Rural Development Act gave jobs and incomes high priority, it also placed significant emphasis on "quality of life," perhaps reflecting a growing national awareness that the attainment of economic well-being does not guarantee a corresponding gain in total well-being.

The Consequences. While much has happened in small towns and on the national scene signaling improvement in the well-being of rural people, what is not clear is how much credit should be given to rural development policy.

A case in point is the recent reversal in the traditional migration of people from rural to urban areas. Calvin Beale (Chapter 3) reports that many rural communities that have traditionally lost population are now showing gains. Rural development programs have probably done more to enhance the turnaround than to cause it. Certainly, a number of other programs have removed obstacles to repopulation. Social Security has helped people retire to rural areas. Increasing rural awareness of urban problems and more limited job opportunities in cities have probably discouraged the outmigration of many farmers and rural laborers.

Similarly, the fact that the nation's farmers in recent years have received over one-half of their income from off-farm employment may be more of a coincidence than a direct result of rural development programs to encourage the location of industry and other sources of employment in rural areas.

If it seems difficult to identify the consequences of rural development policy, an obvious reason is that there is no clear definition of either the policy or its components. Meager and uneven funding of the Rural Development Act, and only nominal support of its provisions by the USDA, raise doubts as to whether a bona fide national rural development policy exists.

A report by the Congressional Research Service of the Library of Congress (1975) criticized the USDA's implementation of the Rural Development Act, pointing out that the Department had not set numerical targets to be accomplished over a period of time. But certain ends stated in the Act, notably improved quality of life, virtually defy measurement. What can be measured is often not what many backers of rural development think it is all about. More miles of sewers and more hospital beds, they argue, are not proof of improved well-being.

Confusion about rural development policy ends could also reflect uncertainty as to what in fact is wanted — the same problem now occurring in the farm policy arena. Many people are concerned that public services in rural America are inferior to those in urban areas. Others are unhappy because good farmland is going into shopping centers. But all have trouble deciding what services should be provided and how our land should be used.

It is ironic that the difficulty of identifying policy ends seems to have accelerated the implementation of policy measures, rather than slowing it down. As Daft (1972) points out, rural development is a case of many "programs" but few "policies." The Executive Office Catalog of Federal Domestic Assistance in 1975 listed over 1,000 separate government programs, at least 500 of which were available to rural communities. Daft comments on this proliferation: "Despite a multitude of programs, each with its own administrative machinery and clientele, there is no overall agreement on end objectives. Each program goes its separate way, sometimes complementing the activities of other programs, sometimes working at cross purposes" (1972:3).

The Policy Process. The 1972 Act gave the Department of Agriculture the job of coordinating rural development activities in all federal agencies (probably an impossible task). But the USDA was an awkward, if not inhospitable, home for this policy. The Butz administration was oriented almost exclusively toward commercial agriculture. They argued that a prosperous agriculture would solve most so-called rural development problems.

USDA officials who were a bit more sympathetic to the need for rural development were frustrated in their efforts to build support for such programs. Others feared that success would dilute USDA programs for agriculture and, as a result, weaken support from the Department's agricultural clientele. The same concern explains much of the difficulty of expanding rural development research and extension in the land-grant colleges of agriculture.

If the proponents of rural development wanted something more than agricultural development, so far they have failed to establish a new home for rural development policy. Nixon recommended creation in the federal government of a new Department of Community Development which would have absorbed the rural development responsibilities of the Department of Agriculture. As his proposal would have dismantled the USDA, the agricultural power cluster successfully opposed it. Since then, a number of organizations have been formed, presumably to speak for rural America, among them the Congressional Rural Caucus, Rural America, Inc., and the Rural Housing Alliance. But their influence has been limited.

Further, there are those within the USDA and outside who feel that an aggressive federal role in the development of local areas is simply inappropriate. The philosophy that too many decisions are made in Washington has many supporters. But if Watergate showed what could happen in Washington it did not necessarily prove that state and local governments could do better.

Many rural people undoubtedly feel that the real issue is not at what level of government rural development efforts should be centered. The real issue is whether rural development is just a nice word for more *planning* and less freedom; whether it is something that is done *to* rather than *for* rural people. The planning of rural land use is often where the battle is fought. To many rural people land use planning conflicts with one of the deepest social values in rural America—the right to do with one's property as he sees fit.

Implications for Rural Society. How will future rural development policy affect rural society? The answer will depend not only on who controls the policy process and the agenda, but also on how two important equity issues are handled:

First, can (and should) rural development policy seek to bring new life to *every* rural community? If policymakers agree that such a goal is unrealistic, the alternative of helping certain communities die gracefully is politically unwelcome. Academicians debate more openly the choice of concentrating versus dispersing development, but so far the criteria for deciding which to pursue are not clear.

Secondly, will the benefits of rural development policy accrue mainly to those communities and to those people who are least in need of assistance? Here, lessons may be learned from farm policy. Family farmers were its intended principal beneficiaries. Yet because farm programs assisted farmers in direct proportion to their production, larger farmers were the actual beneficiaries. Rural development policy, too, could mainly benefit communities and individuals that are able to take advantage of rural development programs. The issue is not whether some benefit and others do not, but whether all have equal access to those benefits. If equality of access is not assured, future analysts of rural development, like today's students of farm policy, will again be documenting the plight of people and communities left behind.

CONCLUSIONS. Until the 1960s one rural policy path dominated—farm policy. Since then, the path has forked. One fork, some say, should be labelled food policy. The other is called rural development policy. Each policy is a response to changing conditions. Each attempts to meet the needs of people who were not the intended beneficiaries of past policies or were not served by those policies. Some of these people are rural residents. Most of them are not. They are consumers, and urban and suburban residents. The well-being of rural people remains an important end for both policies, but it is seen increasingly as a means to the well-being of the rest of society.

Thus, both farm and nonfarm rural interests will be better served by public policy if they recognize and cooperate with nonrural interests in formulating policy. The traditional rural-urban dichotomy has lost most of its relevance. It overlooks many common interests that now cross the rural-urban line—the interests of commercial farmers and businessmen, of workers on farms and in factories, of poor people in rural shanties and urban ghettos, of consumers and taxpayers everywhere, and of those in small towns and big cities who prefer a simpler life. As these common interests are recognized, new and often temporary coalitions will form.

Indeed, many rural people who have not been served by past rural policies—the poor, for example—should fare much better if the traditional geographic focus is replaced by a problem focus.

Cooperation will involve helping nonrural people to understand rural society, not as a way to further purely rural interests, but to increase the enlightenment of policy decisions affecting rural life which will be made by representatives of a largely urban America.

13

Alternative Futures for Rural America: The Cloudy Crystal Ball

C. MILTON COUGHENOUR
LAWRENCE BUSCH

We need to know where we may be going in order to under-stand where we are.

Otis Dudley Duncan

THROUGHOUT history, the actions of men have been guided by their visions of the future (see Meadows, 1971:39–61; Nisbet, 1969). With the advent of modern civilization several centuries ago, however, such visions were given greater substance by more rational bases of thought and decision making. More recently—during this century—the tools of social science data accumulation and analysis have permitted further refinement of rational planning processes as well as the formulation of better socioeconomic forecasts. Although the future remains a riddle, its enigmatic wrappings can be so much removed as to reveal some of its more likely alternatives. This is what we attempt to do here in some degree for rural America.

While different methods may be employed in constructing alternative scenarios of the future rural society, all of these methods involve beliefs about the past and present conditions of society, beliefs which change as a result of new knowledge and different assumptions as to the bases of

C. Milton Coughenour is Professor of Sociology and Lawrence Busch is Assistant Professor of Sociology, University of Kentucky. This chapter is contribution No. 75-14-182 of the Agricultural Experiment Station, University of Kentucky, and is published with permission of the Director.

"truth." Images or scenarios of the future can be constructed by combining beliefs about past and present conditions with beliefs about causal relationships in a dynamic society and about particular valued outcomes (Bell and Mau, 1970). Our beliefs lead us to contend that the principal reference points for the future of rural America are described by the changes occurring in the structure of the rural population, in science and technology, in social organization, in individual expectations or desires, and in man's consciousness of himself and society. The selection of these domains (instead of others which might be used), as well as the identification of critical issues, reflects our belief in the basic importance of these components in the development of society and our observation that with increasing frequency the outcomes of development are contradictory to the original vision of a desirable life for man in society. We explore the effects of change in these five domains in the first section of the chapter. In the second section we sketch two imaginative scenarios of rural America in the decades ahead. The intention is not to forecast the future of rural America, but rather to describe two possible alternative styles of future development.

FIVE DYNAMIC DOMAINS OF CONTEMPORARY RURAL SOCIETY

An Urbanized Population in Dispersed Settlements. A man's image in society is largely cast by his occupation, and where a particular occupational group predominates, as was true of farmers and their families in rural areas of the United States until well into this century, the collective image naturally forms the public image of the society. The orthodox view thus is that rural society is a society of agriculturalists. This image of rural America is beginning to change.

Although farmers and members of their families were one-seventh as numerous in 1970 as in 1900, rural America was more populous by one-seventh than it was seven decades earlier. The rural-nonfarm population has more than doubled in size since 1920. The number is increasing daily. As noted in Chapter 3, since 1970 the rate of growth of the nonmetro population, which includes rural areas and small towns up to 50,000 population, has exceeded that of metropolitan centers. The image of a declining rural America has become clouded.

Agriculture, stock raising, and associated pursuits no longer provide either the principal occupations of rural people nor the socioeconomic basis of rural society in the United States. Rural-nonfarm people spread over the countryside and in small towns predominate by far. Most have little or no connection with agriculture or mining. While they are oriented to rural ways of living, their occupational image is increasingly like that of urban residents. This situation compels us to reshape our conception of the future rural society.

Science, Technology, and the Environment: New Issues. Continuing developments in science and technology have profoundly altered the world in which we live—not only as a result of new discoveries and inventions but also in the very way in which many practitioners perceive their roles as scientists and technicians. Scientists have become much more aware of their own active role in the process of doing science and of the impact of their personal values on the choice of problems to investigate. Whereas a hundred years ago a scientist was forced to dwell on a few problems for which instrumentation was available, the scientist today must actively choose that problem to which attention will be devoted.

In technology, as in science, the choice of project has become an increasingly debatable question. In addition, some of the assumptions underlying the design of technological systems are no longer tacitly accepted. During the nineteenth century, big technology was clearly favored by the economies of scale associated with steam power and the scarcity of skilled labor relative to capital. While many still cling to this assumption, others are beginning to view technology as multiple and adaptable to local circumstances. New "intermediate" technologies, which use a variety of energy sources and smaller scale machines that serve a multiplicity of functions, are being explored. It is not expected that older technologies of production will be replaced by a single new one, but rather that multiple technologies will be developed to meet diverse needs.

The so-called "energy crisis," problems of air and water pollution, the exploration of space, and demands of the developing nations have led to the challenging of many traditional concepts of the relationship between technological systems and our environment. American society has been guided by policies aptly described as "resourceful wastefulness" (Kammen, 1972). Such policies have been based on an illusion of limitless resources (relative to population) and an intense desire, grounded in religious and patriotic beliefs, to remake the world. Our systems of accounting have largely ignored the social and external economic costs of private enterprise, and the exploitation of the environment has continued virtually unchecked and unnoticed for many years.

In response to ecological crises, a new image of our relationship with nature is developing. Instead of a society pitted against nature, we have a society within nature, interacting with nature and receiving sustenance from it. The actions of rural people—farm and nonfarm—are increasingly guided by this perspective.

The Revolution in Organization. Vast changes have occurred in the scale of social organization. In agriculture, industry, and government there have been marked trends toward increased centralization and integration. Moreover, the service sector has come to be the major source of employment for Americans—rural as well as urban (Hines, Brown, and Zimmer, 1975:35).

In agriculture concentration of both ownership and control has markedly increased, as noted by Bertrand in Chapter 5 of this volume. Not only is control of farms becoming concentrated in the hands of large corporations, but the farms themselves are becoming more tightly integrated into the industrial production process. Additionally, the production of farm inputs is increasingly concentrated. Hightower reports that the four largest tractor companies together control 83 percent of the farm machinery market (1975:140). This figure, moreover, does not reflect local market conditions where a single supplier may have a monopoly. Feed, fertilizer, and other input markets are similarly dominated by a handful of companies.

Food manufacturing has also become more concentrated of late. A report of the National Commission on Food Marketing states that

the changes include: A substantial decline in the number of companies involved in food manufacturing generally; an increase in concentration in the food manufacturing industry, particularly since 1951; a substantial increase in the conglomerate nature of leading firms in the industry; a sizeable increase in the number of large acquisitions (companies with assets of $10 million or more) by the larger food producers, starting in about 1952; substantial increases in product differentiation expenditure by large food manufacturers; and a growing differential between the profitability of large vis-a-vis medium-size and small food manufacturers (1966:213).

Indeed, of 32,000 food manufacturing firms, 50 make three-fourths of the industry profits (Hightower, 1975:9).

Rural life has also been markedly affected by the increased concentration of governmental decisions. The federal bureaucracy exercises ever-greater power relative to state and local governments, which in many cases now require federal support. The Committee for Economic Development noted that "local governments tend to become administrative mechanisms for the implementation of national policies, rather than dynamic centers of authority in their own individual rights" (Committee for Economic Development, 1966:9). This decline in local autonomy is the result of state and federal control over financial aid, the standards for public facilities, and the system of public accounts. Of course, local governments do have the option of refusing aid. However, the aid is often allotted in order to resolve very real problems that cannot be met by local revenues. Furthermore, the possibility of getting something "free" often encourages action that otherwise would not be considered.

Increased integration both within and between the agricultural, industrial, and governmental sectors has led to what Duncan and Lieberson (1970) have called the metropolitanization of the country. Unlike the United States of a hundred years ago, substantial regional specialization exists in both industry and agriculture. The distribution system, rather than consisting of a set of loosely linked metropolitan regions, is now national, even international, in scope.

In short, we have witnessed an increase in concentration and integration in agriculture, industry, and government in the United States. While we have produced an increasing variety and abundance of goods and services in both the public and private sectors, we have also created a situation which is inherently unstable. Problems that were once local now tend to be national in scope, and institutional experimentation and change have been rendered more difficult by the need for national planning.

Revolution in Expectations: Quality of Life. Historically in the United States, images of a better life have flowed from the staunch belief in the inevitability of social, economic, and human progress. Whether translated into standards of living or the new notion of quality of life, this belief in progress has included not merely the necessities of life but also a continually expanding array of services which contribute to human development. Rural people have followed their urban brethren in seeking educational opportunities, health services, electrical power, road and water systems, and the incomes with which to gratify their desires (Schuler and McKain, 1949:297).

Nevertheless, during most of this century the gap between rural and urban attainments has been striking. While farm people have enjoyed a feeling of economic security, independence, a close-knit family, and worthwhile work—values associated with the agrarian creed—"urban people have in the past been more amply supplied with material possessions and services" and opportunities for variety in work and cultural expression (Schuler and McKain, 1949:297). Important differences still exist. But many formerly important differences have become less marked or disappeared, and the priorities of rural people today are similar to those of urban residents, as Larson has reported in Chapter 6.

If rural and urban people have similar desires, differences in their attainments would seem to be principally related to differences in incomes, occupations, and participation in the labor force, a conclusion reached by Slesinger (1974) and van Es and Brown (1974).

Lagging incomes in, and economic development of, rural areas slows the movement toward convergence in the quality of life throughout American society. But it does not weaken the motivation of rural people to reduce the gap. The increase in education, use of mass media, and spatial mobility of rural people plays a prominent role in increasing this motivation (De Sola Pool, 1963; Pye, 1963). Improvement in the conditions of life does not breed complacency, rather the opposite. Rural residents today are as dissatisfied as ever (Steelman, 1975; McCann, 1975) and more impatient with the slow course of development than before. Each step forward brings forth new images of future possibilities.

What then will be the future course pursued by rural people in America? It seems that rural people for some time to come are going to want more of the mundane benefits that urban people have heretofore enjoyed—more and better jobs, higher incomes, better schools, medical and dental services, and welfare programs. (Meanwhile, many urban residents desire some of the benefits that rural people have long possessed—greater space in which to live, a slower pace of life, and freedom from the social problems of urban living.) At the same time, images of a new future are emerging out of the confluence of rural and urban ways of life. These images reflect the interest of some people in finding a basis for a more meaningful life and the desire of minority groups for greater respect and equality. The increased interest in community concerns—improvement in the quality of the environment, community pride, land use planning, effective local government and law enforcement and in participation in the decisions that affect these concerns also represent new dimensions of aspirations and expectations in the 1970s.

Revolutions in Consciousness of Self and Society. As late as the mid-1950s, when social scientists sought to describe the social life and mental style of rural people in America they primarily dealt with farmers and farming communities (Beers, 1953; Landis, 1948; Loomis and Beegle, 1950; Taylor et al., 1949; Vogt, 1955; West, 1945). The rhythms of social life were regulated by the seasons and the prevailing type of farming. Similar life experiences, common ethnic backgrounds, relative isolation, and preoccupations with local concerns shaped the homogeneous character of many rural communities.

In this milieu the habits of thought were typically nonreflective and shaped by rigid categories—masculine-feminine, child-adult, guilty-innocent, insiders-outsiders, and so on. The processes of socialization tended to produce introverted personalities and fear of deviation. Man's "essential" nature was taken for granted and the life plan of individual adults—attached to relatively fixed points of reference—was relatively stable. Only God's will could deflect the expected course of one's life if a man had "good" character, a good wife and family, and a good farm.

A generation later, rural sociologists writing in *Our Changing Rural Society* (Copp, 1964) described a quite different type of rural society, one that is still largely prevalent. Today, the farmer employs a highly complex and sophisticated technology, and he has become a businessman with functional ties to large agribusiness firms, national and international markets. Nonfarm people greatly outnumber farmers, and many have similar ties with large-scale industry. In making a living, relationships to nature thus have been supplanted in importance by relationships to socioeconomic institutions and organizations. Formalized, bureaucratic systems linking local people to state and national centers of decision making have become important in nearly every area of social life. For the "modern" farmer faith in "natural" processes has given way to a faith in the efficacy of modern science and technology.

These changes have profoundly altered the consciousness of many rural people. Their immediate world has expanded to encompass manifold layers of "community" at regional, state, and national levels. Through mass media, increased mobility, and higher levels of education, cultural isolation has been reduced, and rural people have come to share in the interests, concerns, and complex imagery of modern society. Rural society has become more heterogeneous and pluralistic. Traditional beliefs and life-styles coexist with romanticized faith in rurality and urban, middle-class life-styles and attitudes. In these respects, rural residents thus participate in an urbanized society regardless of their residential location.

Modern technological, bureaucratic, and pluralistic society manifests a distinctive consciousness and style of mental life (Berger, Berger, and Kellner, 1973). Everyday agricultural and industrial activities are broken up into component parts. They are organized in orderly (technical) sequences based on highly abstract systems of scientific technology. Moreover, the productive processes have become separated from the ends to which many of the products are used. The soybean producer, for example, is no more knowledgeable of the final use of his product than is the producer of alloy steel. In consequence, the ordinary person — farmer or industrial worker — may be only dimly aware of the larger meaning of his productive activities, which must be entrusted to scientists, technicians, and bureaucrats who are often remote, impersonal functionaries. To the degree that this occurs, the problems and difficulties that rural people formerly attributed to their own deficiencies they may now attribute to the larger society.

A fundamental principle of man's relationship to society is that he sees himself mirrored in his images of others. Consequently, man's conception of society as technological and bureaucratic also applies to his concept of himself, that is, he experiences himself as an abstract, anonymous, compartmentalized, and unemotional person.

With the pluralization of experiences in urbanized rural society, standards are relativized. While this breaks the hold traditional institutions have held over the lives of rural people, it also weakens faith in any particular system of values and beliefs. All tend to become relative to the circumstances of particular situations. As Berger, Berger, and Kellner (1973:77) point out, this tends to shift the individual's perception of what is *really meaningful* from the objective institutions of society to his subjective experience. One's personal experience tends to become the paramount reality. But by comparison with the unified subjective experience in traditional society, it is segmented and unstable. Modern man has a continual problem of arranging his private and subjective experiences so as to sustain a coherent personal identity. Both his personal identity and life plan, thus, have the quality of a constructed reality in which there is continual tension within both daily life in society and within one's private, subjective world, and between the two. While many modern men and women develop personally satisfying identities and life plans, others experience personal instability and loss of meaning in life.

A third revolution in the consciousness of self and society has been manifested in the efforts to develop a new — simpler and more stable —

society. Some of the new life-styles have been escapist — seeking withdrawal from society — and others have romanticized primitive life close to "nature." However, the protest against the extremities of modern society has not been confined to the widely publicized endeavors of various radical groups (Kanter, 1972 and 1973; Roberts, 1971; Westhues, 1972). The counter-modernizing movement also includes those who seek to discover and develop a style of social life that retains some of the advantages of modern society while narrowing the gap between the public and private worlds of everyday experience. The aims are to recapture a sense of "wholeness," unity, and comprehensibility, to reduce the impact of large-scale, rationalized organizations, and to give greater emphasis to one's inner spirit and emotionality in the immanent development of the individual's life plan. These developments are too varied and sporadic, too uninstitutionalized as yet to permit a description of the nature of future society or of the characteristics of the consciousness it will engender. Nevertheless, they forecast the development of a potentially different type of social consciousness from that which has characterized American society. We explore some of the implications of the dilemmas the new consciousness elicits in two scenarios on alternative futures for rural society.

ALTERNATIVES FOR RURAL AMERICA. The future of rural society has been a relatively neglected topic with interest limited primarily to the future of farms or the rural economy (for example, see Ball and Heady, 1971; Edwards and De Pass, 1975; and Farmer, 1973:74–84). Thus far, students of rural development have been primarily interested in assessing the current situation and the alternatives for development (Brinkman, 1974; Coward, Beal, and Powers, 1971; North Central Regional Center for Rural Development, 1973 and 1974) rather than constructing images of possible, desirable, or probable futures. (However, the general literature on alternative futures for society is quite voluminous. It is impossible to review — even to list — the most significant of these works here. For recent, brief reviews of selected works see Marien, 1974; Padbury, 1972; and Sheldon and Parke, 1975.) The prevailing trends in American life and the dilemmas and alternatives these evoke suggest that more forthright attempts should be made to look at where rural society might be going.

The coupling of counter-modernizing developments with the intrinsic conditions of rural settings provides the basis for rural society to retain a distinctive character. The quality of rural society always has been shaped by the conditions of space and low population density, by relatively small-scale social organizations, and by distinctive occupations and patterns of consumption. Despite modern transportation systems and electronic media, physical distance and low density of population constrain social activity even as they generate opportunities for a type of social life that more dense settlement makes difficult. This social life promotes relationships based on personal familiarity and trust, in contrast with those of urban centers. This fundamental characteristic of rural society is unlikely to disappear.

The increased employment of rural people in the manufacturing and service industries has reduced the hold that seasonal rhythms of agricultural production had on social life in rural society. Nevertheless, the importance of seasonal conditions has not disappeared, nor will it do so. The increasingly ubiquitous part-time farmer keeps an anxious eye on the weather while scanning the office clock, and the processor suffers from drought along with the farmer. The natural environment continues to regulate and, in combination with the sparsity of settlement, keep slow the pace of social activity. It also slows the pace of social change and eases the adjustment of social institutions. Having fewer opportunities than urban people to "spend" time, rural people have more time to devote to those activities in which they do participate, and value them more (Linder, 1970).

The men and women who choose a rural residence and a rural-based occupation today, or in the immediate future, also accept a slower rate of upward social mobility. Along with this, however, they also may enjoy a greater stability in their occupational career and style of life.

The future rural society will be shaped by the responses of people to the issues of modernization as they attempt to develop satisfactory lives for themselves and their children. Disaffected urbanites will join with rural people in this endeavor as both seek to retain cherished values and to enjoy the benefits and opportunities of modern living (Dillman and Tremblay, Jr., 1977). Their values provide the compass with which they sail an uncharted sea.

Alternative I-Modernized Rurality. In their lives and activities rural men and women have reflected a secure belief in traditional American values—agrarian fundamentalism, conservative religious beliefs, and familism. Though the content of these beliefs has changed, the central themes remain strong in rural areas. They are bolstered too by images of the problems prevalent in urban society (Vidich and Bensman, 1958:30ff), and in some respects by the thrusts of modernization itself. Will men and women in rural America abandon these cherished values when confronted with the issues and opportunities that modernity presents? We do not suppose that they will. It is more likely that the future rural society will be shaped by them.

Agrarian fundamentalism—the belief that farming is the basic industry in America—has lost little of its vitality among rural people. The transformation of American agriculture has not diminished its value as worthwhile work, and the opportunity to acquire the social and psychological benefits from farming activity has increased. The small farm remains a "refuge" for some who are ill-prepared to compete in urban, industrial society. For the large, venturesome farmer, agriculture provides the means by which his needs and those of his family are met. The ranks of agrarians are augmented by part-time farmers—large and small—for whom farming provides supplementary income, an outlet for surplus capital or family labor, and a means of gaining surcease from the pressures of urban living. Relief from complete dependence on farming as a means of livelihood does not lessen its value in other respects, but rather enhances it. In urban as well as in rural society, belief in agrarian fundamentalism is strengthened too by the aura of crisis brought on by food shortages and rising food prices, and the future holds no promised deliverance from this fateful circumstance.

The attachment of rural people to conservative religious beliefs also remains strong, and it cannot be explained merely on the basis of social isolation and the persistence of tradition. Religious beliefs and practices persist because they continue to provide satisfactory explanations of the finitude, fragility, and mortality of the human condition. They are deeply grounded in both the imagery and conditions of the agrarian and pastoral life with which rural people have a special affinity. Their everyday experiences keep alive the symbols and parables by which the nature of man and his relationship to God have been traditionally expressed.

The family today is buffeted by the forces of modern society, which have altered its organization and reduced its stability. However, the institution of marriage has retained its popularity despite the increase in divorce (Hines, Brown and Zimmer, 1975:19-23). One of the ironies of modernization is that the family's traditional functions are strengthened even as the traditional roles of its members are altered. For example, the liberalization of abortion tends to preserve the family's traditional function as the principal reproductive group, which the loss of traditional social control of premarital sexual behavior threatens. The liberation of women from traditional housekeeping roles and from seemingly endless responsibilities for the rearing of numerous children enables them to shoulder greater economic responsibilities, which the increased desire for goods and services stimulates. The psychological stresses of modernization likewise increase the need for intimacy and loyalty in interpersonal relationships through which the tensions of modern life can be released. Consequently, the family today retains its central functions despite a loosening of the traditional relationships that have characterized rural families in the past (Burchinal, 1964:165; Sussman, 1972:145).

Just as the effects of modernization on family functions do not foreshadow the family's disappearance, neither does modernization seem to vitiate the rural system of beliefs undergirding marriage and the nuclear family. Recent studies show that rural people continue to possess basic values with which to maintain the integrity of their families in modern society (Flinn and Johnson, 1974). Familistic themes are embedded in, and reinforced by, the imagery and sentiments of traditional agrarian and conservative religious beliefs and practices. The slower-paced, more personalized basis of social life and the greater prevalence of traditional occupations and life planning are all conducive to the maintenance of the family against the destructive individualizing tendencies of urban society. By contrast, the claim of some radical intellectuals that communal living arrangements provide exemplars of the future is quite unlikely to be realized. Communal forms of living must deal with the same stresses of modern society as do families and have less powerful institutional resources for dealing with them. Moreover, the fundamental changes in related institutions necessary to stabilize communal living arrangements are not even being widely contemplated, much less on the way to being established.

Individual, Family, Community, and the Future Society. Some elitist groups are perennially troubled by what they perceive as the ominous outcomes likely to result from the decisions and activities of ordinary men and women in American society. Their view often seems to be that the common man is some sort of mindless, subservient dolt bent on self-destruction. We do not subscribe to this point of view. Instead, we assume that with respect to the issues and opportunities that modernity presents, people, especially those in rural areas, will make choices that might preserve (1) a relatively large scope for individual freedom, initiative in the pursuit of self-interest, and responsibility for their actions; (2) the integrity of the nuclear family in its main functions and roles; and (3) an expanding, associational basis of social life in community as opposed to the planned, corporate communities of various types. In taking this stance we are not arguing that rural people will rigidly adhere to present-day forms of social life, but rather that they have a secure basis from which to develop satisfactory patterns of living in the future.

One of the fundamental issues of modern life is whether the freedom inherent in greater opportunity for individual choice will be guided by a measured, self-conscious acceptance of responsibility for the collective welfare. That rural people will have greater opportunity for individual choice is a certainty. Those born in rural areas are acquiring more schooling, and their ability to take advantage of opportunities modern society opens to them is increasing. Their numbers will be increased by those with urban-based employment who prefer modern rural to urban life-styles outside of work activity. People in the modern rural society, thus, will have wider and more varied socializing experiences, which tend to relativize traditional standards and erode conventional wisdom. These experiences will result in the development of new types of rural men and women and new patterns of rural living.

We contend that in the modern rural society the fundamental value themes of rural society will provide stable reference points for the development of individual life plans and adaptive social institutions. For the most part the values prevalent in American rural society have always encouraged individual initiative and responsibility for the outcome of one's action (or inaction), but fundamental rural values also encourage the acceptance of collective initiative and responsibility. In the past this has been most in evidence in the creation of voluntary organizations for the attainment of ends beyond the reach of individual men and women.

Acceptance of a broader responsibility for the outcomes of one's action in a community requires acceptance of a different social ethic than that which has characterized rural people in the past. Will rural people grow in their acceptance of a broader concept of social responsibility? We are confident that they may do so as they become better informed and as their capacities for collective activity increase. This is, in fact, the basis on which an increasing number of rural people today have been awakened to the need for environmental planning and other innovative developments by which the benefits of rural living they have heretofore enjoyed can be secured in the future.

Some people today foresee the dissolution and disappearance of the family as the basic social unit in society (Ellis, 1970; O'Neill and O'Neill, 1972; Roy, 1970; Toffler, 1970). We do not. The continuity and well-being of the family is closely linked with institutionalized religion in western civilization, each sustaining the other as the central institutions of moral society. Because of this interdependence, the basic stance of institutionalized religion with respect to the impact of secular society on the family remains conservative.

In consequence, one may expect more continuity than change in the characteristic patterns of family life in rural areas. The trends forecast by Parke and Glick, Nimkoff, and Pollak are consistent with this point of view (these speculations are nicely summarized by Clayton, 1975:527-30). These trends include a smaller family size than in the past and a gradual decline and eventual stabilization in teenage marriage; the continued popularity of marriage; and the maintenance of the principal family functions in reproduction, in providing the basic socioemotional context for the release of tensions, in the stabilization of adult personalities, and in providing a "communal" basis of distributing goods and services essential for individual growth and development.

These continuities, however, allow for change in the relationships between husbands and wives, parents and children, and among kin. Traditional differences between middle-class urban and rural families have become less pronounced (Burchinal, 1964). Among those guided by the conservative values traditional in American life, a syncretic culture of the family is emerging. Thus, it is likely that in a modernized rural society the wage-earning contribution of wives to the family economy would increase, especially before and after the child-rearing period, as well as would joint (husband-wife) decision making in the expenditure of family income and in responsibilities for household maintenance tasks and child rearing. Instead of a fixed pattern of husband-wife roles throughout the family life cycle, the roles of each will be more determined by their interests and needs, which change from early marriage to child rearing to partnership in old age.

In their socioemotional respects, parent-child relationships during childhood and adolescence would take on greater significance in a modern rural society than they have had previously. Rural parents retain greater control over the socialization of their children than do urban and will continue to do so. In part this is because of the lower population density and more limited social relationships outside the family for children growing up in rural areas. But trends in modern rural society serve to increase the importance of socioemotional relationships between parents and their children. Growth in the educational attainments of rural youth prolongs childhood dependency. The erosion of fixed moral standards and greater social consciousness of parents tends to shift the style of parental instruction from "command" to "guidance." With the decline in parental dependence on children for productive activity, along with smaller family size, the social distance between parents and children is reduced and the socioemotional content of their relationship is intensified. This intensity could lead to early rejection of parental authority. But the shift in style of parental instruction from "command" to "guidance" encourages longer childhood dependency, a pattern associated with increased capacity to act autonomously and responsibly in adulthood (Parsons and White, 1961).

The modern rural community is larger in its spatial limits, more differentiated and functionally interdependent in its connections with the larger society than the rural community of yesteryear (Larson and Rogers, 1964; Olsen, 1968:263; Warren, 1963:54). While the wants and expectations of rural people have expanded, locally based services have declined (Ellenbogen, 1974; Fuguitt, 1971), and at least some social costs of obtaining these services in larger centers have increased (Wilkinson, 1974). During this era of adjustment the access of local people to decision makers has declined, along with the ability of local officials to represent their constituencies (Erickson, 1974). These developments have laid to rest that pattern of social life once associated with the isolated, homogeneous rural community. Those who have been unable or unwilling to adapt to life in modern communities, as well as some who have adapted, are often dissatisfied and feel alienated. Apologists of an imagined rural utopia have been dismayed, and some foresee the eclipse of rural society.

This dissatisfaction arises from the development of modern American society, but that development has not been imposed on a supine rural populace. Rural people and their leaders have sought a "better life"—more and better services, the products of a mass consumption society, and increased opportunity for growth and development for themselves and their children—and the majority supports modern institutions by which such desires can be gratified.

In forging rural communities in the future, rural people face a number of issues. One of these is providing a sense of equality, dignity, and opportunity in a society with marked inequalities of income, power, and prestige (Aron, 1969; Bell, 1973). Historically, access to the opportunities to acquire income, power, and prestige in society has been closely tied to one's occupation, which is strongly influenced by one's educational attainments early in life. But the progress of modern technology places those who have not succeeded in this quest at an increasing disadvantage. The present era is characterized by a growing consciousness of disadvantaged groups — the aged, ethnic and racial minorities, the unemployed and the relatively poor, and others. Each at times presses its claims for equal "justice" and coalesces with other disaffected groups in seeking redress of injustice or a greater share of the benefits and opportunities that modern society provides. The challenge of the future in modernized rural society is the development of a social ethic — and effective organization — for distributing those benefits that assure human dignity through access to opportunities, while continuing to provide incentives for creative achievement (see Bell, 1973; and Vickers, 1973). This can take place through the increased commitment of rural people to their communities and, therewith, the capacity of these organic communities to satisfy the needs of their residents.

The number of community needs constantly increases — reduction of the blight of unrestrained urbanization, of environmental pollution, of corruption and mismanagement of public services, and the recapture of power over decisions affecting community institutions. Each calls for public actions by an informed and responsible citizenry. Examples of the power and effectiveness of local communities in obtaining needed services and in dealing with emergent problems are numerous, but far from common. The frequent failure of citizen efforts demonstrates that citizen participation by itself is not sufficient for the development of viable rural communities. As Erickson has recognized, several ingredients are critical, including "the insertion of new information, new alternatives from which to choose," and people who possess a broad sense of "human well-being" (1974:79). Provision of the ingredients for effective citizen action requires the development of relationships between local citizens and "experts" of various kinds. This is not an argument for planned communities, whether designed by hired experts or administered by paternalistic authorities (Gottschalk, 1975:28-33). Planning *for* rural people denies them the will and capacity to undertake action in their own behalf and is out of step with rural traditions. But modernized rural communities can be constructed by local people linked with knowledgeable professionals in relationships of mutual trust and commitment. This implies the involvement of professional experts with local people over the long term and at each step of the development process. In fact, institutionalization of this kind of joint effort appears to be growing through development programs of the Cooperative Extension Service and through federally encouraged multicounty development districts of various types (Doeksen et al., 1975; U.S., Congress, 1971; Hausler, 1974). Unless we have missed the substance of the dynamic in rural society, rural people will not be found wanting in their efforts in the future to develop organized ways for securing a satisfactory social life at local and regional levels of community.

The future provides the opportunity for the men and women in rural America and those who will join them to construct people oriented community organizations. More variable and complex in its patterns of life than in the past, a modernized rural society would possess a distinctively voluntaristic style of social life, more self-conscious and community-conscious, which would preserve a sense of coherence and stability for its individuals and families, and which would be crafted on the basis of its fundamental values.

Alternative II—A Telic Society. The expectations of rural Americans have in the past been similar to those of urban Americans. The image of material abundance, of the good life, has been as important to rural as to urban Americans. At the same time, however, rural consciousness has emphasized individual freedom and initiative. The emergence of large bureaucratic organizations and the integration of agriculture into marketing and processing industries has put these goals at odds. The farmer can insure a stable income only by surrendering a part of his freedom to run his farm his way (see Harris, 1974). The rural merchant must utilize the same marketing methods as the large chain store if he wishes to remain in business. And rural officials must increasingly rely on state and federal aid if they are to provide desired services to rural residents. In short, rural communities must become dependent upon powerful outside organizations if they wish to meet the rising expectations of their residents.

The alternative presented below is an attempt to resolve this dilemma. It is suggested that material abundance and personal freedom need not be antithetical.

The central theme in this image of a future is the telic, or purposive nature of such a society. Put differently, in such a society the construction of the future would be constantly under discussion. Of course, in the past other people in other places have occasionally considered the prospects for their future. The distinction, however, that separates other societies from what one might call "the telic society" lies in striving to make conscious those questions related to what we are becoming. Thus, a telic society must be one within which the construction of images of the future is itself institutionalized. It is a society within which the future is not fixed, or preordained, but remains always open and subject to revision.

In such a society commitment would play a key role, for it is through commitment that images are actualized. The kind of commitment necessary in a telic society would differ substantially from the kind of blind faith that has often been associated with commitment in the past. Instead, it would be an open undertaking; people would attempt to understand the roots of their commitment and would reexamine it in the face of new circumstances.

The socialization process in a telic society would be greatly modified. At present each of us accepts our primary socialization, performed by our parents, as "natural." This, of course, is not likely to change in any society. What can change, however, is our attitude toward this very process.

From our Puritan and liberal tradition we have inherited the mistaken notion that each of us is an autonomous individual (see Ferkiss, 1974). What this means is that we have been so effectively socialized into perceiving ourselves as individuals that the process of becoming an individual has remained opaque to most of us. It has appeared so "natural" for each of us to perceive our views as *merely* our own, that their origin has remained obscured.

However, the individual is a product of society. It is only through others that we, as infants, come to know ourselves. And children who are reared without benefit of human contact are not individuals — indeed, they are barely human (see Polanyi, 1958:296-97). Thus if we perceive ourselves as autonomous individuals, it is only because the society into which we were born has socialized us to believe just that.

In a telic society, the socialization process would be open. People would be encouraged to examine critically the historical roots of the traditions and institutions of society and to remold them constantly to fit new circumstances. Moreover, they would be encouraged to examine the values held by society and to inquire into their meaningfulness.

This is not to say that all tradition would be abandoned. On the other hand, it *is* to say that such a society would retain only those traditions that remained meaningful, that continued to serve real human needs. Commitment would thereby be increased, for it would always include understanding.

A telic society must also be a society that encourages and values the participation of every (normal adult) individual in the decisions affecting that individual. If the future is open and yet to be determined, then decisions regarding the shape of the future are of a moral and ethical nature. Since none of us has a claim to dominion in moral and ethical matters, decisions regarding the future can only be legitimately based on the active participation in decision making by all.

A central characteristic of any society that wishes to encourage the active participation in decision making of all its members is decentralization. Though decentralization is not an end in itself, through it direct participation can be maximized. Hence, we would expect a telic society to encourage the continued movement of population away from metropolitan areas. Moreover, one would expect a general decline in urban dominance as well as a revitalization of small towns and rural areas.

By taking advantage of the potentialities that lie behind new technologies, the web of new relationships between communities would become one best characterized as interdependent. Transportation hubs would be replaced, in part, by communication networks. This is not to suggest that society would return to some modern version of the medieval manor. Unlike the manor, which was entirely self-sufficient, this society would strive for self-sufficiency only in basic goods, while employing the system of exchange to obtain other goods. The relationships within each community would also be interdependent, rather than hierarchical.

Specifically, one might expect each community to be self-sufficient in meeting its food and energy needs. This would entail the employment, in combination, of a variety of decentralized energy sources; for example, wind, tidal, and solar energy. It would also entail the use of a variety of intensive agricultural techniques. Other goods that could not be produced everywhere would be exchanged in a manner similar to the way in which goods are exchanged today. The huge factory, however, in which thousands of workers are employed would become exceedingly rare. It would be replaced by smaller units employing multipurpose equipment and producing a greater variety of product lines. Indeed, much of the equipment necessary for such a decline in scale is already available.

Education would also take on new significance in a telic society. Though it is likely that the trend toward more formal education would continue, the rigid distinctions between education, work, and leisure would be removed. Education would become a lifelong process. Only a part of one's education would take place in classroom settings. More and more, educational activities would take place in settings presently reserved for work or leisure. Instead of attempting to recreate society within the classroom, schools would be more fully integrated into the larger society.

The occupational structure would also be radically altered. The production of goods, presently occupying only a small portion of the labor force, would be of even less significance in a telic society. By eliminating planned obsolescence and the current emphasis on material possessions — indeed, by deliberately producing goods to last — the number of persons engaged in production would decline even further.

Of course, such a transformation would have to be societal and not just limited to rural areas. Yet, it appears that it is in rural areas that such a transformation might begin. The cities are burdened by nineteenth-century physical plants that can only be modified at enormous expense. They are burdened too by entrenched labyrinthine bureaucracies, by high population density, and by fiscal crises. They are far too busy managing crises to actively construct the future.

Moreover, new decentralizing technologies tend to favor small communities. For example, the town of Bridgeport, Texas (population, 5,000) has considered constructing its own solar powered generating plant in order to reduce electricity costs for its residents (National Area Development Institute, 1975). Even the consideration of locally generated electricity would have been considered absurd as little as ten years ago.

Rural communities also offer us the possibility for experimentation with a variety of technological and organizational forms. The smallness of rural communities and their marginal position on the "edges" of modern society make them the most feasible places for experimentation. It is unlikely that any one ideal form of organization or technology will serve the needs of all. Indeed, that assumption is responsible for many of our present-day problems. No energy shortage would exist if we had not relied nearly entirely on fossil fuels to serve us.

In summary, a telic society would be characterized by its self-critical, futurist orientation. Institutional frameworks would be constructed and modified to meet specific, articulate goals. Moreover, those goals themselves would be subject to modification. Thus, a telic society would be exceedingly plastic and diverse. Yet, since its diversity would be anchored in commitment, it could provide a meaningful existence for all.

These scenarios have been written from somewhat different vantage points—two of the many possible perspectives of the social life of people living outside metropolises in the future. The images of alternative futures that we have constructed differ primarily in terms of a more conservative and a more radical ideological perspective with respect to implications of the five ongoing revolutions. The first alternative adopts the perspective that the future will be molded out of traditional themes, while the second alternative conceives of a more revolutionary course of technological and organizational development under the guidance of different value priorities.

But considerable similarity unites the perspectives, too. They are similar in the sense that they are hopeful, even optimistic, about the capacity of mankind to shape a future society that permits the realization of fundamental human needs for sustenance, human development, and well-being in society. Neither perspective envisions the decay and disappearance of rural society or its development into some monstrous form of technological and bureaucratized machine operated by a meritocratic elite. Neither portrays a future rural America as totalitarian on either the right or left, or as a collection of ad hoc groups. Rural people are not assumed to be in the process of becoming uncompromising "activist" revolutionaries, free-wheeling "anarchist" individualists, or "gnostics" withdrawn from society (Zijderveld, 1971:92–119). All of these are *possible* alternatives. However, none seems to us either desirable or within the range of real possibilities when considering the transactional relationships between man and society within his culture and environment.

The realm of the realistically possible is quite spacious and likely to become more so. Its boundaries are mobile and permeable, shaped by the contingent conditions of man in society. As human capacities have expanded, the given conditions have become less fixed and permanent, and with this development the possibilities for both good and ill have increased. The future rural society will be shaped by the images of desirable futures that guide the decisions and actions of today. At present, many alternatives engage the imagination of rural people as they seek to transcend their immediate problems. These images of the future must be carefully examined if the probability of favorable outcomes is to be increased. The need to do so is no longer debatable. It is essential that this examination be undertaken by people and groups at all levels in society.

NOTES

CHAPTER 1

Bailey, Liberty H. 1913. *The Country-Life Movement.* New York: Macmillan.
Bender, Thomas. 1975. *Toward an Urban Vision: Ideas and Institutions in Nineteenth-Century America.* Lexington: Univ. Press of Kentucky.
Commission on Country Life. 1911. Reprinted 1944. *Report of the Commission on Country Life.* Chapel Hill: Univ. of North Carolina Press.
Fischer, Claude S. 1975a. "The Effect of Urban Life on Traditional Values." *Social Forces* 53 (Mar.): 420-32.
_____. 1975b. "Toward a Subcultural Theory of Urbanism." *American Journal of Sociology* 80 (May): 1319-41.
Friedman, John, and John Miller. 1965. "The Urban Field." *Journal of the American Institute of Planners* 31 (Nov.): 312-20.
Fuguitt, Glenn V., and James J. Zuiches. 1975. "Residential Preferences and Population Distribution." *Demography* 12 (Aug.): 491-504.
Haren, Claude C. 1974. "Current Spatial Organization of Industrial Production and Distribution Activity," in U.S. Senate, Committee on Agriculture and Forestry, Subcommittee on Rural Development, *Rural Industrialization: Prospects, Problems, Impacts, and Methods.* 93rd Cong., 2nd sess., Committee Print, Apr. 19.
Harshbarger, C. Edward, and Sheldon W. Stahl. 1974. "Economic Concentration in Agriculture: Trends and Developments." Federal Reserve Bank of Kansas City *Monthly Review* (Apr.): 21-28.
Hines, Fred K.; David L. Brown; and John M. Zimmer. 1975. *Social and Economic Characteristics of the Population in Metro and Nonmetro Counties.* Economic Research Service, U.S. Department of Agriculture. AER-272.
Larson, Olaf F., and Everett M. Rogers. 1964. "Rural Society in Transition: The American Setting," in James H. Copp (ed.), *Our Changing Rural Society: Perspectives and Trends.* Ames: Iowa State Univ. Press.
Martin, Roscoe C. 1957. *Grass Roots. University, Alabama:* Univ. of Alabama Press.
Rogers, Everett M., and Rabel J. Burdge. 1972. *Social Change in Rural Societies.* New York: Appleton-Century-Crofts.
Sorokin, P. H.; Carle C. Zimmerman; and C. J. Galpin. 1930. *A Systematic Source Book in Rural Sociology.* Vol. 1. Minneapolis: Univ. of Minnesota Press.
U.S. Bureau of the Census. 1975. *Statistical Abstract of the United States: 1975.* 96th ed. Washington: USGPO.
U.S., Congress, Senate, ERS, USDA, 1975. *The Economic and Social Condition of Nonmetropolitan America in the 1970's.* 94th Cong., 1st sess., Committee Print, May 30.

CHAPTER 2

Barrows, Richard. 1974. Use-Value Taxation: The Experience of Other States. Department of Agricultural Economics, University of Wisconsin, Madison. Staff Papers Series no. 73.
Becker, Catherine, and Rabel J. Burdge. 1971. "The Effects of Familism, Traditionalism and S.E.S. on Attitude toward Reservoir Construction in an Eastern Kentucky County." Paper presented at Rural Sociological Society meetings, August, Denver.
Bennett, Hugh Hammond. 1964. "Soil," in Roderick Nash (ed.), *The American Environment.* Reading, Mass.: Addison-Wesley.

Bultena, Gordon L. 1974. "Dynamics of Agency-Public Relations in Water Resources Planning," in Donald Field, James C. Barron, and Burl F. Long (eds.), *Water and Community Development*. Ann Arbor: Ann Arbor Science.

Burch, William R., Jr. 1974a. "In Democracy It's the Preservation of Wilderness." *Appalachia*, December, pp. 89-101.

_____. 1974b. "The Response to the Changing Needs and Values of People." *The Forestry
Chronicle* 50 (Dec.):1-4.

Buttel, Frederick H., and William L. Flinn. 1974. "The Structure and Support for the Environmental Movement, 1968-1974." *Rural Sociology* 39 (Spring): 56-59.

Catton, William, Jr. 1974. "Depending on Ghosts." *Humboldt Journal of Social Relations*
2 (Fall/Winter): 45-49.

Caudill, Harry M. 1971. *My Land is Dying*. New York: E. P. Dutton.

Cheek, Neil H., Jr. 1972. "Variations in Patterns of Leisure Behavior: An Analysis of
Sociological Aggregates," in William R. Burch, Jr., Neil Cheek, Jr., and Lee Taylor
(eds.), *Social Behavior, Natural Resources, and the Environment*. New York: Harper
and Row.

Clark, Roger N., and George H. Stankey. 1976. "Analyzing Public Input to Resource
Decisions: Criteria, Principles and Case Examples of the Codinvolve System." *Natural
Resources Journal* 16 (Jan.): 213-36.

Clawson, Marion. 1972. *America's Land and Its Uses*. Baltimore: Johns Hopkins Univ.
Press.

Cooper, Rollin B. 1973. Upper Great Lakes Regional Recreational Planning Study. Institute for Environmental Studies, University of Wisconsin, Madison.

Cottrell, Fred. 1955. *Energy and Society: The Relation between Energy, Social Change
and Environmental Development*. New York: McGraw-Hill.

Council on Environmental Quality. 1974. *Environmental Quality—1974*. Fifth annual
report. Washington: USGPO.

Dasgupta, Satadal. 1967. Attitudes of Local Residents toward Watershed Development.
Social Science Research Center, Mississippi State University, State College, Miss.
Preliminary Report 18.

Dillman, Don A., and James A. Christenson. 1972. "The Public Value for Pollution Control," in William R. Burch, Jr., Neil Cheek, Jr., and Lee Taylor (eds.), *Social
Behavior, Natural Resources, and the Environment*. New York: Harper and Row.

Dunlap, Riley, E., and R. B. Heffernan. 1975. "Outdoor Recreation and Environmental
Concern: An Empirical Examination." *Rural Sociology* 40 (Spring): 18-30.

Extension Committee on Organization and Policy, Subcommittee on Environmental Quality, National Association of State Agencies and Land-Grant Colleges. 1974, Report.
Cooperative Extension Service, University of Georgia, Atlanta.

Ekirch, Arthur A., Jr. 1973. *Man and Nature in America*. Lincoln: Univ. of Nebraska
Press.

Fortney, Charles T., et al. 1972. Attitudes of South Dakota Farm Operators toward
Wetlands and Waterfowl Protection. Agricultural Experiment Station, South Dakota
State University, Brookings. Bull. 592.

Foss, Phillip. 1960. *Politics and Grass: The Administration of Grazing on the Public Domain*. New York: Greenwood.

Frey, John C. 1952. Some Obstacles to Soil Erosion in Western Iowa. Agricultural Experiment Station, Iowa State University, Ames. Res. Bull. 391.

Frutchey, Fred P., and W. K. Williams. 1965. *Motivations of Small Woodland Owners: Summary of Nine State Studies*. Federal Extension Service, U.S. Department of Agriculture.

Gale, Richard P. 1972. "From Sit-in to Hike-in: A Comparison of Civil Rights and Environmental Movements," in William R. Burch, Jr., Neil Cheek, Jr., and Lee Taylor
(eds.), *Social Behavior, Natural Resources, and the Environment*. New York: Harper
and Row.

Gray, L. C., et al. 1923. "The Utilization of Our Lands for Crops, Pastures and Forests," in
U.S. Department of Agriculture, *Yearbook of Agriculture*.

Hardin, Charles. 1952. *Politics of Agriculture*. Glencoe, Ill.: Free Press.

Harry, Joseph; Richard Gale; and John Hendee. 1969. "Conservation: An Upper-Middle
Class Social Movement." *Journal of Leisure Research* 1 (Summer): 246-54.

Heberlein, Thomas E. 1972. "The Land Ethic Realized: Some Social Psychological Explanations for Changing Environmental Attitudes." *Journal of Social Issues*
28 (Dec.): 79-87.

_____. 1975. "Social Norms and Environmental Quality." Paper presented at American
Association for the Advancement of Science meetings, January, New York.

———. 1976. "Some Observations on Alternative Mechanisms for Public Involvement: The Hearing, the Public Opinion Poll, the Workshop, and the Quasi-Experiment." *Natural Resources Journal* 16 (Jan.): 197-212.

Heichel, G. H. 1973. Comparative Efficiency of Energy Use in Crop Production. Agricultural Experiment Station, University of Connecticut, New Haven. Bull. 77.

Hornback, Kenneth. 1975. "Overcoming Obstacles to Agency and Public Involvement: A Program and Methods." Manuscript. Denver Service Center, National Park Service, Denver, Colo.

Howard, Walter E., and William M. Longhurst. 1956. "The Farmer-Sportsman Problem and a Solution," in *Transactions of the 21st North American Wildlife Conference.* Wildlife Management Institute, Washington, D.C.

Huth, Hans. 1957. *Nature and America: Three Centuries of Changing Attitudes.* Berkeley: Univ. of California Press.

Johnson, Sue, and Rabel Burdge. 1975. "Sociologists—Environmental Impact Statements: What Are We Doing Here?" Paper presented at Rural Sociological Society meetings, August, San Francisco.

Klessig, Lowell L. 1970. Hunting in Wisconsin: Initiation, Desertion, Activity Patterns and Attitudes as Influenced by Social Class and Residence. Center for Resource Policy Studies, University of Wisconsin, Madison. Working Paper 3.

———. 1973. Recreational Property Owners and Their Institutional Alternatives for Resources Protection: The Case of Wisconsin Lakes. Inland Lake Demonstration Project, University of Wisconsin, Madison.

Kronus, Carol, and Jon C. van Es. 1972. "Pollution Attitude, Knowledge and Behavior of Farmers and Urban Men." Paper presented at Rural Sociological Society meetings, August, Baton Rouge, La.

Lambert, Virginia, et al. 1974. Public Services, Programs and Policies in Far Northwestern Wisconsin Counties. Institute for Environmental Studies, University of Wisconsin, Madison. Report 41.

Leopold, Aldo. 1949. *A Sand County Almanac,* New York: Oxford Univ. Press.

McEvoy, James III. 1972. "The American Concern with Environment," in William R. Burch, Jr., Neil Cheek, Jr., and Lee Taylor (eds.), *Social Behavior, Natural Resources, and Environment.* New York: Harper and Row.

McIntosh, Kenneth D. 1967. Posting of Land in West Virginia and Landowner Attitudes Regarding Posting, Hunting Fees, and the Hunter. Agricultural Experiment Station, West Virginia University, Morgantown. Bull. 542.

Marsh, George Perkins. 1864. Reprinted 1965. David Lowenthal, ed. *Man and Nature.* Cambridge: Harvard Univ. Press, Belknap Press.

Morrison, Denton; Kenneth E. Hornback; and W. Keith Warner. 1972. "The Environmental Movement: Some Preliminary Observations and Predictions," in William R. Burch, Jr., Neil Cheek, Jr., and Lee Taylor (eds.), *Social Behavior, Natural Resources, and the Environment.* New York: Harper and Row.

Munger, James. 1968. *Public Access to Public Domain Lands: Two Case Studies of Landowner-Sportsman Conflict.* Economic Research Service, U.S. Department of Agriculture. Misc. Publ. 1122.

National Wildlife. 1975. "Sixth Environmental Quality Index: The Year of the Trade-off" 13 (Feb.): 3-10.

Pampel, Fred Carroll, Jr. 1974. "The Social Basis of Environmental Protection: Innovativeness among Illinois Farmers." Master's thesis, University of Illinois, Urbana.

Peterson, John H., Jr., and Peggy J. Ross. 1971. Changing Attitudes toward Watershed Development. Social Science Research Center, Water Resources Institute, Mississippi State University, State College, Miss.

Public Land Law Review Commission. 1970. *One Third of the Nation's Land.* Washington: USGPO.

Ragatz, Richard L. and Associates. 1974. *Recreational Properties: An Analysis of the Markets for Privately-Owned Recreational Lots and Leisure Homes.* National Technical Information Service, Springfield, Va.

Real Estate Research Corporation. 1974. *The Costs of Sprawl: Environmental and Economic Costs of Alternative Residential Development Patterns at the Urban Fringe.* Washington: USGPO.

Saitta, William W., and Richard L. Bury. 1973. "Local Economic Stimulation from Reservoir Development: A Case Study of Selected Impacts." *Journal of Soil and Water Conservation* 28 (Mar./Apr.): 80-83.

Smith, Cortland L. 1974. "Groups and Human Emotions as Adaptive Mechanisms," in Donald R. Field, James Barron, and Burl F. Long (eds.), *Water and Community Development*. Ann Arbor: Ann Arbor Science.

Smith, Cortland L.; Thomas C. Hogg; and Michael J. Reagan. 1971. "Economic Development: Panacea or Perplexity for Rural Areas?" *Rural Sociology* 36 (June): 173–86.

Solberg, Erling D. 1961. *New Laws for New Forests*. Madison: Univ. of Wisconsin Press.

Steinhart, John S., and Carol E. Steinhart. 1973. "Energy Use in the U.S. Food System." *Science* 184 (Apr. 19): 307–16.

Stoddard, Charles H., and Albert M. Day. 1969. "Private Lands for Public Recreation: Is There a Solution?" in *Transactions of the 34th North American Wildlife and Natural Resources Conference*. Wildlife Management Institute, Washington, D.C.

Twight, Ben W. 1975. "Public Involvement as a Cooperative Strategy in Natural Resource Decision Making." Paper presented at Rural Sociological Society meetings, August, San Francisco.

Udall, Stewart L. 1963. *The Quiet Crisis*. New York: Avon.

Wengert, Norman. 1955. *Natural Resources and the Political Struggle*. Garden City, N.Y.: Doubleday.

Wengert, Norman, and Thomas Graham. 1974. "Transferable Development Rights and Land Use Control." *Journal of Soil and Water Conservation* 29 (Nov./Dec.): 253–57.

Wilkening, Eugene A., and Cecil Gregory. 1941. Planning for Family Relocation: Preliminary Report on Practices Followed and Results Obtained in Evacuation of the Basin of the Wappappelo Dam, Wayne County, Missouri. Agricultural Experiment Station, University of Missouri, Columbia. Bull. 427.

Wilkening, Eugene A., et al. 1973. Quality of Life in Kickapoo Valley Communities. Institute for Environmental Studies, University of Wisconsin, Madison. Report 11.

Wilkinson, Kenneth P. 1966. Local Action and Acceptance of Watershed Development. Social Science Research Center, Mississippi State University, State College, Miss. Report 12.

Wolfe, C. P. 1974. *Social Impact Assessment: The State of the Art*. in C. P. Wolfe (ed.) 2: *Social Impact Assessment*, Environmental Design Research Association, Inc.

Wong, Elaine. 1974. "Agri-business Plows Under the Family Farm: A New Endangered Species." *Environmental Action* 6 (9): 3–6.

Yoesting, Dean R., and Dan L. Burkhead. 1971. Sociological Aspects of Water-Based Recreation in Iowa. Department of Sociology and Anthropology, Report 94. Iowa State University, Ames.

Zuiches, James J., and Glenn V. Fuguitt. 1974. "Residential Preferences: Implications for Population Redistribution in Nonmetropolitan Areas," in Sara Mills Mazie (ed.), *Population Distribution and Policy*. Commission on Population Growth and the American Future. Research Reports, vol. 5. Washington: USGPO.

CHAPTER 3

Banks, Vera J. *Farm Population Estimates for 1975*. 1976. U.S. Department of Agriculture. AER-352.

Banks, Vera J., and Calvin L. Beale. 1973. *Farm Population Estimates, 1910–70*. Rural Development Service, U.S. Department of Agriculture. Stat. Bull. 523.

Fuguitt, Glenn V., and Calvin L. Beale. 1976. *Population Change in Nonmetropolitan Cities and Towns*. Economic Research Service, U.S. Department of Agriculture. AER-323.

Fuguitt, Glenn V., and James J. Zuiches. 1975. "Residential Preferences and Population Distribution." *Demography* 12 (3): 491–504.

Grabill, Wilson H.; Clyde V. Kiser; and Pascal K. Whelpton. 1958. *The Fertility of American Women*. New York: Wiley.

Johansen, Harley E. 1974. "Recent Changes in Population and Business Activity in Rural Villages in the United States." Ph.D. dissertation, University of Wisconsin.

Kitagawa, Evelyn M., and Philip M. Hauser. 1973. *Differential Mortality in the United States: A Study in Socioeconomic Epidemiology*. Cambridge: Harvard Univ. Press.

Sauer, Herbert I. 1974. "Geographic Variation in Mortality and Morbidity," in C. L. Erhardt and J. E. Berlin (eds.), *Mortality and Morbidity in the United States*. Cambridge: Harvard Univ. Press.

Truesdell, Leon E. 1960. *Farm Population: 1880–1950*. U.S. Bureau of the Census. Techn. Paper 3.

U.S. Bureau of the Census. 1970. U.S. Census of Population: 1970, and also *Current Population Reports*. Washington: USGPO.
_____. 1973. U.S. Census of Population: 1970. *Subject Reports*. Final Report PC(2)-3A, "Women by Number of Children Ever Born." Washington: USGPO.
_____. 1944. 16th Census of the U.S.: 1940. *Special Reports*. "Population-Differential Fertility 1940 and 1910: Women by Number of Children Ever Born." Washington: USGPO.
U.S., Congress, House. 1921. *Congressional Record*. 66th Congress, 3d sess., vol. 60, p. 1633.

CHAPTER 4

Beale, Calvin L. 1975. *The Revival of Population Growth in Nonmetropolitan America*. Economic Research Service, U.S. Department of Agriculture. ERS-605.
Bogue, Donald J. 1959. *The Population of the United States*. Glencoe, Ill.: Free Press.
Brown, David L. 1975. *Socioeconomic Characteristics of Growing and Declining Nonmetropolitan Counties*. Economic Research Service, U.S. Department of Agriculture. AER-306.
_____. 1976. "Metropolitan Reclassification: Some Effects on the Characteristics of the Population in Metropolitan and Nonmetropolitan Counties." Paper presented at Population Association of America meetings, April, Montreal.
Ducoff, Louis J., and Margaret Jarmon Hagood. 1949. "Occupational Patterns of Rural Population," in Carl C. Taylor, et al., *Rural Life in the United States*. New York: Knopf.
Fredrickson, Carl R. 1974. The Characteristics of In-Migrants to Nonmetropolitan Urban Places, 1955-1960. Center for Demography and Ecology, University of Wisconsin, Madison. Working Paper 74-10.
Fuguitt, Glenn V., and James J. Zuiches. 1975. "Residential Preferences and Population Distribution." *Demography* 12 (3): 491-504.
Grabill, Wilson H. 1955. "Progress Report on Fertility Monograph," in *Current Research on Human Fertility, 1954*. New York: Milbank Memorial Fund.
Hauser, Robert M., and David L. Featherman. 1974. "White-Nonwhite Differentials in Occupational Mobility in the United States, 1962-1972." *Demography* 11 (2): 247-65.
Hines, Fred K.; David L. Brown; and John M. Zimmer. 1975. *Social and Economic Characteristics of the Population in Metro and Nonmetro Counties, 1970*. Economic Research Service, U.S. Department of Agriculture. AER-272.
Kirschenbaum, Alan. 1971. "Patterns of Migration from Metropolitan to Nonmetropolitan Areas: Changing Ecological Factors Affecting Family Mobility." *Rural Sociology* 36 (3): 315-25.
National Center for Health Statistics. 1970. *Life Tables*. Vol. 2, Section 5. Public Health Service, U.S. Department of Health, Education, and Welfare, Rockville, Md.
National Office of Vital Statistics. 1954. *Vital Statistics of the United States 1950*. 1: 149-50. Washington: USGPO.
Taylor, Carl C. 1949. "Significant Trends and Direction of Change," in Carl C. Taylor, et al., *Rural Life in the United States*. New York: Knopf.
Tucker, C. Jack. 1976. "Changing Patterns of Migration between Metropolitan and Nonmetropolitan Areas in the United States: Recent Evidence" *Demography* 13 (4): 435-43.
U.S. Bureau of the Budget. 1964. *Standard Metropolitan Statistical Areas*. Washington: USGPO.
U.S. Bureau of the Census. 1973. U.S. Census of Population: 1970. *Subject Reports*. Final Report PC(2)-2C, "Mobility for Metropolitan Areas." Washington: USGPO.
_____. 1975. *Current Population Reports*. Series P-20, No. 285, "Mobility of the Population of the United States: March 1970 to 1975." Washington: USGPO.
U.S. Department of Labor. 1971. *Autumn 1970 Urban Family Budgets and Comparative Indexes for Selected Urban Areas*. Washington: USGPO.

CHAPTER 5

Annas, Carl E. 1970. "Problems and Advantages of Rural Locations by Labor-Intensive Industries," in *Rural Development: Problems and Advantages of Rural Location for Industrial Plans*. Agricultural Policy Institute, North Carolina State University, Raleigh. API Series 49.

Bailey, Warren R., and John E. Lee, Jr. 1970. "The New Frontier of Finance," in U.S. Department of Agriculture, *Contours of Change: Yearbook of Agriculture.*

Banks, Vera J., and Calvin L. Beale. 1973. Farm Population Estimates, 1910–70. Rural Development Service, U.S. Department of Agriculture. Stat. Bull. 523.

Barrons, Keith C. 1971. "Environmental Benefits of Intensive Crop Production." *Agricultural Science Review* 9 (2): 34–35.

Bertrand, Alvin L. 1948. "The Social Processes and Mechanization of Southern Agricultural Systems." *Rural Sociology* 13 (1): 31–39.

Byerly, T. C. 1970. "Systems Come, Traditions Go," in U.S. Department of Agriculture, *Contours of Change: Yearbook of Agriculture.*

Council for Agricultural Science and Technology. 1974. Report 35. Department of Agronomy, Iowa State University, Ames.

Durant, Thomas J., Jr. 1973. "The Impact of Industrial Development on the Farm Enterprise." Ph.D. diss., University of Wisconsin.

Durest, Donald D., and Warren R. Bailey. 1970. "What's Happened to Farming?" in U.S. Department of Agriculture, *Contours of Change: Yearbook of Agriculture.*

Economic Research Service, U.S. Department of Agriculture. 1974. *American Agriculture: Its Capacity to Produce.* ERS 544.

Fulton, Maurice. 1970. "Problems and Advantages of Selecting Rural Areas for Plant Location." in *Rural Development: Problems and Advantages of Rural Locations for Industrial Plants.* Agricultural Policy Institute, North Carolina State University, Raleigh. API Series 49.

_____. 1974. "Industry's Viewpoint of Rural Areas," in North Central Regional Center for Rural Development, *Rural Industrialization: Problems and Potentials.* Ames: Iowa State Univ. Press.

Garrison, Charles B. 1970. *The Impact of New Industry on Local Government Finances in Five Small Towns in Kentucky.* Economic Research Service, U.S. Department of Agriculture. AER-191.

_____. 1972. "The Impact of New Industry: An Application of the Economic Base Multiplier to Small Rural Areas." *Land Economics* 48 (Nov.): 329–37.

Gray, Irwin. 1969. "Employment Effect of a New Industry in a Rural Area." *Monthly Labor Review* 92 (6) (June): 26–30.

Gray, Ralph. 1962. "Community Impact of New Industry." *Arkansas Economist* 4 (3) (Spring): 21.

Hardin, Clifford M. 1970. "Foreword" in *Contours of Change: Yearbook of Agriculture.* U.S. Department of Agriculture. 1974. *Agricultural Statistics.*

Haren, Claude C. 1974. "Location of Industrial Production and Distribution," in North Central Regional Center for Rural Development, *Rural Industrialization: Problems and Potentials.* Ames: Iowa State Univ. Press.

Heady, Earl O., and Steven T. Sonka. 1975. Farm-Size Structure and Off-Farm Income and Employment Generation in the North Central Region. North Central Regional Center for Rural Development, Iowa State University, Ames.

Holmes, Joy, ed. 1973. "Energy, Environment, Productivity," in *Proceedings of the First Symposium on RANN: Research Applied to National Needs,* National Science Foundation, Washington, D.C.

Holt, Kenneth, and Jerry Pratt. 1974. "Company Officials and Community Leaders," in North Central Regional Center for Rural Development, *Rural Industrialization: Problems and Potentials.* Ames: Iowa State Univ. Press.

Kotter, Herbert. 1962. "Economic and Social Implications of Rural Industrialization." *International Labour Review* 86 (Jan.): 1–14.

Lindow, Howard E. 1974. "Decision Making for Locating Industry," in North Central Regional Center for Rural Development, *Rural Industrialization: Problems and Potentials.* Ames: Iowa State Univ. Press.

Lonsdale, Richard, and C. E. Browning. 1971. "Rural-Urban Locational Preferences of Southern Manufacturers." *Annals of Association of American Geographers.* 6 (2) (June): 255–68.

Maitland, Sheridan, and James Cowhig. 1958. "Research on the Effects of Industrialization in Rural Areas." *Monthly Labor Review* 81 (10) Oct.: 1122.

Manny, T. B., and Wayne C. Nason. 1934. *Rural Factory Industries.* Division of Farm Population and Rural Life, BAE, U.S. Department of Agriculture. Circ. 312.

Martin, A. Wade. 1974. "Problems and Advantages of Rural Labor for Industrial Operations," in *Rural Development: Problems and Advantages of Rural Locations for Industrial Plants.* Agricultural Policy Institute, North Carolina State University, Raleigh. ADI Series 49.

Mesthene, Emanuel G. 1970. *Technological Change: Its Impact on Man and Society.* Cambridge: Harvard Univ. Press.

Scott, John T., Jr., and C. T. Chen. 1973. "Expected Changes in Farm Organization When Industry Moves into a Rural Area." *Illinois Agricultural Economics* (January): 43-44.

Scott, John T., Jr., and Gene F. Summers. 1974. "Problems in Rural Communities after Industry Arrives," in North Central Regional Center for Rural Development, *Rural Industrialization: Problems and Potentials.* Ames: Iowa State Univ. Press.

Summers, Gene F., et al. 1974. Industrial Invasion of Non-metropolitan America: A Quarter Century of Experience. Center of Applied Sociology, Department of Rural Sociology, University of Wisconsin, Madison. Final Report to the Office of Economic Research, EDA, U.S. Department of Commerce.

Till, Thomas E. 1974. "Industrialization and Poverty in Southern Non-metropolitan Labor Markets." *Growth and Change.* (Jan.): 20.

CHAPTER 6

Beale, Calvin L. 1975. *The Revival of Population Growth in Nonmetropolitan America.* Economic Research Service, U.S. Department of Agriculture. ERS-605.

Beers, Howard W. 1953. "Rural-Urban Differences: Some Evidence from Public Opinion Polls." *Rural Sociology* 18 (Mar.): 1-11.

Buttel, Frederick H., and William L. Flinn. 1975. "Sources and Consequences of Agrarian Values in American Society." *Rural Sociology* 40 (Summer): 134-51.

Campbell, Angus; Philip E. Converse; and Willard L. Rodgers. 1976. *The Quality of American Life: Perceptions, Evaluations and Satisfactions.* New York: Russell Sage.

Christenson, James A. 1973. *Through Our Eyes. Vol. 1: Peoples Goals and Needs in North Carolina.* Agricultural Extension Service, North Carolina State University, Raleigh. Misc. Publ. 106.

_____. 1974a. *Through Our Eyes. Vol. 3: Who Wants What in North Carolina.* Agricultural Extension Service, North Carolina State University, Raleigh, Misc. Publ. 111.

_____. 1974b. *Through Our Eyes. Vol. 5: Rural-Urban Problems in North Carolina.* Agricultural Extension Service, North Carolina State University, Raleigh. Misc. Publ. 113.

Christenson, James A., and Choon Yang. 1975. "Dominant Values in American Society: An Exploratory Analysis." Paper presented at Rural Sociological Society meetings, August, San Francisco.

Clark, John P., and Eugene P. Wenninger. 1963. "Goal Orientations and Illegal Behavior among Juveniles." *Social Forces* 42 (Oct.): 49-59.

Copp, James H., ed. 1964. *Our Changing Rural Society: Perspectives and Trends.* Ames: Iowa State Univ. Press.

Dillman, Don A. 1971. Public Values and Concerns of Washington Residents. Agricultural Experiment Station, Washington State University, Pullman. Bull. 748.

Flinn, William L., and Donald E. Johnson. 1974. "Agrarianism among Wisconsin Farmers." *Rural Sociology* 39 (Summer): 187-204.

Folkman, William S. 1962. Attitudes and Values in a Rural Development Area: Van Buren County, Arkansas. Agricultural Experiment Station, University of Arkansas, Fayetteville. Bull. 650.

Fuguitt, Glenn V., and James J. Zuiches. 1975. "Residential Preferences and Population Distribution." *Demography* 12 (Aug.): 491-504.

Gallup Opinion Index. 1965-75. Reports 1-118. Princeton, N.J.

Glenn, Norval D., and Jon P. Alston. 1967. "Rural-Urban Differences in Reported Attitudes and Behavior." *Southwestern Social Science Quarterly* 47 (Mar.): 381-400.

Gulley, James L. 1974. *Beliefs and Values in American Farming.* Economic Research Service, U.S. Department of Agriculture. ERS-558.

Jerome, Judson. 1974. *Families of Eden.* New York: Seabury.

Larson, Olaf F. 1961. "Basic Goals and Values of Farm People," in Iowa State University Center for Agricultural and Economic Development, *Goals and Values in American Agriculture.* Ames: Iowa State Univ. Press.

Larson, Olaf F., and Everett M. Rogers. 1964. "Rural Society in Transition: The American Setting," in James H. Copp (ed.), *Our Changing Rural Society: Perspectives and Trends.* Ames: Iowa State Univ. Press.

Lowe, George D., and Charles W. Peek. 1974. "Location and Lifestyle: The Comparative Explanatory Ability of Urbanism and Rurality." *Rural Sociology* 39 (Fall): 392-420.

National Geographic Society. 1974. *Life in Rural America.* Washington: National
    Geographic Society, Special Publications Division.
Nelsen, Hart M., and Raytha L. Yokley. 1970. "Civil Rights Attitudes of Rural and Ur-
    ban Presbyterians. *Rural Sociology* 35 (June): 161-74.
Nelsen, Hart M.; Raytha L. Yokley; and Thomas W. Madron. 1971. "Rural-Urban Dif-
    ferences in Religiosity." *Rural Sociology* 36 (Sept.): 389-96.
Rokeach, Milton. 1973. *The Nature of Human Values.* New York: Free Press.
———. 1974. "Change and Stability in American Value Systems, 1968-1971." *Public
    Opinion Quarterly* 38 (Summer): 222-38.
Schwarzweller, Harry K. 1960. "Values and Occupational Choice." *Social Forces*
    39 (Dec.): 126-35.
van Es, J. C., and J. E. Brown, Jr. 1974. "The Rural-Urban Variable Once More: Some
    Individual Level Observations." *Rural Sociology* 39 (Fall): 373-91.
Wigginton, Eliot, ed. 1972. *The Foxfire Book.* Garden City, N.Y.: Doubleday.
Williams, Robin M., Jr. 1967. "Individual and Group Values." *Annals of the American
    Academy of Political and Social Science* 371 (May): 20-37.
———. 1970. *American Society: A Sociological Interpretation.* 3rd ed. New York: Knopf.
———. 1975. "Race and Ethnic Relations." *Annual Review of Sociology* 1:125-64.
Willits, Fern K.; Robert C. Bealer; and Donald M. Crider. 1973. "Leveling of Attitudes
    in Mass Society: Rurality and Traditional Morality in America." *Rural Sociology*
    38 (Spring): 36-45.

CHAPTER 7

Adams, Bert N. 1969. "The Small Trade Center: Processes and Perceptions of Growth or
    Decline," in Robert Mills French (ed.), *The Community: A Comparative Perspective.*
    Itasca, Ill.: F. E. Peacock.
Allport, Gordon. 1955. *Becoming.* New Haven: Yale Univ. Press.
Beale, Calvin L. 1974. "Rural Development: Population and Settlement Prospects." *Jour-
    nal of Soil and Water Conservation* 29 (Jan./Feb.): 23-27.
———. 1975. *The Revival of Population Growth in Nonmetropolitan America.* Economic
    Research Service, U.S. Department of Agriculture. ERS-605.
Berry, Brian J. L. 1970. *Urban Relationships and Regional Growth.* Economic Develop-
    ment Administration, U.S. Department of Commerce. COM-74-11241.
Brokensha, David, and Peter Hodge. 1969. *Community Development: An Interpretation.*
    San Francisco: Chandler.
Brownell, Baker. 1950. *The Human Community.* New York: Harper.
Buck, Roy. 1963. "An Interpretation of Rural Values," in U.S. Department of
    Agriculture, *A Place to Live: Yearbook of Agriculture.*
Clelland, Donald A., and William H. Form. 1964. "Economic Dominants and Community
    Power: A Comparative Analysis." *American Journal of Sociology* 69 (Mar.): 511-21.
Clemente, Frank; Dean Rojek; and E. M. Beck. 1974. "Trade Patterns and Community
    Identity: Five Years Later." *Rural Sociology* 39 (Spring): 92-95.
Cottrell, W. F. 1951. "Death by Dieselization: A Case Study in the Reaction to
    Technological Change." *American Sociological Review* 16 (June): 358-65.
DeJong, Gordon F., and Trudy L. Bush. 1974. "Residential Preference Patterns and
    Population Redistribution," in Wilbur Zelinsky, et al., *Population Change and
    Redistribution in Nonmetropolitan Pennsylvania, 1940-1970.* Population Issues
    Research Office, Pennsylvania State University, University Park. Report to The
    Center for Population Research, National Institute of Child Health and Human
    Development, National Institutes of Health, Department of Health, Education and
    Welfare, under Contract NIH-NICHO-72-2743.
Eberts, Paul R. 1974. Trends in Inequality in the Northeast: Major Empirical Dimen-
    sions. Paper presented at Northeast Rural Sociology Committee meetings, June,
    Ithaca, N.Y.
Etuk, Efiong. 1973. "Community Development as a Theoretical Construct." Master's
    thesis, Pennsylvania State University.
French, Robert Mills. 1970. "Economic Change and Community Power
    Structure: Transition in Cornucopia," in Michael Aiken and Paul E. Mott (eds.), *The
    Structure of Community Power.* New York: Random House.
Fuguitt, Glenn V. 1965. "The Growth and Decline of Small Towns as a Probability
    Process." *American Sociological Review* 30 (June): 403-11.

_____. 1971. "Places Left Behind: Trends and Policy for Rural America." *Rural Sociology* 36 (Dec.): 449-70.

_____. 1972. "Population Trends of Nonmetropolitan Cities and Villages in the United States." Sara Mills Mazie (ed.), *Population Distribution and Policy.* Commission on Population Growth and the American Future. Research Reports, vol. 5. Washington: USGPO.

Haga, William J., and Clinton L. Folse. 1971. "Trade Patterns and Community Identity." *Rural Sociology* 36 (Mar.): 42-51.

Hawley, Amos. 1950. *Human Ecology: A Theory of Community Structure.* New York: Ronald.

Hillery, George A., Jr. 1968. *Communal Organizations: A Study of Local Societies.* Chicago: Univ. of Chicago Press.

Hunter, Albert. 1975. "The Loss of Community: An Empirical Test through Replication." *American Sociological Review* 40 (Oct.): 537-52.

Johnson, Ronald L., and Edward Knop. 1970. "Rural-Urban Differentials in Community Satisfaction." *Rural Sociology* 35 (Dec.): 544-48.

Kasarda, John D. 1972. "The Theory of Ecological Expansion: An Empirical Test." *Social Forces* 51 (Dec.): 165-75.

Kaufman, Harold F. 1975. Community Development Working Papers: Conceptualization for Practice in Town and Country. Social Science Research Center, Mississippi State University, State College, Miss. Report 45.

Kaufman, Harold F.; Satadal Dasgupta; and Avtar Singh. 1975. *Villages Upward Bound: Community Structure and Development in Selected Indian Villages.* Calcutta: Editions Indian.

König, René. 1968. *The Community.* Translated by Edward Fitzgerald. New York: Schocken.

Nisbet, Robert. 1953. *The Quest for Community.* New York: Oxford Univ. Press.

Pellegrin, Roland J., and Charles Coates. 1956. "Absentee-Owned Corporations and Community Power Structure." *American Journal of Sociology* 61 (Mar.): 413-19.

President's National Advisory Commission on Rural Poverty. 1967. *The People Left Behind.* Washington: USGPO.

Rodefeld, Richard. 1975. "Evidence, Issues and Conclusions on the Current Status and Trends in U.S. Farm Types." Paper presented at Rural Sociological Society meetings, August, San Francisco.

Sanders, Irwin. 1970. "The Concept of Community Development," in Lee J. Cary (ed.), *Community Development as a Process.* Columbia: Univ. of Missouri Press.

Schulze, Robert O. 1961. "The Bifurcation of Power in a Satellite City," in Morris Janowitz (ed.), *Community Political Systems.* Glencoe, Ill.: Free Press.

Smith, Ronald W. J. 1975. "Community Environment and Levels of Voluntary Association Activity." Master's thesis, Pennsylvania State University.

Speight, John F. 1973. "Community Development Theory and Practice: A Machiavellian Perspective." *Rural Sociology* 38 (Winter): 477-90.

Stein, Maurice R. 1960. *The Eclipse of Community: An Interpretation of American Studies.* Princeton, N.J.: Princeton Univ. Press.

Summers, Gene F.; Lauren H. Seiler; and John P. Clark. 1970. "The Renewal of Community Sociology." *Rural Sociology* 35 (June): 218-31.

Veblen, Thorstein. 1969. "The Case of America: The Country Town," in David W. Minar and Scott Greer (eds.), *The Concept of Community: Readings with Interpretations.* Chicago: Aldine.

Vidich, Arthur J., and Joseph Bensman. 1958. *Small Town in Mass Society: Class, Power and Religion in a Rural Community.* Princeton, N.J.: Princeton Univ. Press.

Vogt, Evon Z., and Thomas F. O'Dea. 1953. "A Comparative Study of the Role of Values in Social Action in Two Southwestern Communities." *American Sociological Review* 18 (Dec.): 645-54.

Voth, Donald E. 1975. "An Evaluation of Community Development Programs in Illinois." *Social Forces* 53 (June): 635-47.

Walton, John. 1967. "The Vertical Axis of Community Organization and the Structure of Power." *Social Science Quarterly* 48 (Dec.): 353-68.

Warren, Roland L. 1970. "Toward a Non-Utopian Normative Model of the Community." *American Sociological Review* 35 (Apr.): 219-28.

_____. 1972. *The Community in America.* 2d ed. Chicago: Rand McNally.

Whiting, Larry R., ed. 1974. *Communities Left Behind: Alternatives for Development.* Ames: Iowa State Univ. Press.

Wilkinson, Kenneth P. 1970. "The Community as a Social Field." *Social Forces* 48 (Mar.): 311–22.

———. 1972. "A Field-Theory Perspective for Community Development Research." *Rural Sociology* 37 (Mar.): 43–52.

Young, Frank W., and Ruth C. Young. 1973. *Comparative Studies of Community Growth.* Rural Sociological Society Monograph 2. Morgantown: West Virginia Univ. Press.

Zuiches, James J., and Glenn V. Fuguitt. 1972. "Residential Preferences: Implications for Population Redistribution in Nonmetropolitan Areas," in Sara Mills Mazie (ed.), *Population Distribution and Policy.* Commission on Population Growth and the American Future. Research Reports, vol. 5. Washington: USGPO.

CHAPTER 8

Alonso, William. 1971. "The Economics of Urban Size." *Papers of the Regional Science Association* 26: 67–83.

American Medical Association. 1972. *Health Care in Rural Areas.* Chicago.

Federal Bureau of Investigation, U.S. Department of Justice. 1975. "Crime in the United States, 1974." Washington: USGPO.

Georgia Regional Executive Directors Association. 1971. Georgia's APDC's: What They Are and Why. Institute of Community and Area Development, University of Georgia.

Goldmark, Peter C. 1972. "Tomorrow We Will Communicate to Our Jobs." *The Futurist* 6 (Apr.): 55–58.

National Academy of Sciences. 1971. *The Quality of Rural Living: Proceedings of a Workshop.* Washington.

New England Municipal Center. 1975. *Multi-Town Management in Maine Communities.* Durham, N.H.

President's National Advisory Commission on Rural Poverty. 1967. *The People Left Behind.* Washington: USGPO.

Real Estate Research Corporation. 1974. *The Costs of Sprawl.* Washington: USGPO.

Richardson, Harry W. 1973. *The Economics of Urban Size.* Lexington, Mass.: Lexington Books.

Schumacher, E. F. 1973. *Small Is Beautiful.* New York: Harper and Row, Harper Torchbook.

Sundquist, James L. 1969. *Making Federalism Work.* Washington: Brookings Institution.

U.S. Bureau of the Census. 1974a. *Census of Governments, 1972.* Vol. 5, "Local Government in Metropolitan Areas." Washington: USGPO.

———. 1974b. *Census of Governments, 1972.* Vol. 6, Topical Studies. No. 5, "Graphic Summary of the 1972 Census of Governments." Washington: USGPO.

———. 1975. *Current Population Reports,* Series P-23, No. 55, "Social and Economic Characteristics of the Metropolitan and Nonmetropolitan Population: 1974 and 1970." Washington: USGPO.

CHAPTER 9

Black Americans

Beale, Calvin L. 1970. "Rural-Urban Migration of Blacks: Past and Future." *American Journal of Agricultural Economics* 53 (May): 302–7.

———. 1966. "The Negro in American Agriculture," in J. P. Davis (ed.), *The American Negro Reference Book.* Englewood Cliffs, N.J.: Prentice-Hall.

Campbell, Rex R.; Daniel M. Johnson; and Gary Stangler. 1974. "Return Migration of Black People to the South." *Rural Sociology* 39 (Winter): 514–28.

Finney, Henry C. 1973. "Problems of Local, Regional and National Support for Rural Poor Peoples' Co-operatives in the United States: Some Lessons from the 'War on Poverty' Years." Paper presented at European Society for Rural Sociology meetings, July, Rome, Italy.

Howze, Glenn R. 1970. "The Black Farmer and the USDA." Paper presented at Association of Southern Agricultural Workers meeting, February, Memphis.

Johnson, Daniel M. 1971. "Black Return Migration to a Southern Metropolitan Community: Birmingham, Alabama." Ph.D. dissertation, University of Missouri.

Jones, Lewis W., and Everett S. Lee. 1974. "Rural Blacks—A Vanishing Population."

Paper presented at W. E. B. DuBois Institute for the Study of the American Black, October, Atlanta University, Atlanta, Ga.

Lee, Ann S., and Gladys K. Bowles. 1974. "Policy Implications of the Movement of Blacks out of the Rural South." *Phylon* 35 (Sept.): 332–39.

Lee, Everett S. 1966. "A Theory of Migration." *Demography* 3 (2): 47–57.

Marshall, Ray, and Lamond Godwin. 1971. *Cooperatives and Rural Poverty in the South.* Baltimore: Johns Hopkins Press.

President's National Advisory Commission on Rural Poverty. 1967. *The People Left Behind.* Washington: USGPO.

———. 1968. Rural Poverty in the United States. Washington: USGPO.

Price, Daniel O. 1968. "The Negro Population of the South," in President's National Advisory Commission on Rural Poverty, *Rural Poverty in the United States.* Washington: USGPO.

Reid, John D. 1974. "Black Urbanization of the South." *Phylon* 35 (Sept.): 259–67.

Shryock, Henry S. 1964. Population Mobility within the United States. Chicago: Community and Family Study Center.

Tucker, Charles Jackson. 1974. "Changes in Age Composition of the Rural Black Population of the South 1950 to 1970." *Phylon* 35 (Sept.): 313–22.

U.S. Bureau of the Census. 1920. 14th Census of the U.S. *Characteristics of the Population.* Vol. 2. Washington: USGPO.

———. 1930. 16th Census of the U.S. *Characteristics of the Population.* Vols. for 15 southern states. Washington: USGPO.

———. 1960. U.S. Census of Population: 1960. *Social and Economic Characteristics.* "U.S. Summary." Washington: USGPO.

———. 1970a. U.S. Census of Population: 1970. *Characteristics of the Population.* "U.S. Summary." Washington: USGPO.

———. 1970b. U.S. Census of Population: 1970. *Characteristics of the Population.* Vols. for 15 southern states. Washington: USGPO.

———. 1970c. U.S. Census of Population: 1970. *Social and Economic Characteristics.* "U.S. Summary." Washington: USGPO.

———. 1971, 1972, 1973, and 1974. *The Social and Economic Status of the Black Population in the United States.* July of each year. Washington: USGPO.

Wadley, Janet K., and Everett S. Lee. 1974. "The Disappearance of the Black Farmer." *Phylon* 35 (Sept.): 276–83.

Weintraub, Dov. 1970. "Rural Periphery, Societal Center, and Their Interaction in the Process of Agrarian Development: A Comparative Analytical Framework." *Rural Sociology* 35 (Sept.): 367–76.

Mexican-Americans

Cleland, Robert G. 1959. *From Wilderness to Empire: A History of California,* pp. 60–73. Rev. ed. New York: Knopf.

Day, James M., et al. 1968. Six Flags of Texas, pp. 57–68. Waco: Texas Press.

Grebler, Leon; Joan W. Moore; and Ralph Guzman. 1970. *The Mexican-American People.* New York: Free Press.

McWilliams, Carey. 1949. Reprinted 1968. *North from Mexico, the Spanish Speaking People of the United States.* New York: Greenwood.

Meinig, Donald W. 1971. *Southwest: Three Peoples in Geographical Change, 1600–1970.* New York: Oxford Univ. Press.

Moore, Joan W. 1970. *Mexican-Americans.* Englewood Cliffs, N.J.: Prentice-Hall.

Pitt, Leonard. 1966. *The Decline of the Californios,* pp. 167–80. Berkeley: Univ. of California Press.

Richardson, Rupert N.; Ernest Wallace; and Adrian N. Anderson. 1970. *Texas, the Lone Star State.* 3rd ed. Englewood Cliffs, N.J.: Prentice-Hall.

Stoddard, Ellwyn R. 1973. *Mexican-Americans.* New York: Random House.

U.S. Bureau of the Census. 1973. *Current Population Reports.* Series P-20, No. 250, "Persons of Spanish Origin in the United States." Washington: USGPO.

———. 1970a. *Subject Reports.* Final Report PC(2)-C1, "Persons of Spanish Origin." Washington: USGPO.

———. 1970b. *Detailed Characteristics.* Final Report PC(1)-D1, "U.S. Summary." Washington: USGPO.

U.S. Civil Rights Commission. 1974. *Counting the Forgotten. The 1970 Census Count of Persons of Spanish-Speaking Background in the United States.* April.

Weems, John E. 1971. *Dream of Empire.* New York: Simon and Schuster.

Indian Americans

Johnson, Helen W. 1975. *American Indians in Transition.* Economic Development Division, Economic Research Service, U.S. Department of Agriculture. AER-283.
_____. 1969. *Rural Indian Americans in Poverty.* Economic Research Service, U.S. Department of Agriculture, AER-167.
Levine, Stuart, and Nancy O. Lurie. 1968. *The American Indian Today.* Baltimore: Penguin.
Lurie, Nancy Oestreich. 1966. "The Enduring Indian." *National History,* November, pp. 1-4.
Tyler, S. Lyman. 1974. *A History of Indian Policy.* Pp. 54-69, 125-49, 151-88, and 169-253. Department of the Interior, Washington: USGPO.
U.S. Bureau of the Census. 1960. *Subject Reports.* PC(2)-1C, "Nonwhite Population by Race." Washington: USGPO.
_____. 1970. *Subject Reports.* PC(2)-1F, "American Indians." Washington: USGPO.
Wax, Murray L., and Robert W. Buchanan. 1975. *Solving "The Indian Problem,"* pp. 78-79 and 189-90. New York: New Viewpoints.
Wise, Jennings C., and Vine Deloria, Jr. 1971. *The Red Man in the New World Drama,* pp. 357-62; 375; and 377-78. New York: Macmillan.

CHAPTER 10

Blood, Robert O., Jr., and Donald M. Wolfe. 1960. *Husbands and Wives.* New York: Free Press.
Burchinal, Lee G. 1964. "The Rural Family of the Future," in James H. Copp (ed.), *Our Changing Rural Society.* Ames: Iowa State Univ. Press.
Kahn, Kathy. 1973. *Hillbilly Women.* Garden City, N.Y.: Doubleday.
Kuvlevsky, William P., and Angelita S. Obordo. 1972. "A Racial Comparison of Teen-Age Girls' Projections for Marriage and Procreation." *Journal of Marriage and the Family* 34 (Feb.): 75-84.
National Geographic Society. 1974. Life in Rural America. Washington: National Geographic Society, Special Publications Division.
New Land Review. 1975. 1 (Winter): 1, 11.
Nietzke, Ann. 1975. "The Media/. . . Doin' Somebody Wrong." *Human Behavior* 4 (Nov.): 66-68.
Rice, Rodger R., and J. Allan Beegle. 1972. *Differential Fertility in a Metropolitan Society.* Rural Sociological Society Monograph 1. Morgantown: West Virginia Univ. Press.
Roper Public Opinion Research Center. 1974. *National Data Program for the Social Sciences.*
Smuts, Robert W. 1959. *Women and Work in America.* New York: Columbia Univ. Press.
Stokes, C. Shannon, and Fern K. Willits. 1974. "A Preliminary Analysis of Factors Related to Sex-Role Ideology Among Rural-Origin Females." Paper presented at Rural Sociological Society meetings, August, Montreal.
U.S. Bureau of the Census. 1940. U.S. Census of Population: 1940. Second Series, *Characteristics of the Population.* "U.S. Summary." Washington: USGPO.
_____. 1950a. *Marital Status.* Washington: USGPO.
_____. 1950b. U.S. Census of Population: 1950. Vol. 1, *Characteristics of the Population.* Part 1, "U.S. Summary," Washington: USGPO.
_____. 1960a. *Marital Status,* Washington: USGPO.
_____. 1960b. U.S. Census of Population: 1960. Vol. 1, *Characteristics of the Population.* Part 1, "U.S. Summary," Washington: USGPO.
_____. 1970a. *Marital Status.* Washington: USGPO.
_____. 1970b. U.S. Census of Population: 1970. Vol. 1, *Characteristics of the Population.* Part 1, "U.S. Summary." Washington: USGPO.
_____. 1970c. U.S. Census of Population: 1970. *Detailed Characteristics.* Final Report PC(1)-D1, "U.S. Summary." Washington: USGPO.
_____. 1975. *Current Population Reports.* Series P-20, No. 277, "Fertility Expectations of American Women: June 1974." Washington: USGPO.
Wilkening, Eugene A. 1958. "Joint Decision-Making in Farm Families as a Function of Status and Role." *American Sociological Review* 23 (Apr.): 187-92.

CHAPTER 11

Blau, Peter M., and Otis Dudley Duncan. 1967. *The American Occupational Structure.* New York: Wiley.

Borland, Melvin, and Donald E. Yett. 1967. "The Cash Value of College for Negroes and Whites." *Trans-Action* 5 (Nov.): 44–49.

Clinton, Lawrence; Bruce A. Chadwick; and Howard M. Bahr. 1975. "Urban Relocation Reconsidered: Antecedents of Employment among Indian Males." *Rural Sociology* 40 (Summer): 117–33.

Duncan, Otis Dudley; David L. Featherman; and Beverly Duncan. 1972. *Socioeconomic Background and Achievement.* New York: New York Seminar Press.

Fogel, Walter. 1966. "The Effect of Low Educational Attainment on Incomes: A Comparative Study of Selected Ethnic Groups." *Journal of Human Resources* 1 (Fall): 22–40.

Gans, Herbert J. 1969. "Culture and Class in the Study of Poverty: An Approach to Anti-Poverty Research," in Daniel P. Moynihan (ed.), *Understanding Poverty.* New York: Basic Books.

Harrington, Michael. 1962. *The Other America: Poverty in the United States.* Baltimore: Penguin.

Hines, Fred K.; David L. Brown; and John M. Zimmer. 1975. *Social and Economic Characteristics of the Population in Metro and Nonmetro Counties, 1970.* Economic Research Service, U.S. Department of Agriculture. AER-272.

Jencks, Christopher, et al. 1972. *Inequality: A Reassessment of the Effect of Family and Schooling in America.* New York: Basic Books.

Leacock, Eleanor Burke. 1971. *The Culture of Poverty: A Critique.* New York: Simon and Schuster.

Lewis, Oscar. 1968. *The Study of Slum Culture—Background for La Vida.* New York: Random House.

Marshall, Ray. 1973. Rural Workers and Rural Labor Markets. Center for the Study of Human Resources, University of Texas, Austin. Report.

McPherson, W. W. 1968. "An Economic Critique of the National Advisory Commission Report on Rural Poverty." *American Journal of Agricultural Economics* 50 (5): 1362–72.

Miller, Herman P. 1960. "Annual and Lifetime Income in Relation to Education: 1939–1959." *American Economic Review* 50 (Dec.): 962–86.

Morrison, Peter A., et al. 1974. *Review of Federal Programs to Alleviate Rural Deprivation.* Prepared for the Edna McConnell Clark Foundation. Santa Barbara, California: Rand Corp.

Office of the Federal Register, National Archives and Records, General Services Administration. 1971. "Annual Message to the Congress on the State of the Union," January 22, 1970 in *Public Papers of the Presidents of the United States, RICHARD NIXON: Containing the Public Messages, Speeches, and Statements of the President.* Washington: USGPO.

Orshansky, Mollie. 1969. "Perspectives on Poverty: How Poverty Is Measured." *Monthly Labor Review* 20 (Feb.): 32–41.

President's National Advisory Commission on Rural Poverty. 1967. *The People Left Behind.* Washington: USGPO.

_____. 1968. *Rural Poverty in the United States.* Washington: USGPO.

Rainwater, Lee. 1969. "The Problem of Lower-Class Culture and Poverty-War Strategy," in Daniel P. Moynihan (ed.), *Understanding Poverty.* New York: Basic Books.

Schiller, Bradley R. 1973. *The Economics of Poverty and Discrimination.* Englewood Cliffs, N.J.: Prentice-Hall.

Starnes, Charles E. 1976. "Contemporary and Historical Aspects of Officially Defined Poverty in the United States," in Don H. Zimmerman (ed.), *Understanding Social Problems.* New York: Praeger.

U.S. Bureau of the Census. 1973a. U.S. Census of Population: 1970. *General Social and Economic Characteristics.* Final Report PC(1)-C1, "U.S. Summary." Washington: USGPO.

_____. 1973b. U.S. Census of Population: 1970. *Detailed Characteristics.* Final Report PC(1)-D1, "U.S. Summary." Washington: USGPO.

Vallentine, Charles A. 1968. *Culture and Poverty.* Chicago: Univ. of Chicago Press.

CHAPTER 12

Congressional Research Service, Library of Congress. 1975. *Rural Development Goals: Critique of the Second Annual Report of the Secretary of Agriculture to Congress.* Prepared at the request of the Congressional Rural Caucus. Washington, D.C.

Daft, Lynn M. 1972. "Toward a Possibly Practical Framework for Rural Development Policies and Programs." *Southern Journal of Agricultural Economics* 4 (July): 1–8.

Heady, Earl O. 1970. Preface to Iowa State University Center for Agricultural and Economic Development, *Benefits and Burdens of Rural Development: Some Public Policy Viewpoints.* Ames: Iowa State Univ. Press.

Kaldor, Donald R. 1975. "Rural Income Policy in the United States," in Earl O. Heady and Larry R. Whiting (eds.), *Externalities in the Transformation of Agriculture: Distribution of Benefits and Costs from Development.* Ames: Iowa State Univ. Press.

North Central Regional Extension. 1972. Who Will Control U.S. Agriculture? Policies Affecting the Organizational Structure of U.S. Agriculture. College of Agriculture, Cooperative Extension Service, University of Illinois at Urbana. Ext. Publ. 32.

Ogden, Daniel M., Jr. 1972. "How National Policy Is Made," in *Increasing Understanding of Public Problems and Policies, 1971.* Chicago: Farm Foundation.

Paarlberg, Don. 1976. "The Farm Policy Agenda," in *Increasing Understanding of Public Problems and Policies, 1975.* Chicago: Farm Foundation.

President's Task Force on Rural Development. 1970. *A New Life for the Country.* Washington: USGPO.

Rasmussen, Wayne D.; Gladys L. Baker; and James S. Ward. 1976. *A Short History of Agricultural Adjustment, 1933–75.* Economic Research Service, U.S. Department of Agriculture, Agric. Inf. Bull. 391.

Schickele, Rainer. 1954. *Agricultural Policy: Farm Programs and National Welfare.* New York: McGraw-Hill.

Schnittker, John A. 1970. "Distribution of Benefits from Existing and Prospective Farm Programs," in Iowa State University Center for Agricultural and Economic Development, *Benefits and Burdens of Rural Development: Some Public Policy Viewpoints.* Ames: Iowa State Univ. Press.

Spitze, R. G. F. 1976. "Agricultural and Food Policy Issues and the Public Decision-making Environment," in *Agricultural and Food Price and Income Policy—Alternative Directions for the United States and Implications for Research.* Report of a Policy Research Workshop, Washington, D.C., January 15–16. Agricultural Experiment Station, University of Illinois at Urbana. Special Publ. 43.

U.S. Congressional Budget Office. 1976. *Agricultural Price Support Programs—A Layman's Guide.* Washington: USGPO.

U.S., Congress, House. 1972. *Program of Rural Development.* President of the United States. Doc. 92-240. Washington: USGPO.

U.S., Congress, Senate, Committee on Agriculture and Forestry. 1973. *Agriculture and Consumer Protection Act of 1973: Report Together with Additional Views on S. 1888.* Report 93-173. Washington: USGPO.

U.S., Congress, Senate, Committee on Agriculture and Forestry. 1975. *1975 Revised Guide to the Rural Development Act of 1972.* Prepared for the Subcommittee on Rural Development. Washington: USGPO.

Wood, William W., Jr. 1976. "Domestic Food and Farm Policy—A Reaction," in *Increasing Understanding of Public Problems and Policies, 1975.* Chicago: Farm Foundation.

CHAPTER 13

Aron, Raymond. 1969. *Progress and Disillusion: The Dialectics of Modern Society.* New York: Mentor.

Ball, A. Gordon, and Earl O. Heady, eds. 1971. *Size, Structure, and Future of Farms.* Ames: Iowa State Univ. Press.

Beers, Howard. 1953. "Rural Urban Differences: Some Evidence from Public Opinion Polls." *Rural Sociology* 18 (Mar.): 1–11.

Bell, Daniel. 1973. *The Coming of Post-Industrial Society: A Venture in Social Forecasting.* New York: Basic Books.

Bell, Wendell, and James Mau. 1970. "Images of the Future," in James C. McKinney and E. A. Tiryakian (eds.), *Theoretical Sociology: Perspectives and Developments.* New York: Appleton-Century-Crofts.

Berger, Peter; Brigitte Berger; and Hansfried Kellner. 1973. *The Homeless Mind: Modernization and Consciousness.* New York: Random House.

Brinkman, George L. 1974. "The Condition and Problems in Nonmetropolitan America," in George L. Brinkman (ed), *The Development of Rural America.* Lawrence: Univ. Press of Kansas.

Burchinal, Lee G. 1964. "The Rural Family of the Future," in James H. Copp (ed.), *Our Changing Rural Society: Perspectives and Trends.* Ames: Iowa State Univ. Press.

Clayton, Richard R. 1975. *The Family, Marriage, and Social Change.* Lexington, Mass.: D. C. Heath.

Committee for Economic Development. 1966. *Modernizing Local Government.* Committee for Economic Development, New York.

Copp, James H., ed. 1964. *Our Changing Rural Society: Perspectives and Trends.* Ames: Iowa State Univ. Press.

Coward, E. Walter, Jr.; George M. Beal; and Ronald C. Powers. 1971. "Domestic Development: Becoming a Post-Industrial Society," in George M. Beal, Ronald C. Powers, and E. Walter Coward, Jr. (eds.), *Sociological Perspectives of Domestic Development.* Ames: Iowa State Univ. Press.

De Sola Pool, Ithiel. 1963. "The Role of Communication in the Process of Modernization and Technological Change," in Bert F. Hoselitz and Wilbert E. Moore (eds.), *Industrialization and Society.* UNESCO-Mouton.

Dillman, Don A., and Kenneth R. Tremblay, Jr. 1977. "The Quality of Life in Rural America." *The Annals of the American Academy of Political and Social Science* 429 (Jan.): 115–29.

Doeksen, Gerald, et al. 1975. *The Role of Multicounty Development Districts in Rural Areas.* Economic Research Service, U.S. Department of Agriculture. AER-307.

Duncan, Beverly, and Stanley Lieberson. 1970. *Metropolis and Region in Transition.* Beverly Hills: Sage Publications.

Edwards, Clark, and Rudolph De Pass. 1975. *Alternative Futures for Nonmetropolitan Population, Income, Employment and Capital.* Economic Research Service, U.S. Department of Agriculture. AER-311.

Ellenbogen, Bert T. 1974. "Service Structure of the Small Community: Problems and Options for Change," in North Central Regional Center for Rural Development, *Communities Left Behind: Alternatives for Development.* Ames: Iowa State Univ. Press.

Ellis, Albert. 1970. "Group Marriage: A Possible Alternative," in Herbert A. Otto (ed.), *The Family in Search of a Future.* New York: Appleton-Century-Crofts.

Erickson, Eugene. 1974. "Consequences for Leadership and Participation," in North Central Regional Center for Rural Development, *Communities Left Behind: Alternatives for Development.* Ames: Iowa State Univ. Press.

Farmer, Richard N. 1973. *The Real World of 1984: A Look at the Foreseeable Future.* New York: McKay.

Ferkiss, Victor. 1974. *The Future of Technological Civilization.* New York: Braziller.

Flinn, W. L., and D. E. Johnson. 1974. "Agrarianism among Wisconsin Farmers." *Rural Sociology* 39 (Summer): 187–204.

Fuguitt, Glenn V. 1971. "The Places Left Behind: Population Trends and Policy for Rural America." *Rural Sociology* 36 (Dec.): 449–70.

Gottschalk, Shimon S. 1975. *Communities and Alternatives: An Exploration of the Limits of Planning.* New York: Schenkman Pub. Co. of John Wiley and Sons.

Harris, Marshall. 1974. *Entrepreneurial Control in Farming.* Economic Research Service, U.S. Department of Agriculture. ERS-542.

Hausler, Richard. 1974. "The Emergence of Area Development," in George Brinkman (ed.), *The Development of Rural America.* Lawrence: Univ. Press of Kansas.

Hightower, Jim. 1975. *Eat Your Heart Out.* New York: Crown.

Hines, Fred K.; David L. Brown; and John M. Zimmer. 1975. *Social and Economic Characteristics of the Population in Metro and Nonmetro Counties, 1970.* Economic Research Service, U.S. Department of Agriculture. AER-272.

Kammen, Michael. 1972. *People of Paradox.* New York: Knopf.

Kanter, Rosabeth Moss. 1972. *Commitment and Community: Communes and Utopias in Sociological Perspective.* Cambridge: Harvard Univ. Press.

_____. 1973. *Communes: Creating and Managing Collective Life.* New York: Harper and Row.

Landis, Paul H. 1948. *Rural Life in Process.* 2d ed. New York: McGraw-Hill.

Larson, Olaf F., and Everett M. Rogers. 1964. "Rural Society in Transition: The American Setting," in James H. Copp (ed.), *Our Changing Rural Society: Perspectives and Trends.* Ames: Iowa State Univ. Press.

Linder, Staffan Burenstam. 1970. *The Harried Leisure Class.* New York: Columbia Univ. Press.

Loomis, Charles P., and J. Allan Beegle. 1950. *Rural Social Systems.* New York: Prentice-Hall.

McCann, Glenn C. 1975. "Perceptions of the Nature of Society in the Rural South," in *Rural Sociology in the South: 1975.* Proceedings Rural Sociology Section, Southern Association of Agricultural Scientists meetings, February. New Orleans.

Marien, Michael. 1974. "Views of Society's Next Stage." *Fields within Fields, within Fields . . .,* 13 (Fall): 81-95.

Meadows, Paul. 1971. *The Many Faces of Change.* Cambridge, Mass.: Schenkman.

National Commission on Food Marketing. 1966. *The Structure of Food Manufacturing.* Techn. Study 8. Washington: USGPO.

National Area Development Institute. 1975. "Development Briefs." *Area Development Interchange* 5 (24) (Dec.): 4.

Nisbet, Robert A. 1969. *Social Change and History.* New York: Oxford Univ. Press.

North Central Regional Center for Rural Development. 1973. *Rural Development: Research Priorities.* Ames: Iowa State Univ. Press.

————. 1974. *Communities Left Behind: Alternatives for Development.* Ames: Iowa State Univ. Press.

Olsen, Marvin E. 1968. *The Process of Social Organization.* New York: Holt, Rinehart and Winston.

O'Neill, Nena, and George O'Neill. 1972. "Open Marriage: A Synergic Model." *Family Coordinator* 21 (Oct.)21: 403-409.

Padbury, Peter. 1972. *The Future: A Bibliography of Issues and Forecasts.* Council of Planning Librarians, Monticello, Ill.

Parsons, Talcott, and Winston White. 1961. "The Link Between Character and Society," in Seymour Martin Lipset and Leo Lowenthal (eds.), *Culture and Society.* Glencoe, Ill.: Free Press.

Polanyi, Michael. 1958. *Personal Knowledge.* London: Routledge and Kegan Paul.

Pye, Lucien W. 1963. *Communications and Political Development.* Princeton, N.J., Princeton Univ. Press.

Roberts, Ron E. 1971. *The New Communes: Coming Together in America.* Englewood Cliffs, N.J.: Prentice-Hall.

Roy, Rustrum, and Della Roy. 1970. "Is Monogamy Outdated?" *Humanist* 30 (Mar./Apr.): 19-26.

Schuler, Edgar A., and Walter C. McKain, Jr. 1949. "Levels and Standards of Living," in Carl C. Taylor et al., *Rural Life in the United States.* New York: Knopf.

Sheldon, Eleanor Bernert, and Robert Parke. 1975. "Social Indicators." *Science* 188 (May): 693-99.

Slesinger, Doris P. 1974. "The Relationship of Fertility to Measure of Metropolitan Dominance: A New Look." *Rural Sociology* 39 (Winter): 350-61.

Special Task Force. 1973. *Work in America.* Report to the Secretary of Health, Education, and Welfare. Cambridge: MIT Press.

Steelman, Virginia P. 1975. "Income and Welfare: Change between 1960 and 1972 and Current Situation. Summary Results of Preliminary Data," in *Rural Sociology in the South: 1975.* Proceedings Rural Sociology Section, Southern Association of Agricultural Scientists meetings (Feb. 2-5), New Orleans.

Sussman, Marvin B. 1972. "Family, Kinship, and Bureaucracy," in Angus Campbell and Philip E. Converse (eds.), *The Human Meaning of Social Change.* New York: Russell Sage.

Taylor, Carl C., et al. 1949. *Rural Life in the United States.* New York: Knopf.

Toffler, Alvin. 1970. *Future Shock.* New York: Bantam.

U.S., Congress, Senate, ERS, USDA. 1971. *The Economic and Social Condition of Rural America in the 1970s.* 92d Cong., 1st sess., May, 1971.

van Es, J. C., and J. E. Brown, Jr. 1974. "The Rural-Urban Variable Once More: Some Individual Level Observations." *Rural Sociology* 39 (Winter): 373-91.

Vickers, Geoffrey. 1973. *Making Institutions Work.* New York: Wiley.

Vidich, Arthur J., and Joseph Bensman. 1958. *Small Town in Mass Society.* Garden City, N.Y.: Anchor.

Vogt, Evon Z. 1955. *Modern Homesteaders.* Cambridge: Harvard Univ. Press.

Warren, Roland. 1963. *The Community in America.* Chicago: Rand-McNally.

West, James. 1945. *Plainville, USA.* New York: Columbia Univ. Press.

Westhues, Kenneth. 1972. *Society's Shadow: Studies in the Sociology of the Countercultures.*
    Toronto: McGraw-Hill-Ryerson.
Wilkinson, Kenneth P. 1974. "Consequences of Decline and Social Adjustment to It," in
    North Central Regional Center for Rural Development, *Communities Left Behind:
    Alternatives for Development.* Ames: Iowa State Univ. Press.
Zijderveld, Anton. 1971. *The Abstract Society.* Garden City, N.Y.: Anchor.

INDEX

U.S. Federal Bureau of Investigation, 135
U.S. Forest Service, 29, 32, 34
U.S. Office of Economic Opportunity, 14, 140, 192
U.S. Office of Management and Budget, 135
U.S. Senate Committee on Agriculture and Forestry, 200
U.S. Soil Conservation Service, 29
U.S. Supreme Court, 105, 203
Universities and community development, 122
Urbanization, 3, 4, 13, 54, 117, 155, 224
Utah, 27, 161–65

Vallentine, Charles A., 183
Values and value orientations. *See also* Beliefs
  achievement, 92, 94–95
  activity and work, 92, 94–95
  agrarian, 215, 219–20
  changes, 8–9, 14, 92, 96–97, 110–11, 226
  conformity, 92
  culture component, vii
  definition, 92
  democracy, 92, 94, 226
  efficiency and practicality, 92, 94, 111
  farmers', 107–8, 111
  freedom, 92
  group superiority, 92, 99
  honesty, 94
  humanitarianism, 92, 94, 98, 106, 108
  individualism, 92, 94
  leisure and recreation, 94
  materialism, 94
  maternal, 172
  moral orientations, 92, 95, 97
  nationalism-patriotism, 92, 94, 95
  persistence, 3, 112, 179, 219, 220
  personal, 93
  rural, 91–99, 106–7, 109–12
  rural-urban differences, 8, 9, 14, 16, 94–98, 110–11
  science and rationality, 92, 111
  social, 93
  Williams' categories, 91, 93
van Es, Jon C., 33, 95, 215
Veblen, Thorstein, 119
Vegetable production, 10
Vermont, 161–162
Vickers, Geoffrey, 224
Vidich, Arthur J., 120, 219
Virginia, 146, 161
Vogt, Evon Z., 120, 216
Voth, Donald E., 121

Wadley, Janet K., 151
Walden Two, 124
Wallace, Ernest, 153
Wallace, Jerry, 170
Walton, John, 120
Warner, W. Keith, 29
War on Poverty, 151, 182–83

Warren, Roland L., 120
Washington, 112, 161–64
Washington, D.C., 41, 61, 208
Waste disposal, 5, 20, 139–40
Water supply, 139–40
Wax, Murray L., 165
Weems, John E., 153
Weintraub, Don, 152
Welfare programs and services, 138–39, 185–86, 191
Wengert, Norman, 27, 32
Wenninger, Eugene P., 94
West, 27, 81, 150, 155
West, James, 216
Westhues, Kenneth, 218
West Virginia, 5, 87, 141, 161, 194
Wheat production, 77–78
Whelpton, Pascal K., 45
White, Winston, 223
White House Conference on Conservation (1908), 29
Whiting, Larry R., 118–19
Who Will Control U.S. Agriculture? (1972), 205
Wigginton, Eliot, 108
Wilderness Act (1964), 25
Wilderness Society, 29
Wilkening, Eugene A., 25–27
Wilkinson, Kenneth P., 26, 121, 123, 223
Williams, Robin M., 92–93, 98–99, 106, 111
Williams, W. K., 26
Willits, Fern K., 95–97, 179
Wisconsin, University of, 29, 32, 41, 52, 80, 107, 161, 163–64
Wise, Jennings C., 165–66
Wolfe, C. P., 34
Wolfe, Donald M., 169
Women
  employment, 63, 85, 174–77, 179, 188–89
  rural, vii, 13, 98–99, 168–81
Wong, Elaine, 22
Wood, William W., Jr., 203
World War I, 37
World War II, 39, 155, 165
Wyoming, 27, 161–62

Yang, Choon, 93–94, 106
Yearbook of Agriculture
  1923, 21
  1970, 76
  1971, 82
Yett, Donald E., 187
Yoesting, Dean R., 29
Yokley, Raytha, 98–100
Young, Frank W., 118
Young, Ruth C., 118

Zijderveld, Anton, 228
Zimmer, John M., 8, 61, 185–86, 220
Zimmerman, Carle C., 9
Zoning, 33, 143
Zuiches, James J., 15, 24, 71, 109, 117